YOU
AND
YOUR
anxious
CHILD

ANNE MARIE ALBANO, PH.D.

with

Leslie Pepper

A Lynn Sonberg Book

AVERY   A MEMBER OF PENGUIN GROUP (USA) INC.   NEW YORK

YOU
AND
YOUR
anxious
CHILD

Free Your Child from Fears
and Worries and Create a
Joyful Family Life

Published by the Penguin Group
Penguin Group (USA) Inc., 375 Hudson Street,
New York, New York 10014, USA

USA · Canada · UK · Ireland · Australia
New Zealand · India · South Africa · China

Penguin Books Ltd, Registered Offices:
80 Strand, London WC2R 0RL, England
For more information about the Penguin Group visit penguin.com

Most Avery books are available at special quantity discounts for bulk purchase for
sales promotions, premiums, fund-raising, and educational needs. Special books or
book excerpts also can be created to fit specific needs. For details, write Penguin
Group (USA) Inc. Special Markets, 375 Hudson Street, New York, NY 10014.

Library of Congress Cataloging-in-Publication Data

Albano, Anne Marie.
You and your anxious child : free your child from fears and worries and
create a joyful family life / Anne Marie Albano with Leslie Pepper.
        p.   cm.
Includes index.
ISBN 978-1-58333-495-9
1. Anxiety in children.   2. Fear in children.   I. Pepper, Leslie.   II. Title.
        BF723.A5A53   2013   2012039976
                155.4'1246—dc23

Printed in the United States of America
3   5   7   9   10   8   6   4

BOOK DESIGN BY ELLEN CIPRIANO

For my mom and dad, Katie and Joe, for giving us a home filled with opportunity, choice, and much, much love; and to all the children, adolescents, and parents with whom I've worked over the years —you inspire me . . . you are my heroes!

—Anne Marie Albano

Contents

YOU
AND
YOUR
anxious
CHILD

1

You and Your Child's Anxiety

Timmy, a seven-year-old boy, came with his parents, Jon and Linda, to the Columbia University Clinic for Anxiety and Related Disorders, where I am the director. Timmy was a handsome boy with big blue eyes and a mop of curly hair, but his furrowed brow revealed the ever-present worry that preoccupied his mind. He leaned forward in his chair, elbows on his knees and hands wringing whenever he uttered a word.

As the story of Timmy and his parents unfolded, I thought of the classic children's book *Goodnight Moon*. On one page, there is a drawing of the little bunny in bed, alone in the dark. It's a primal scene in a heartwarming book, but there's also something poignant about seeing the little fellow all alone in a big, big room. Timmy wasn't good at being alone, in the dark or otherwise. He always wanted to be wherever his parents were, and he trailed them around the house like a shadow. More than once, Linda stepped back from the stove or sink and right onto her son, not realizing that he had slipped up quietly behind her and was sitting on the floor.

School was a daily battle. Many days, Timmy threw tantrums that caused him to miss the bus, so Linda was chronically late for work. Once at school, Timmy often complained of tummy aches, and although he usually managed to stay through the last bell, other times he begged the nurse to call his mother, who would leave work early to come pick him up.

Although Linda only worked part-time hours at the office, while home she often stayed quite busy on her laptop with consulting work. Jon and Linda thought perhaps Timmy's problems stemmed from her work schedule, and after much deliberation they decided she'd leave her job. If she were home to spend more quality time with Timmy, they thought, his troubles would diminish.

But instead, they got worse. Now that Linda was home all the time, Timmy stuck to her like glue. Even when he was in the bathroom, the door was always open. At night, Timmy shared a room with his four-year-old brother. Yet, more nights than not, he sneaked down the hall and climbed into his parents' bed.

Jon and Linda consulted their pediatrician, who told them separation anxiety was normal. Timmy would grow out of it, he said reassuringly, so they resigned themselves to wait for that magical day and make the best of things in the meantime.

Then, one weekend, Timmy's parents invited another couple over for a visit. Timmy was so engrossed in playing with the couple's eight-year-old son that he didn't notice when everyone else went down to the basement. When Timmy realized that he couldn't hear his parents' voices, he began to frantically search for them, screaming and crying as he ran from room to room. When he reached the top of the basement stairs, he heard his parents talking below and rushed down toward them. At that same moment, his little brother was making his way up the stairs. In his desperation, Timmy pushed the younger boy, who tumbled backward.

Timmy's little brother lay crumpled at the foot of the stairs. Yet even as his parents hurried to help their younger son, Timmy pulled at their sleeves, wailing, "Where *were* you?" Fortunately, Timmy's brother was fine. But his parents were not. They finally understood that his separation anxiety was not just a normal, passing phase but a serious problem.

When I interviewed Timmy, he explained that every time his parents were out of sight, he was terrified that he'd never see them again. And the school bus? He was consumed by fear that the driver would forget he was there. When I pressed for details, he described an imagined scenario in which the driver would drop off all the other children but skip his house. "Then the bus driver will go to the big parking garage and put the bus away and go home. And I'll still be on the bus alone. It will get dark, and no one will know where I am."

This is when I thought of the little bunny in bed, alone and scared. Timmy never considered how easy it would be to simply speak up and let the driver know he was there. Nor did he realize how remote the chances were that the driver would park the bus overnight with a student still in it. In his mind, the threat was very real—and very frightening. It was just one fear among many that fueled Timmy's anxiety disorder.

Classic Anxiety, Typical Parents

Although Linda and Jon tried everything to help their son, and Linda even quit her job to try to calm her son's fears, we saw in Timmy's case that it did not help the problem and in fact made it even worse. I hear stories like this every day in my office, from the richest to the poorest families, from single moms to two-dad households. Though the specifics may change, the overarching problem is similar with every parent who comes through my doors.

Do you remember what it was like to go to sleep at night before you had your children? After a hard day at work, maybe after a night on the town, your head hit the pillow and you slept all night long. A marching band could have played right through your room and you still would have slept, right?

But the minute you have a child, that all changes. You probably had a baby monitor in your child's room, but I'll bet you didn't need it. All it took was a little squeak and you'd sit bolt upright in bed, awake and alert. This is the natural instinct that parents have: to protect their children and keep them safe. Your child's cry puts you on high alert in a flash, and you're ready for whatever comes your way.

Although Timmy wasn't literally crying in the middle of the night, in a figurative sense he was. Linda and Jon heard his cries of distress through his clinging behaviors, and they wanted to rush in and rescue him. As Timmy's anxiety spun more and more out of control, they began to swoop in more and more often, faster and faster, and as you saw from their story, this only intensified the anxiety.

Let me say something front and center: Anxiety disorders are *not* caused by bad parenting. This is a concern I hear over and over from distraught moms and dads. Ironically, however, the very instinct that makes for *good* parenting—the instinct to protect—may play a key role in perpetuating and deepening your child's anxiety.

It's natural for a parent to want to soothe a child who's upset. And in many circumstances, that makes good parenting sense. But with an anxiety disorder, a parent's reassurance actually has the opposite effect of what you expect. Instead of soothing the child, the reassurance makes him grow even more anxious, forcing the parent to hold on even tighter. Eventually, they may end up in a vicious cycle, with an overprotective parent feeding the fears of an overanxious child.

It's all too easy to fall into this type of unhealthy pattern. Imagine that your kindergartner comes home from school crying, telling you, "Sasha and Amy wouldn't sit with me today. They were mean! I don't have any friends." Your first instinct is to hug her and tell her you're going to take care of it. You pick up the phone the next day and find out from the teacher what happened. If the problem continues, you may even call the other girls' parents and enlist their help as well. For the child in kindergarten, who can't reason well by herself, this may make sense. But what if you continue to do it through first grade, second grade, third grade? What if your daughter is in fifth grade and still relying on you to mend fences for her?

When you have a child who tends to get distressed, has difficulty soothing herself, and is anxious and afraid, a certain parenting style evolves. From early on, you're always in comfort, protect, and reassurance mode. And your child never has an opportunity to learn the skills for handling her own friendships, nor does she get a chance to see that she's blowing her fears out of proportion. So those fears remain in her, while you, slowly but surely, cross the line from concerned parent to over-involved.

It's a vicious cycle—but also a breakable one. By reading this book, you can learn how to stop rescuing and, instead, start empowering your child. One of the main goals I have for you is to help you begin to stop, think, and ask, "How much more have I taken on for my child, rather than let her handle this situation herself?"

Let me tell you something that may not sit well right away. You're not going to always feel, as my niece used to say, that this is a rainbow and unicorn world. You're going to have to sit through the upset and anguish your child is feeling. In order to master anxiety, your child will have to face his fears, which will upset him. But he has to experience this anxiety in order to learn that whatever he's afraid of, it's not as bad as he thinks it is. And while he's learning that, it's going to take all the strength you can summon to watch your child go through it. You're asking him to face the fears he's been running from, probably for years, and we hope the practical tools and insights in this book will provide guidance and support along the way.

But when a child faces his fears, what will come out on the other end is a more confident child: one who has overcome his worries instead of fleeing from them, and who now has skills and abilities to manage his own emotions and the challenges of everyday life. When you take a step back and let your child take control, it doesn't make you any less important in his life. In fact, it's made you more important because you've helped him see that he can do it all on his own. And that is something you can all be proud of.

A Look in the Mirror

When parents continue to help too much for too long, it's typically because of their own worries:

"Without me, she will fail."

"She won't know what to do."

"She needs my help."

This type of thinking is conveyed to the child by word or deed, reinforcing the child's fears, worries, and self-doubts. I've found that almost every parent in this situation eventually asks one question: "What did I do wrong?" I want you to stop blaming yourself right now, and instead replace that question with a more constructive one: "What can I do to empower my child?" In this book I'll offer plenty of realistic answers that will help you reclaim your self-confidence and hope.

One rule of thumb I emphasize: If you fear that your child cannot handle a situation alone, then that's precisely when you need to let him or her do so. I recommend a 1:2 formula. Have your child handle the situation once with your guidance and then twice without you. And even when offering guidance, remember, you don't need to solve every aspect of the problem for your child. Instead, you will guide your child to come up with solutions independently. But how? In the pages that follow, I will show you step-by-step how to accomplish this.

All children have some fears and worries. These are normal, adaptive responses to challenging or dangerous situations. It's only when such responses become irrational and excessive that they are transformed from anxiety into an anxiety *disorder*. To help you determine what's normal and what's not for your child at various ages, I'll describe the hundred years of research categorizing typical childhood fears. From animals and blood to thunderstorms and darkness, I'll outline the ages at which these fears are most likely to occur and tell you how to distinguish a normal fear from one that may signal a lasting problem.

Of course, it's important to recognize when outside professional help is needed. For more intractable anxiety, professional treatment is an important part of the solution and I will provide you with a clear understanding of how to tell when it's advisable to seek outside help. The good news is that anxiety disorders at any age are highly treatable. Parents play a crucial role by seeking professional help when needed, supporting therapy goals, giving any necessary medication as prescribed, getting the family on board, working with teachers, and helping prevent relapse. In the process, they can reclaim their own lives.

QUIZ: COULD YOU BE CONTRIBUTING TO YOUR CHILD'S ANXIETY?

Answer yes or no to the following questions.

- Your nine-year-old has been practicing for his piano recital for months. He's been so excited about it, yet on the day of the recital, he says that he feels ill. He doesn't have a fever, but he's complaining of not feeling well. Do you let him stay home? After all, he can't perform when sick. Yes/No

- You're walking with your seven-year-old and you see a small dog being walked up the block toward you. Do you cross to the other side of the street because you know your daughter is afraid of dogs? Yes/No

- Your teenager says no to every party his classmates invite him to. When you question him, he says he doesn't want to go because his "whole grade drinks and does drugs." Are you thrilled that he's making good choices, so you don't question him further? Yes/No

- Your twelve-year-old is consistently having trouble with her math homework. You've helped her as much as you can, but when you suggest that she speak to the teacher, she says that she'd rather you help her. Are you happy that you have such a good relationship that she's coming to you for help? Yes/No

- Your kindergartner has been invited to a few drop-off birthday parties, but you always go, too. After all, that's the only way to make sure she stays safe. Yes/No

- While watching the news, your thirteen-year-old gets very upset about what she's seeing. You quickly change the channel. After all, she's too young to be worried about this sort of stuff. Yes/No

If you've answered yes to two or more of these questions, you may be unwittingly contributing to your child's anxiety.

What Causes Anxiety?

We are preprogrammed from birth to develop certain fears at certain ages in order to survive. Nature is ingenious when you think about it. When learning to crawl, an infant develops a fear of heights, keeping him from tumbling down the stairs. Separation anxiety first comes into play right around the same time as a child is learning to walk—a natural course correction so he doesn't venture too far from Mom or Dad. These innate fears have an evolutionary function: to keep us safe from harm.

Fears come with a physiological component. When confronted with the threat of danger, the brain sends a warning signal to the central nervous system and the adrenal glands begin to overproduce the stress hormones adrenaline and noradrenaline. This causes our hearts to pound more quickly and our breath to get more shallow. Our muscles begin to tense; we shake, sweat, or tremble; and our pupils even dilate. This instinctive reaction—known as the fight-or-flight response—is, again, a stroke of nature's brilliance. Our body is prepping to either confront and combat the threat, or turn and run like the wind. Once the danger disappears, the body returns to normal.

For some children, this natural instinct isn't operating correctly, and their hair-trigger alert system signals danger when there isn't any. A situation that would mean nothing to most children—an airplane ride, a math quiz, an hour with a new babysitter—sounds the alarm bell and their amygdala, the region of the brain that sets the fight-or-flight response in motion, begins firing wildly.

The Anxious Brain

Let's take a minute to discuss this amygdala and the brain. Let's say you're walking down the street and you hear a loud BANG! *Was it a gunshot? A car backfiring?* The amygdala, a small, almond-shaped structure deep within your brain, doesn't wait to find out the answer—in an instant it begins prepping for disaster. This microcircuit of neurons (nerves in the brain) sends a series of signals to other brain circuits that triggers the release of hormones (such as adrenaline) to get you ready to fight or flee from the (presumed) gun.

Your heart starts to pump blood faster so that your muscles are getting more blood flowing to them while you increase your breathing to deliver oxygen to these muscles to help you deal with the situation, and many other physical responses occur, including the narrowing of your attention to focus on finding that threat and dealing with it in a way that keeps you safe. The amygdala is sort of a sentry, on the watch for immediate danger.

Ever notice that the physical feelings of fear (the startling "Uh-oh!" experience of clenching your stomach, catching your breath, and jumping) happen seemingly before or simultaneously with your conscious awareness of the loud bang? Well, in a way, the amygdala is always on and ready to react. As soon as it senses a potential problem, it sends a signal to another brain circuit, the hypothalamus, which then sets off the fight-or-flight response. Since the amygdala is also associated with memory, particularly memories of highly emotional experiences, it signals alarm before you even have a chance to process. Hence, you jump at the sound of a bang as if it's something that will harm you, even if it's just a car backfiring.

But it's not that simple and, in fact, two people can be in the same place at the same time and react to the same situation quite differently. Some time back, I was at a hotel pool in Santa Monica taking a break from attending the annual meeting of the Anxiety Disorders Association of America. After grabbing a towel at the cabana, I noticed my friends were clutching their beach chairs and yelling at me. We were experiencing some aftershocks of an earthquake, but other than a momentary unsteadiness, I hardly gave a second thought to the trembling below my feet. My mind was focused on getting a towel and getting into that pool, while my conference friends were practically panicking. So, you see, in the same situation, some people were frightened, some laughed, some were simply astonished, and others proceeded on their merry way, as I did without so much as a second thought.

Why did some of us react so intensely and others hardly noticed? There is yet another circuit in the brain (actually, many others) that sends signals to the sensory cortex, the region of the brain responsible for interpreting the meaning of what's happening in and around you. The sensory cortex is responsible for making sense of the situation. In the case of a loud bang on the street, the cortex is processing where you are, what you're doing, and how likely it is that this is something dangerous. In a way, the cortex is asking *What else might be happening here? Where have I heard this sound before? How can I handle it?* You'll learn more about this later, but examining a situation in context and realistically is at the heart of the type of therapy I do, a therapy that is effective for treating problematic anxiety. Because the reasoning within the circuits of the cortex takes a little bit more time, there's that initial twinge of fear, but then the cortex rapidly processes the information and sends a signal to the amygdala to tamp down and turn off the fight-or-flight response. "It's just a car backfiring" or in my case at the poolside, "Okay, it's an aftershock but we're all okay, so let's go swimming!"

When Fear Goes Awry

As we've just seen, fear is an innate, human, and reasonable response to impending danger, a signal from within the brain to seek immediate safety or to protect yourself by fighting or fleeing something that could harm you. Fear becomes problematic when nothing is objectively dangerous, yet your child reacts as though there's a saber-toothed tiger bearing down on him. When a child panics at the thought of taking a spelling test, or when you ask him to sleep in his own bed and he breaks down shaking and in tears, or when she is so frightened of speaking to new kids at camp that she freezes and can't speak, their inborn alarm systems are firing for no good reason.

There's one more system in the brain that works to protect us in a longer-term sense. Whereas fear is focused on an immediate threat, anxiety is focused on future threatening possibilities. As the child's brain develops the capacity to reason and understand the future, worry comes into play as he comprehends the notion that everything may be safe today but may change down the road. Whereas the amygdala is in the oldest part of our brain, anxiety is mostly processed in the cerebral cortex, the part of the brain that is uniquely developed in humans. The cortex allows us to imagine scenarios, plan our course of action, and think through and reason all sorts of possibilities.

For example, you're driving somewhere you've never been before and find that you've taken a wrong turn. At the first twinge of fear (*Oh no, I'm lost!*), the anxiety system can step in and reason with *Well, this is a new area that I've not been to before. Let me look at the GPS and take in the scenery while I have the chance.* That's very different from going with the *Oh no!* response and following a different set of thoughts, such as, *What if this is a dangerous area? What if I can't find my way back to the main road!?!* Those thoughts rev up anxiety and help to keep active the fight-or-flight response. The anxiety system in the brain is mostly mediated by a neurotransmitter called GABA (gamma-aminobutyric acid), which inhibits firing of neurons that excite the brain and keep a person on edge.

In contrast to the panic sensations of fear, anxiety is that feeling of unease and tension that reflects the idea that *something wicked this way comes*, but you might not be sure of what and when or whether you can deal with the imagined wickedness or not. Anxiety is future-oriented: *What if the teacher turns out to be mean? What if you or Dad get sick and die? What if there's an earthquake and our house falls apart?* A child with anxiety is always on "orange alert," waiting for the other shoe to drop.

Brief and normal levels of anxiety help us to prepare for future events and manage well: A test is assigned, so a child studies, college applications have deadlines so a teenager can prepare the material to submit in time. Normal levels of anxiety, which we call "worry," have no long-term effects beyond motivating you to act responsibly and problem solve accordingly when things go wrong.

However, persistent anxiety, which often shows itself in the form of *What if, what if, and what if,* keeps the child in an ever-ready stance of apprehension and tension. In this state, the child can be consumed with worry, which takes his attention away from the tasks at hand, impairs his ability to problem-solve, and wears him down physically with muscle aches, headaches, and stress.

The Anxious Family

We don't know exactly why some children's alert response and anxiety systems are stuck in overdrive and not processing the realistic

aspects of a situation and how to handle it, but we have several the-
ories. And in fact, there's probably not one reason, but a number of
contributing factors that increase the likelihood of anxiety taking
hold. Genetics plays a part, although the same anxiety disorders
don't always appear in children and their family members. In other
words, while your mother may have had a phobia about spiders,
your son may have a more generalized anxiety. Your aunt may have
generalized anxiety and your daughter may have separation anxiety.

Work by my colleague Deborah Beidel, Ph.D., and others has
shown, though, that children of anxious parents are seven times
more likely to develop an anxiety disorder than children of non-
anxious parents. But don't despair if you have anxiety in your
family, because while genes may transfer a vulnerability to the child,
sort of like an Achilles' heel, other factors, such as the way his
brain processes information and his experiences as he grows and
matures, also factor into whether the anxiety becomes problematic or not. We also know that infant temperament—their early
"personalities"—also may render a child vulnerable to certain forms
of anxiety. The baby who is difficult to soothe, slow to warm to
others, and hesitant to crawl around and explore his immediate surroundings away from Mom or Dad has a tendency toward being
anxious. And, if anxiety does take hold, it is malleable—that is, your
child can learn to get control over the anxiety and learn how to
cope with the situations that challenge him.

The Ultimate Cycle

Anxiety tends to be self-perpetuating. Often an event triggers the
initial anxiety. A boy is called on in class, his face gets hot and red,

THE ANXIOUS MIND

Children who are anxious have some glitch in their thinking. Their thoughts always fall into the same traps. Instead of focusing on the positive or neutral, they go straight to the negative. The most common thinking traps were first identified by the preeminent psychiatrist Aaron T. Beck, M.D., one of the founders of cognitive therapy. These include the following:

All-or-none thinking: "It's all my fault." . . . "Things will never get better."

Disqualifying the positive: "Those kids were only nice because they had to be."

Mind reading: "My teacher must think I'm such a dummy."

Fortune-telling: "I just know I won't have any fun if I go to camp."

Catastrophizing: "That girl turned me down for the dance. I'm never going to have a girlfriend."

Shoulds, can'ts, won'ts: "I can't do this." . . . "I should be perfect; if I was, bad things wouldn't happen." . . . "I won't ever feel better about this."

Overgeneralization: "I'm a loser at everything I do."

his stomach churns, and he feels like he's going to throw up. He gives a short, clipped answer and quickly sits down in his seat and finds that—voilà!—the uncomfortable feeling has vanished. He didn't like that hot, red, stomach-churning feeling, so he doesn't want to get called on in class again. The next day he tells his mother he doesn't feel well. She doesn't want him to go to school feeling sick, so she keeps him home. Or he may even confess the truth—he hates being called on in class—and Mom, unable to bear the thought of her son being uncomfortable, speaks to the teacher to ask that he not call on him.

And this is how easily the anxiety gets perpetuated. The longer your child can avoid the anxiety-provoking situations, the longer the anxiety will persist and, over time, get worse. All children experience those butterflies in their stomach from time to time when called on in class, going to sleepaway camp for the first time, or asking someone on a date. Every child has thoughts race through his mind: *What if I mess up? What if the kids laugh at me? What if nobody likes me? What if she says no?* But most take a deep breath, power through it, and come out the other end unscathed.

For the child with anxiety, however, the combination of physical signals and negative thinking brings them to a standstill. They retreat to a safe, nonthreatening place and their questions go unanswered, they never venture to a new camp, and instead of asking for a date on Friday night, they spend the night home alone.

The end result is that the child who's prone to anxiety never has the chance to discover that the feeling will go away. It is only by persevering into and through the challenging situation that your child will have the opportunity to manage that anxious feeling rising in his body, and not obsess over it, but instead pay attention to the activity itself. Once focused on the oral report, or the smiles on his new friends' faces, or the clarity the teacher provides in answering his question, the anxiety will subside and be replaced with feelings of accomplishment, fun, and a boost in self-confidence.

Your Role as a Parent

Parenting style may also play a major role in perpetuating anxiety. The two parenting styles associated with anxiety disorders are overprotection and overcontrol. Take, for example, five-year-old Sophie, who comes home from school crying, "The other kids in my class don't like me, they're mean!" An overprotective parent will react with something like, "You stay away from those kids!" Instead of finding out what's really going on, and coaching Sophie to find the friends in the crowd, Mom is teaching Sophie to withdraw.

The overcontrolling parent might march into the school the next morning, demanding a change of classroom for Sophie. And so again Sophie learns nothing about how to turn the situation to her advantage or how to figure out the kids who would make good friends. Instead, the message she's getting is, "You can't handle this situation." She switches classes; perhaps another friendship goes sour, and another.

We will revisit overprotection and overcontrolling parenting throughout this book. These are parenting styles that have been studied and found to contribute to the maintenance of anxiety in children. We can't and won't blame parents for the way they approach managing their child's emotions. I can't say that if my child cried night after night about sleeping in his bed, I, too, wouldn't scoop him up and comfort him in mine. But we now know that this overprotection is an anxiety trap. And, if my child was fearful of being separated from her friends in the new school year, I, too, might walk into the principal's office and beg, borrow, and steal to get her placed in the same class with her friends and the warmest of teachers. But that overcontrol is now known to deprive my daughter of learning to roll with the chance happenings of daily life.

What we can, and I hope to do, in this book is enlighten you about the way you interact with your child and his world, and ask you to examine whether what you do is helping or hindering him.

IS HELICOPTER PARENTING LEADING TO MORE ANXIOUS CHILDREN?

When I was a child, every day after school I'd go home, do my homework, then run out the door and across the street to the Dunns' house. After I rang the bell Mrs. Dunn would appear and I'd ask, "Can Karen come out to play?" A simple act on the surface, and yet, so much is packed into it. I had to muster up social skill and positive manners to ask Mrs. Dunn the question. If Karen was available, the next challenge was for us to figure out something fun and creative to do. Perhaps we'd sew some clothes for our dolls, maybe we'd play some games or call on our other friends and put a play together, all of which involved a host of social interaction skills including cooperative play, sharing, engaging, listening, and activating verbal skills.

If Mrs. Dunn told me that Karen wasn't available, I then needed to learn how to regulate my emotions as I handled disappointment ("I wanted to play with Karen!"), excuse myself calmly (a mix of emotion regulation and more social skill), and move into problem solving ("What do I do next?"). This may have meant dealing with boredom if no one else was around (I had to self-soothe and be creative in finding a solitary task), or search for other friends to play with, or, heaven forbid . . . get my little sister and brother to play with me.

In short, the simple task of asking a friend to come play was loaded with developmental challenges and lessons and, when repeated day after day, helped to solidify a series of very important skills that carried through adulthood: social skills, assertiveness, creative thinking, problem solving, and emotion regulation, among others.

Now, imagine if instead of my running across alone, my mother had called Mrs. Dunn for me. All of those skills that I honed day after day would have been lost. And so, here we find ourselves today, arranging our children's playdates, managing their soccer schedules, and fielding all their phone calls. While it may seem like we're doing right by our children, we're depriving them of a plethora of rich learning and skill-building experiences. Is it any wonder that it seems as though our children are having more difficulty now than ever before?

How to Use This Book

As you have seen from this chapter, you may be inadvertently contributing to your child's anxiety through overprotecting and overcontrolling. In the chapters that follow, I'll offer practical, hands-on, evidence-based advice on how to break out of the cycle you've found yourself in and, instead, give your anxious child a chance to confront and conquer his own fears. I will show you how your anxiety may be affecting your child, and vice versa. I'll show you when and how to take a step back. And I will help you to see what's normal and what's worrisome.

I will also describe the three most common types of anxiety disorders, and with each one I'll give specific advice tailored to the type of anxiety your child is facing. The rest of the book is devoted to diagnosis, treatment, and living with a child who has an anxiety disorder.

Let's take a quick look at these disorders that are so widespread and so devastating.

Clingers, Worrywarts, and Fraidy-Cats: An Introduction

Anxiety disorders, characterized by excessive fears or worries that are recurring or long lasting, are *the* most common of all emotional illnesses in youth. They're both more distressing and more disruptive than the milder fears and worries that all children experience from time to time. But the good news is that they are also the most treatable of all psychiatric conditions, and groundbreaking clinical research has led to the development of evidence-based treatments that really work.

Fears and worries can take many forms. Prevalence estimates vary from study to study, depending on the research methods used. But we know for certain that anxiety disorders are extremely widespread, affecting a minimum of 10 percent of youth, with most experts accepting that some 13 percent to 20 percent of children and young teens are affected.

There are a number of anxiety disorders that can affect children and adolescents, from specific phobias to obsessive-compulsive disorder (OCD) to panic disorder. But most often, these disorders are expressed in one of three forms in youth: separation anxiety, generalized anxiety, and social phobia. These are the disorders that we will focus on in this book.

Separation anxiety refers to fear and worry focused on being away from home or separated from parents and caregivers that is excessive and inappropriate for the child's age. Timmy's story, which you heard earlier, is a classic example. From interviews with thousands of children and adolescents over the years, my colleagues and I have learned that youngsters with separation anxiety are tormented by one belief: Something bad will happen—maybe they'll be lost or kidnapped, or perhaps a parent will have an accident or die—and this event will keep them forever separated from a loved one. The scenes these children imagine are overwhelming for them and drive their unrelenting efforts to never be apart from those they love. For example, an elementary school–aged child with separation anxiety might always play within eyesight of a parent, resist staying with a sitter, and refuse to sleep over at a friend's house.

Generalized anxiety refers to a pattern of excessive worry and anxiety over a number of different things, such as friends, school, health, and sports. Sometimes the worry may focus on a particular concern, such as failing in school. Other times, the child feels tense and uneasy all the time, about many different things, but nothing you or he can really put a finger on. I often hear parents refer to children with generalized anxiety as "little adults" or "worrywarts." The children are relentless with their "what if" questions:

"What if we go on vacation and someone gets sick and there's not a doctor nearby?"
"What if Dad loses his job, like it's happened to other people?"
"What if someone breaks into our house while we're out to dinner?"

No amount of reassurance stops the questions for long. Parents begin to feel worn out by the child's demands and may go to great lengths to quell the child's anxiety. But try as they might, it never seems to go away.

Social phobia refers to a strong fear of social situations involving being the focus of attention, being around unfamiliar people, or possibly being scrutinized by others. For example, a child with social phobia might be afraid of talking in class, walking across a crowded cafeteria, and being introduced to new peers. The fear goes well beyond ordinary shyness or self-consciousness. Terrified of doing something that will lead to ridicule or embarrassment, the child starts avoiding the feared situation or enduring it only with great distress.

In young children, social phobia occasionally takes the form of selective mutism—an inability or refusal to speak in front of anyone outside the immediate family. With teachers, classmates, extended family, and others, the child is literally frozen with fear and unable to talk, so parents and even classmates begin speaking for the child and making excuses for the silence. Parents of children with this condition often tell me how confused and helpless it makes them feel.

In older children and teens, social phobia is quite insidious and can go unrecognized for many years. Parents may be lulled into a false sense of security because their child is never in any trouble. To the contrary, teachers may say things such as, "I don't even know she's in my class." While other parents bemoan teens who are always on the go and never off the phone, teens with social phobia are almost always at home. Parents may be grateful for having such a quiet child—at least, until they realize that their child is also isolated and anxious. That's when parents start to notice that they're the ones who always order in restaurants, talk to cashiers in stores, and call for missed homework while their child hangs back quietly.

Although the majority of children with an anxiety disorder will present with one of these three conditions, the information and treatment strategies in this book also apply to children and teens with any anxiety disorder, including the following:

Panic disorder: Children with panic disorder experience bursts of heart palpitations, sweating, trembling, shortness of breath, nausea, and dizziness. These panic or anxiety attacks come on suddenly and for no obvious reason. Panic disorder is diagnosed if your child suffers at least two attacks followed by at least one month of concern over having another attack, losing control, or "going crazy." While panic attacks can happen at any age, panic disorder is rare in young children and most often onsets in mid- to late adolescence.

Specific phobias: Children who suffer from a specific phobia have an intense, illogical fear of a particular object or situation. Children will avoid it at all costs, or they'll experience it with extreme uneasiness. They'll cry, throw a tantrum, cling to the parent, or complain of headaches or stomachaches to avoid contact with the feared situation. Common childhood phobias include animals, the dark, storms, bugs, vomit or vomiting, going in the water, costumed characters, blood, and medical and dental procedures. Specific phobias start early, around age four or five, and often stay long-term.

Obsessive-compulsive disorder: Children with OCD experience persistent, intrusive, and somewhat strange thoughts, such as feeling they're contaminated with germs or they've done something terribly wrong. They feel compelled to repeatedly perform rituals and routines to rid themselves of those thoughts. Most children are diagnosed with OCD around age ten, although children as early as age two or three can show signs of the disorder.

Post-traumatic stress disorder: While most children who experience or witness a traumatic or life-threatening event will not develop any clinically impairing problems, 25 percent may develop post-traumatic stress disorder (PTSD). They experience an intense fear and anxiety, become emotionally numb or easily irritable, or avoid places, people, or activities that remind them of the event. Children most at risk are those who directly witnessed a traumatic event, who suffered directly (such as injury or abuse), who had emotional issues before the event, and who lack a strong support network. Violence at home also increases a child's risk of developing PTSD after a traumatic event.

RIGHT NOW YOU MAY FEEL WORRIED, alarmed, sad, overcome, defeated, or all of the above. I've seen hundreds of parents just like you and I can say without question that things will get better. That's why I wrote this book: to help parents who are consumed with worry about their worried children. Armed with coping strategies that really do work, your child can look forward to freer, easier days ahead. And so can you.

I'll show you how to restructure your own thinking in a more realistic and constructive direction. And I'll explain that, when you do this, the benefits rub off on your child. Anxiety is a vicious cycle—but also a breakable one. By reading this book, you can learn how to stop rescuing and, instead, start empowering your child.

2

What's Normal—and What's a Warning Sign

One of the great joys of being a parent is watching your child master firsts: the first word, the first step, the first time getting dressed without help. As your child grows, the challenges become more complicated and the stakes can seem higher, and scarier: the first time your child walks to school alone, the first time your son asks a girl on a date, your daughter's first dance. Mastering age-appropriate challenges—and overcoming any anxieties they stir up—is crucial for your child's maturation process.

In this chapter, I'll offer guidelines on the age at which your child should be passing specific developmental milestones. Of course, children mature at different rates. But if your son or daughter is lagging far behind in certain areas for no obvious reason, it could be a sign that anxiety is the cause. The types of lags you notice can help you identify the particular type of anxiety your child may be struggling with.

In this chapter you'll learn some of the major developmental tasks that children should be learning to do for themselves at various ages. For example:

- By fifth grade, children should be handling their own friendships
- By seventh grade, talking with teachers when they have a question about schoolwork
- By ninth grade, arranging their own social schedule
- By twelfth grade, visiting nearby colleges without parents

After covering what's expected for each stage and age, I'll also address in this chapter the common fears at various ages, with guidelines on how to distinguish normal childhood fears from ones that may signal a problem that needs attention. This will help you to determine when you should take action and, if necessary, seek professional help. I'll also discuss some other conditions occurring in childhood that can look like anxiety but be something quite distinct, warranting a different approach to overcome them. You'll learn how to make the distinction among conditions.

Fear: Not Always Something to Be Afraid Of

All children have fears. We have a saying in our field: "Research is Me-Search," and my parents can attest that my work in the area of childhood anxiety comes from personal experience. I was an anxious child with many, many fears, and at least two were at the level of a phobia. Most severe were my fears of doctors and of needles. Every year when I visited Dr. Horn on Staten Island, both my parents and a nurse had to hold me down just to be examined. My fear

Questions to Ask Yourself:
Is My Child's Anxiety Just a Passing Phase?

❖ Are your child's reactions in proportion, or too extreme, in relation to what's going on in front of him? Do your child's fears diminish when you answer his questions, or do they just seem to
lead to more questions?

❖ When your child is scared to do something, is he able to push
through it and learn from it? Or does he avoid the situation at all
costs?

❖ Are his reactions specific to the situation, or does he generalize
and get worse over more situations?

❖ When you explain to your child that he needs to face what he's
afraid of, does he understand and agree? Or does he do whatever
possible to avoid the situation?

of shots was so intense that once when I was six, in order to avoid a
shot, I ran out of the office, through several streets, and into my
grandparents' house. I bolted upstairs and hid silently under their
queen-size bed until my parents found me. I refused to come out,
and my dad and grandfather had to take the bed apart to pull me out
from underneath. My fear of needles remained with me until I was
seventeen, but that's another story for later. (If you really can't wait,
thumb through chapter 3 for what happened in high school.)

My cowardice didn't end at doctors and needles. I was also
terror-stricken by thunder, loud noises, dogs, bees, and costumed
characters. Most of these fears eventually passed, but to this day I'm
not fond of loud noises and I still have to psych myself up to get
blood drawn and usually ask for the butterfly needle. So I may be

walking evidence that some intense fears in childhood can be managed over time with maturation and an accidental, naturally occurring exposure situation.

Fears have been the subject of study by developmental psychologists for well over a century. As a result of a large number of studies looking at several groups of children as they aged into adulthood, we know quite a bit about normal childhood fears. We know that fears in children and adolescents are common. In fact, children between six and twelve years of age may experience an average of eleven different fears, all at the same time.

My colleague Thomas Ollendick, Ph.D., a professor at Virginia Tech, has studied fears extensively in children. His work has shown that girls consistently own up to more fears than boys (with girls having upward of thirteen different fears and boys around nine) and that girls report a higher intensity of fear than boys. Whether the girls actually experience fear at a greater intensity or they're just more likely to report their fear as more intense is still in question. In this culture, boys are taught pretty early to tough it out and not express fear or anxiety, whereas girls are encouraged to be expressive. So it may well be that even in reporting their fears, neither gender quite tells the truth: boys hold back on what they are feeling and girls elaborate.

We also know that certain fears are expected at various ages. Infants are scared of strangers, preschoolers fear the dark, and early-school-age children are scared of doctors and dentists, for example. And, while having more than one fear is normal, the number of fears declines with age. So, for instance, when Mary was in kindergarten, she was terrified of small animals, the dark, and loud noises. By middle school she still didn't like small animals, but the dark and loud noises didn't faze her anymore. And by high school she actually asked her mother to buy her a hamster. From research, we also know that the focus of fear changes with age and moves from a fear of certain

WHEN DO COMMON FEARS BEGIN?

Infants/Toddlers (birth to two years): Separating from parents, sudden loud noises, strangers, water (e.g., taking a bath), large objects.

Preschoolers (three to five years): Dark, small animals; imaginary figures (like ghosts, monsters); sleeping alone; nighttime noises; costumed characters and masks; thunder and lightning.

School age (six to twelve years): Insects, snakes and other animals, injections, doctors and dentists, death and dying. Eventually children develop fears that move away from just physical pain or separation and are grounded in reality, particularly as they see things in the media like natural disasters, plane crashes, war, terrorism, and crime. Children in this age group may also show some momentary fear of homeless people, authority figures (e.g., police, principal), and people with observable illnesses or disabilities.

Adolescents (thirteen to eighteen years): Fear of rejection, embarrassment, humiliation; fear of conflict with others, negative feedback, making mistakes, taking tests; fear of the unknown in relation to one's future (e.g., getting into college, holding a job). Fears in this age often relate to more abstract ideas of inclusion, safety, happiness, and stability over the course of one's life.

things, such as costumed characters and getting shots, to fears of situations where the person may be the focus of attention or evaluation.

Anxiety: What's Everyday and What's Excessive?

Seven-year-old Phillip has always wanted to go to Chuck E. Cheese's, and he's thrilled when the invitation to a friend's party arrives. Before leaving for the party, Phillip asks, "Will there be a lot of people there?" His mom, Lanie, answers, "Probably, but stick close to me and you'll be fine," which satisfies the boy.

When they arrive, a mob of people flank the entryway, and Phillip clings to Lanie as they make their way through the crowd. He sees the room full of video games and slowly but surely leaves Lanie's side to find his friends. Lanie hangs back as Phillip surveys the room. He spots his friends and turns back to Lanie with a wave. A few minutes later the room lights dim, music begins to blare, and Chuck E. Cheese appears onstage. Phillip screams and runs to Lanie as he covers his ears. Lanie hugs her son tight, then bends down to get to eye level with Phillip. "Honey, look, it's Chuck E. Cheese—your favorite!" As she points to the stage, Phillip warily turns around and sees the character. His crying subsides and after a few seconds, with Lanie's hand in his, he begins to walk a bit closer to the stage. Within a few minutes he's close to the stage, watching the show, and his tearstained face has an ear-to-ear grin.

When the invitation gets to seven-year-old Mason's house, she doesn't want to go to Chuck E. Cheese's. "Mom, what if I can't find my friends?" Mom, Penny, tells her that she'll help her find them.

"But what if I get lost?"

"You won't get lost, I'll be with you."

"But what if you walk away?"

"I promise to stay close."

"But what if one of the moms starts talking to you and you forget about me?"

After a long-drawn-out conversation, Penny finally convinces Mason to agree to go to the party. When they arrive, Mason sees the crowd gathered around the door and refuses to go inside. "Please, let's go in, Mason," Penny begs. "I'll make sure you get extra tokens and some extra ice cream!" Mason timidly goes in the door, then, seeing the lights of the video games, clings to her mother even tighter.

Penny suggests they find Mason's friends, but Mason clutches Penny's leg so tightly she can't take a step. Suddenly the lights dim, music begins to blare, and Chuck E. Cheese appears onstage. Mason screams at the top of her lungs. Penny tries to shush her but Mason's screams only get louder by the second. Nothing Penny does settles Mason, and finally Penny scoops Mason up, puts her in the car, and collapses in the front seat in utter exhaustion. Through her tears, she backs the car out of the parking spot and out of the lot. She'll call the party host later and explain it away somehow.

So, if you're Lanie or Penny, how do you know if your son's or daughter's fears are typical? If fears naturally occur as a child develops, how do you know when yours is having a typical childhood fear that will pass in time and when the fear is problematic?

In general, we focus on four features, which are typical tip-offs that the anxiety is out of hand. Let's take a walk through each.

1. The fear reaction occurs immediately. This *spontaneity* feature tells us that your child does not need any time to think it through, she simply reacts with fear when she's confronted by the scary situation, or when she starts to think about it, or when she's made aware that it's going to happen.

   • Your daughter overhears you talking about Hawaii on the phone and immediately bursts into tears. "Why are you leaving me? Don't go!" she screams. Mind you, the conversation may be with your friend who just returned from Hawaii, but your child's mind instantly jumps to a separation from you. A typical child might sit and stew, then later come back with, "Hey, Mom, I heard you talking on the phone with someone about Hawaii. Are you going away?" The child with anxiety makes a beeline straight to *You're leaving this minute and something awful will happen when you do.*

• Your son's fifth-grade teacher calls to let you know that she assigned a book report in his class, which is due in three weeks. As soon as she gave out the assignment, your child put his head down and began to cry. He was sure he couldn't get this done in time and begged her for extra time. A typical child might be worried, and might even talk to you about it. But it would be later, after he came home and thought about it a bit. The anxious child jumps right to *I'm going to fail miserably.*

2. The intensity of the fear reaction is excessive. Your child's reaction is way out of proportion to the actual threat of the situation. That is, he's acting as if the situation will result in a major catastrophe or tremendous pain and suffering, when actually it may be just a bit uncomfortable.

• Okay, I'll own up to this one . . . a six-year-old girl should not be running out of an office, through a neighborhood, and eventually need three adults to hold her down for a booster shot. The threat of that injection and how much it actually would hurt does not warrant that level of fear. (Okay, okay! I've been apologizing to Mom and Dad for decades!)

- You're going away for the weekend to help a relative who's been ill. Your spouse will be home with the children but your twelve-year-old son is inconsolable. He's sobbing, begging you to stay, and every time you try to pack your bag, he pulls out your clothes and in a panicky state so you are torn between comforting him and having to start packing again. "What if something happens to you, Mommy? Please, please don't go! You can catch what Aunt Joanie has and you'll die!" A typical child might be upset, too, she might even cry. But she'd be asking questions like, "How long are you going to be gone?" The anxious child will be sobbing, hyperventilating, and throwing himself at your feet to hold on and keep you in place.

3. The fear is in response to an innocuous, nonthreatening situation. This is fear that comes from a very active imagination, because the situation itself is harmless.

  - While walking down the street with your five-year-old son, you spot a woman carrying a tiny dog (what we in New York City call "accessory pets"), *on the other side of the street.* Your son sees the dog, screams at the top of his lungs, and runs away to escape this tiny canine that can fit into a purse.
  - Not long after you dropped off your seven-year-old daughter at a friend's birthday party, the birthday girl's mom calls. Your daughter is hysterical and cannot be consoled after a clown arrived at the party.

4. No amount of reassurance can calm your child. Try as hard as you might, nothing settles your child. In fact, as your child has gotten older she seems even more afraid than she had been when she was younger, and no amount of practice is helping. You've tried to cajole her, comfort her, bribe her, and you're at the point where you're thinking of punishing her because you don't know what else to do. This fear is fixed, her distress is increasing, and you're losing your patience, fast. A typical child might be afraid of thunderstorms. But as it rains more and more, she's learned how to manage. The anxious child doesn't get better with experience, and, in fact, ramps up the anxiety even more with every storm.

If any of the four scenarios I describe above fits your child, you may well have problematic anxiety and fear on your hands. For example, there may be an excessive reaction that keeps happening despite your attempts at reassurance and bribes to get your child to settle and manage the fear. The majority of the children we see in our clinic show two, three, or all four of these features at once. In this book, I'm hoping we can help you to spot the signs of excessive anxiety as it starts to build, so that you might intervene early and stop it before it gets out of hand.

When Does Anxiety or Fear Become a Disorder?

I'm not sure why, but I tend to like things in fours. So in addition to the four features for determining if anxiety is typical or excessive, let's look at four other features to determine if anxiety warrants concern.

- Is she avoiding the situation the majority of the time? Does she do everything she can to elude or escape what she's afraid of? Does she hide, run away, feign being ill, and otherwise not make herself available in situations where she's afraid?

- Is the anxiety causing a disruption or interference in your child's daily life? Does it spoil activities and his ability to function in school, with peers, at home, and with taking care of himself? Is he losing ground in his class work, not making or keeping friends, losing sleep and becoming irritable, and are you always struggling with him over his anxieties?

- Is your child's distress getting the best of her? Is she shaking, crying, begging, having physical symptoms such as headaches or stomachaches, all because of the anxiety? Is your child having meltdowns that cause her to give up and for you to step in and rescue her . . . so that you're becoming really good at writing lab reports for her high school biology class and you know practically all of the kids on her Facebook page because you respond to their postings for her?

- Has this anxiety settled in and made a home in your child? That is, has the anxiety taken hold and is not getting any better with time and experience? Is your child just as frightened of going into the classroom each November morning as he was in September? We expect that children and adolescents should get more comfortable with any of the challenges they meet within a few weeks to a few months at the most. So, every time a child masters a situation, he conquers his fear and moves to the next developmental challenge.

Let's make sure we understand a very important notion: Fleeting fears are expected and should cause very little disruption in your child's life and in her ability to function. These hiccups, so to speak, are associated with specific events—sleeping in his big-boy bed, meeting new kids at the new school, going away to camp for the first time, giving an oral report for the first several times, getting gently teased by friends, the sound of thunder in the middle of the night, asking someone on a date, sticking up for oneself, going on an interview—and each of these events and others like them are normal and part of every child's life.

This is very important for you to understand: If your child sticks with it, if he stays in these situations and does them again and again, he will get used to the situation (he will what we call "habituate" to it) and the overall positive attention he receives from peers, from teachers, and from you will overshadow the momentary anxiety. Positive reinforcement from others and then the internal, self-satisfied feeling of *I can do this!* will take over so that your child becomes accustomed to the situation and fear fades away.

Bear this in mind: Allowing him to escape and avoid the situation will only serve to set the anxiety in place. Again, let me emphasize, when you allow your child to escape from or avoid an anxiety-provoking situation, you allow that anxiety to take hold and set in. Most of the situations that cause anxiety are harmless, are normal, and happen day in, day out through our lives. So he has to learn to stick with it and adjust to normal anxious arousal. Throughout this book we'll talk about how to help your child stick with the situation he's afraid of so that he can get used to and learn to effectively manage anxiety.

Fears Through the Years

When your child was younger, the pediatrician probably asked you about developmental milestones during each visit. These are a set of age-specific tasks that most children can do within a certain age range—most children will walk by eighteen months, for instance, and be potty trained between two and a half and three years. But there's something very important you need to know: Milestones don't end in early childhood with being potty trained and sleeping in a big bed. There are milestones that your child will need to reach throughout life that relate to your child's ability to reason, take initiative, act independently, and form a solid self-identity.

Doctors don't often ask about this later set of milestones, but they're just as important. These are the cognitive-social-developmental milestones, and they're critical to your child's maturation and staying in step with what is expected for success with the ever-more-challenging aspects of school, the social world, and independence in adulthood. Although every child will not reach every milestone at the exact same time, this is a good guideline of where your child should be in terms of these milestones in relation to managing anxiety.

- **Ages birth to two years:** The baby learns to recognize different states of comfort and discomfort. Comfort comes from being held, from smiling faces of others and soothing talk, from interacting with others, and from repetitive behaviors and activity ("Do it again!"). The baby stumbles on self-comfort behaviors like sucking his hands and fingers, snuggling into a favorite blanket or stuffed toy, playing with rattles and toys, and using his voice to coo, babble, and sing. Over time, these self-soothing behaviors become part of his routine to calm himself as well as put himself to sleep. In general, routines relax him. While separations may be difficult, positive interactions when his parents return help the child to learn to cope and to develop object permanence—the idea that just because something is out of sight does not mean that it is gone forever.

- **Ages three to five:** Now that he's walking and running about, the child is exploring his world more freely. And he starts to understand there are scary things that may harm him but he's not clear about what's real or not. Is there a monster under the bed? Can a burglar crawl in through the chimney? What's that noise I hear in the middle of the night!? Can the Grinch come and get me? Limits help a child learn to manage his feelings, explore his environment with safety ("No, Justin, the stove is hot!"), and interact with others in a positive way ("Let's share nicely with Matthew"). On the flip side, he also needs to develop age-appropriate independence and the ability to voice his opinions. Choices are important ("Would you like the red shirt or the blue shirt today?") and give him a sense of control over his world so he learns that he has an effect on what happens to him throughout the day. Playing make-believe games helps children distinguish between fantasy and reality ("If a cat gets stuck in a tree, who can save him? Daddy or Superman?"). Imaginary play helps the child to understand roles and the upcoming challenges of development ("Let's play school! I'll be the teacher and Mommy, you play me!" "Now, I'm going to be the daddy and I have to go to work, so you be good while I'm gone!"). Parents can use "if-then" statements to teach the child self-control, such as "If you go to sleep while we are out to dinner, then tomorrow we will bake cookies together." The child begins to understand that his behavior is linked to consequences.

- **Ages six to eleven:** Earlier fears of childhood (the dark, monsters, small animals) start to give way to concerns about world events, natural disasters, and more sophisticated ideas of what can cause harm to himself and his loved ones. These worries will dissipate with time and having been met with calm and rational thinking. Children can understand the consequences of their actions and anticipate events. "What if" questions come into play as the child is capable of greater reasoning and searching for more meaning than simple "Because I said so" statements. They are more curious and seek information from many sources. With maturing cognitive capacities, the child can also imagine more frightening scenarios ("What if a terrorist attacks our town when I'm at school and you're home?"). Teaching reasoning through Socratic questioning ("Tommy, tell me what you know about safety and who is working to keep you, your daddy, and me safe?") helps the child learn to reason with himself to understand realistic outcomes and scenarios. Your child takes over managing his friendships as he progresses through this age. He asks for play-dates and makes efforts to contact his friends outside of school. He wants to visit them at their homes and have them come to his. Sleepovers happen by third grade and many children progress from day camp to sleepaway camp. Independence is starting to become important to your child.

· **Ages twelve to eighteen:** Younger adolescents are taking on greater responsibility for managing their schoolwork and for interacting with authority figures. By seventh grade, your child is asking the teacher for help and speaking up if she thinks there's been a mistake in grading her test. By ninth grade your child is in control of his social schedule. He's telling you (or asking you) where he's going with friends and he's attending more social outings and school activities. She negotiates a curfew with you, and over time you'll give more privileges as your daughter demonstrates responsibility and good choices. Adolescents can answer their own "what if" questions with more clarity and rationality, and are able to think more hypothetically than in earlier childhood. Their ability to think abstractly allows them greater understanding of concepts such as trust, democracy, faith, and beliefs. And yet, adolescents are self-centered and those with anxiety may fall prey to *Yet, I might be the one kid who is attacked in my home if Mom is out.* This contrasts with the typically developing teen, who believes *I'm invincible* and that nothing could go wrong for her. Social activity and friendships become paramount, so peer acceptance and inclusion warrants social skill development and the ability to make and keep friendships. There is greater reliance on the self for problem solving, self-soothing, managing emotional issues, and making choices related to academic and career goals. Adolescents crave independence and often prefer time alone, away from the scrutiny of family members. Tasks such as scheduling and keeping routine medical appointments, negotiating with others (e.g., teachers, employers), and managing one's own schedule assist with preparing for the self-reliance needed in college and the transition to adulthood. In fact, you might go with your daughter on one or two college visits, but she takes up several schools' offers of staying in a dorm and doing some visits on her own, something that most colleges make available for the prospective student. The formation of positive romantic relationships is linked to self-identity and self-esteem, and the not unexpected breakups of adolescent romantic relationships help the teen to learn to manage her emotional upheavals.

Could It Be Something Else?

You may be thinking at this point that your child has a problem with anxiety. Before we go any further, I want to discuss some other disorders that can be confused with anxiety. In fact, these other conditions may mimic anxiety, or anxiety may mimic these other conditions. In other words, your child could have something that looks like anxiety, but in reality it is something very different. And the opposite is true as well—your child could be anxious, but his symptoms are making it look like he has something else. Your child can also have more than one condition at a time (called comorbidity), so he could have anxiety along with one—or more—of these conditions. Let's take a look at some of the common conditions that share symptoms with anxiety.

Attention-Deficit/Hyperactivity Disorder

All children occasionally have difficulty sitting still, paying attention, or controlling impulsive behavior. But for children with attention-deficit/hyperactivity disorder (ADHD), the problem is so severe that it interferes with their daily lives at home, at school, and with friends. When considering whether your child has ADHD, we ask parents to think about whether the behavior is *much, much, much more pronounced than the typical child* would exhibit and whether it occurs not just at home, but also at school and in other settings.

Anxious children can appear impulsive. If, for instance, your child has a specific phobia and there's a spider crawling on the sidewalk, he may run into the road without looking. An anxious child may interrupt your conversation again and again because he needs reassurance about something he's nervous about. However, children with ADHD will display certain behaviors at all times and not just when facing an anxiety-provoking situation.

QUIZ: COULD IT BE ADHD?

When going through this list of behaviors common to children with ADHD, think about whether your child is very, very much different from other children. Answer yes or no.

- Always seems to be losing or misplacing things.

- Has trouble concentrating on schoolwork and tasks you give him, but can play a video game for hours.

- Always seems to be distracted by any little sound coming from any little place.

- Loses his place when reading or forgets what he's doing.

- Has a lot of trouble listening to conversations and goes off on his own tangents.

- Makes many little mistakes in schoolwork and tasks at home that you have to constantly point out.

- Jumps on every piece of furniture you own.

- Has trouble sitting still in class and is always out of his seat.

- Has trouble playing quietly or sitting alone calmly.

- Starts one thing but then moves on to another without finishing the first, or the second, or the third thing.

- Upsets his friends because he doesn't wait his turn in games and at play.

- Talks constantly and can't seem to stop talking to listen!

- Interrupts conversations, despite your telling him again and again not to do this.

- Answers questions before you can even finish a sentence.

- Eats his meals at home standing up.

If your answers were mostly yes, consult a psychologist or developmental pediatrician about testing for ADHD. Anxiety and ADHD can go together, and often do, but the ADHD will necessitate a separate approach to help your child manage the challenges of organization and self-control that come with ADHD.

Sensory Processing Disorder (SPD)

Children with SPD (formerly known as sensory integration dysfunction, or SID) misinterpret information coming in from the five senses. For hyposensitive, or low sensory children, the senses don't register as much as they should—an elbow banging into the wall feels more like the brush of a feather. Hypersensitive children are high sensory, registering more sensation than what is really coming in, so even the seams of their socks can trouble them endlessly.

When the brain doesn't properly integrate the onslaught of information coming in through the senses, it can cause anxiety and behavior problems. A child with SPD might shy away from a group of friends, which could look like social anxiety, when in reality it's because she doesn't want to get bumped in the crowd. A boy with SPD could throw a tantrum about his shirt being on the wrong way, which could look like obsessive-compulsive disorder (OCD), but in reality the shirt's tag is bothering him. SPD affects motor planning, so children are often clumsy, fidgety, and unable to sit still not because they're nervous but because they're trying to get the sensory input they're lacking.

QUIZ: COULD IT BE SENSORY PROCESSING DISORDER?

Answer yes or no to the following questions.

- Does your child become anxious when he is touched lightly or without warning? Does your child avoid standing near other people? Yes/No

- Does your child throw a tantrum or get very upset at the sound of a vacuum cleaner, the toilet flushing, or other common noises? Yes/No

- Does your child either overreact or underreact to cuts, scrapes, and bumps? Yes/No

- Does your child either avoid or seek out being on playground equipment like slides, swings, or merry-go-rounds? Yes/No

- Does your child chew on pens or his sleeve? Yes/No

- Does your child seem too distracted or generally unaware of background noise? Yes/No

- Is it difficult for your child to be in crowded places and he covers his ears when you take him places? Yes/No

- Does your child have extreme food preferences or aversions? Yes/No

If you answered yes to more than two of these questions, your child could have an issue with sensory processing. This is a highly difficult condition to accurately diagnose, as it could be part of several different clinical syndromes or developmental problems. So it's best to start with a pediatric neurologist or a child neuropsychologist for a complete and accurate evaluation. Treatment usually involves sessions with an occupational therapist who, using activities and games (from shaving cream to swings), will help the child adapt to and accept the various sensory stimuli that we encounter (and for the most part don't even notice) throughout the twenty-four-hour day.

Depression

Everyone has bad days. As I often explain to parents, depression isn't a simple moodiness that you chalk up to being a teenager or to an event such as the death of a beloved pet. Depression is an unrelenting sadness or heaviness that simply will not lift. When most people think of depression they imagine someone lying in bed, listless, crying, unable to go anywhere. While it's true that depression often looks this way in adults, in children and teenagers it usually takes the form of irritability and being easily frustrated. Other symptoms of depression include dramatic changes in appetite and sleep habits, a decline in their grades and interest in social activities, and the loss of interest in things that would normally bring them pleasure.

Children who are depressed lose interest in almost everything they cherished before—friends, school, sports, hobbies. While children with anxiety may be afraid to participate in these areas and do their best to avoid them, they are still interested and will complain about not being comfortable enough to join in. And they will find other things to do instead of what they are afraid of. The child or teen with depression, however, gives up doing things and doesn't replace the activity with something else. Instead he withdraws from you and all social contact. Older children may lose themselves for hours at a time in video games or their computer, while younger children may be clingy and regress to early and immature behavior.

Depression is less common in younger children, more common among adolescents, but we do see it starting in children who are very young. A family history of depression, some very unsettling family or living circumstances, and having a parent with depression are all risk factors for depression in youth.

QUIZ: IS IT DEPRESSION OR ANXIETY?

1. Does your child shy away from activities because
   a. he seems afraid to join in?
   b. he seems too sad or lacks the energy to join in?

2. Does your child seem irritable
   a. some of the time?
   b. most of the time?

3. Does your child lose sleep
   a. because his mind is filled with anxious thoughts?
   b. for no apparent reason?

4. Does your child's anger or irritability seem unprovoked?
   a. no
   b. yes

5. Does your child have a change in appetite
   a. due to specific circumstances (e.g., he has a test coming up)?
   b. for no apparent reason?

6. Does your child have concentration issues in school, to the point where it affects his grades *and* he doesn't really seem to care?
   a. no
   b. yes

7. Does your child tell you that his life is not worth living or that he wishes he had never been born?
   a. no
   b. yes

If your answers were mostly A, your child's symptoms are more likely due to anxiety. If your answers were mostly B, your child's symptoms could be due to depression. But again, these two syndromes tend to occur together and much research evidence suggests that anxiety usually starts first and may lead to depression, at which point they are co-occurring and doubly disabling your child. Depression is a serious issue by itself and should be taken as such. I would caution you that depression is not just a phase and not something you will be able to handle on your own. Please check with a child psychiatrist or a clinical child and adolescent psychologist if you think your child is depressed.

SO, now you've gotten a sense of what's typical and what may be troubling conduct that needs attention. As I said earlier, if you've picked up this book, my guess is that you think your child's behavior is not just a passing phase, but something he's been experiencing for a while now, and nothing you've tried to do so far has helped. In the next few chapters I'm going to introduce you to a type of therapy and a basic attack strategy that will help you manage your child's anxiety. I'm also going to explain the three most common types of anxiety disorders—what they are, how to spot them in your child, and how they may have developed. And I'll give you detailed advice on how you can deal with each type of disorder so you all can start living healthier lives.

There's something I want to lay out for you right here, right now. I say this to all the parents and children who come to my clinic who are suffering with anxiety. Whether your child is seven or seventeen, it's not too early and it's not too late to make a difference for them. Whether your child has one anxiety, two different types of anxieties, or more than you wish to count, it's never too much to overcome. Through the steps in this book, we will figure out ways to cope with your child's concerns and give him skills and strategies that will both relieve his anxiety and help him to feel better about himself.

Anxiety is a normal, basic emotion that every child—and every adult—has throughout their lives. As I wrote in chapter 1, anxiety helps to motivate you to pay the bills on time and your child to look both ways before crossing the street. Your child needs anxiety; we all do. However, if your child happens to have too much of it, it's caused a lot of upset. Fortunately, researchers have learned a lot about how to corral that anxiety and shrink it down to a reasonable and helpful level. We're going to use what researchers have learned to put your child back in control of the anxiety, so that she makes choices based on what she *wants* to do, and not what she is *afraid* to do.

As I have done with hundreds of children in my office, I'll lay out the basics of how to manage anxiety and cope with situations that stop your child in his tracks. Anxiety is treatable and we'll go through the different options to help turn your child around and open him up to a full and happy life. And, in the process, we'll examine some of the ways that anxiety has made its way into your home and caused you to experience frustration and upset. We'll work on some strategies for soothing yourself and how you can disengage from the anxiety trap!

3

Why Cognitive Behavioral Therapy Is Best

Through my training and development as a clinical psychologist, I became convinced early on that I wanted to align with a system of therapy that

- was grounded in principles that make sense to the patient;
- produced observable, measurable change;
- was subject to testing that proves it works.

And so I embraced training in cognitive behavioral therapy, or CBT. Unlike traditional therapy, where the patient does most of the talking, CBT is interactive and collaborative. The child, parents, and therapist are all involved and the therapy focuses on teaching the child skills to take control of his anxieties as well as to develop healthy, coping-focused attitudes and behaviors. In addition, the CBT therapist will help you adjust your parenting approach so that you can help your child to cope, rather than continue the cycle of anxiety (and lose patience and compassion in the process).

Often when you see people in therapy in movies or on television, you see a client lying prone on a couch, narrating stories about their past, their conflicts with their parents (usually their mother), trying to connect with their deepest, darkest feelings. The therapist sits off to the side, clipboard in hand, raising an eyebrow here and there, asking questions such as "How did you feel about that?" and "Tell me more."

In my opinion, that type of long-term talk therapy isn't the way to go for children with anxiety problems. It does not define reasonable, visible goals, give an explanation of the therapy process, or provide an expected time frame for when goals should be achieved. While there certainly are reasons for long-term therapy, and I myself do have long-term patients, we need to tread very lightly when it comes to children and adolescents. Their formative years should not be spent in unstructured therapies that neither they nor their parents understand a whit about.

A History Lesson

Let's go back in time a bit so I can show you how CBT came about. It began to take root in the 1920s with Mary Cover Jones, an aspiring psychologist who was conducting her dissertation project. At that time, John B. Watson, Ph.D., the founder of behaviorism, had already established that emotional responses, including fear, could be conditioned in children. In his famous experiment, a young child named Albert, who had no fear of animals, was taught to be scared of them when researchers paired the animals with unpleasant stimuli (loud noises).

So, if fear could be conditioned, could it be deconditioned as well, Cover Jones wondered? To that end, she took very young children who were afraid of animals and paired them with pleasant stimuli (food). Slowly but surely, she was able to move the children closer and closer to the animals, proving that positive reinforcement could help teach a child to remain calm and overcome fear.

The work of Mary Cover Jones laid the foundation for the treatment of anxiety and fears, but it wasn't until the 1950s that Joseph Wolpe, M.D., developed a method called "systematic desensitization," which outlined a clinical approach and strategy for treating patients with phobias and anxiety. Dr. Wolpe reasoned that if a person was in a relaxed state, she could not at the same time be afraid of something. Therefore, he first outlined the idea of breaking down a feared situation into a series of steps, starting with the least fearful aspects of the situation and moving up to the more overwhelming fear.

So, for example, thinking about flying on a plane produces some fear, and visiting an airport is a bit more fearful, purchasing a ticket ups the ante, and waiting to board a plane is worse, followed by getting on the plane, buckling in, and . . . taking off! By having the patient with flying phobia first get into a totally relaxed state by doing deep breathing and guiding the patient to think of the most relaxing scene that calms her mind, Dr. Wolpe then would begin talking about the idea of taking a trip. The patient would listen and would signal when she began to feel anxiety by raising her hand, at which point Dr. Wolpe switched back to talking about being relaxed and calm.

Back and forth they would go, from imagining the feared step (thinking about a trip) and the relaxing scene (for example, lying on a beach) until that step no longer caused any fear. At that point, the next step was tackled in the same way, switching back and forth between visiting an airport and lying on the beach. This was repeated until the patient reported minimal fear all the way to the top of the hierarchy (staircase). Dr. Wolpe extended this procedure from using the imagination to "in vivo" desensitization, where patients practiced the relaxation while entering the feared situation in a step-by-step way, and this proved to be effective and formed the basis of the procedures we now use, called "in vivo exposure" to feared situations. And so, the field of clinical behavioral therapy was born with Dr. Wolpe's work, and literally thousands upon thousands of studies were conducted to perfect these methods with the range of types of anxiety and also for different populations, from children to adolescents, to older adults.

Later, in the early 1990s, my good friend and colleague Philip C. Kendall, Ph.D., from Temple University, developed and tested a comprehensive approach for anxious children in two large, randomly controlled clinical studies of children. His work was among the first to be funded by the National Institute of Mental Health (NIMH), focused on treating separation anxiety, social anxiety, and generalized anxiety disorders in children seven to twelve years of age. Using the image of a "Scaredy-Cat" who learns the skills of CBT and develops into a brave "Coping Cat," the resulting guide, entitled *Coping Cat,* became the first step-by-step treatment manual for anxiety in children, involving some sixteen sessions that brought together the key components of CBT.

In his initial studies, Dr. Kendall found that children and their parents reported significant improvement coping with anxiety using the Coping Cat method. In addition, clinical staff called "raters" who did not know whether the children had received treatment or not (called "blind raters") interviewed the children and parents and found that the children's behavior improved and anxiety decreased as compared to the non-treated children.

Dr. Kendall's group continued to follow these children over time and found that for most of the children who received the CBT, the improvements made during the treatment study continued to remain seven to ten years later. The Kendall studies ushered in a whole range of studies of CBT for anxiety in youth, which consistently found that treatment was effective for the majority of children. The methods put together by Dr. Kendall were adapted and extended for adolescents and for group and family therapy, and even caught on in many different cultures and countries (e.g., Canada has the "Coping Bear" and in Australia there's the "Coping Koala"). Other investigators, including yours truly, then developed their own CBT programs for the triad of separation anxiety disorder (SAD), social anxiety, and generalized anxiety disorder (GAD), and other types of anxiety disorders we haven't gone into detail about in this book, such as obsessive-compulsive disorder (OCD), panic disorder, post-traumatic stress disorder (PTSD), and the specific phobias.

Precise Proof

I will go into far more detail about medication to treat anxiety in a later chapter, but for purposes of this chapter, I'm going to touch on medication briefly in the context of the research comparing it to CBT therapy, and how well it works in conjunction with CBT.

Around the same time as Dr. Kendall's work was catching on, a new class of antidepressants emerged that had a better safety record and fewer side effects for treating adults with anxiety. Clinical trials found that the selective serotonin reuptake inhibitors (SSRIs), including fluoxetine (Prozac), fluvoxamine (Luvox), and sertraline (Zoloft), were effective in treating a number of anxiety disorders in adults. Then, after the Food and Drug Administration (FDA) approved the use of these medications for adults, doctors began to prescribe them for children. In 1997 the FDA gave the pharmaceutical companies an incentive to conduct controlled clinical trials of medications in children by extending the length of the pharmaceutical company's market exclusivity by six months for any already patented medication or one under development.

You see, when a drug company develops a new drug for a condition, they have a limited number of years of being the sole company to market and sell the drug. After that time, the patent expires and other companies are allowed to develop generic and alternate forms of the medication. It's only when a company holds the sole patent that they stand to gain much from the sale of the drug. So simply conducting clinical trials in children and adolescents allowed companies to keep exclusive control over the production and sale of certain medications for an extra six months.

Studies continued to evaluate how well these medications worked (known as "efficacy") compared to a placebo for children with social phobia, GAD, OCD, and SAD. One specific study, sponsored by a division of the NIMH called the Research Units in Pediatric Psychopharmacology, is considered a landmark in the treatment of the triad of SAD, social phobia, and GAD. Led by Daniel Pine, M.D. (who is at the NIMH), and a team of child psychiatrists and psychologists, the RUPP study found that after eight weeks of treatment, fluvoxamine (Luvox) was significantly better than a placebo in reducing the symptoms of separation, social, and generalized anxiety disorders in children and adolescents ages seven to seventeen years.

And so, by the year 2001, we knew that CBT was an effective psychotherapy for children and adolescents with anxiety, and that the SSRIs were also effective in treating these disorders. But key questions remained unanswered. Which is better, CBT or medication? And how about both? Are children who receive CBT plus a medication better off than those who receive just one form of treatment at a time or no treatment at all?

With these questions in mind, the NIMH sponsored the Child/Adolescent Anxiety Multimodal Study (CAMS), a six-year clinical trial conducted at six sites across the country. This study brought together leading clinical investigators studying the treatment of childhood anxiety: Dr. Kendall; John March, M.D., from Duke; John Piacentini, Ph.D., at UCLA; John Walkup, M.D., from Johns Hopkins; Boris Birmaher, M.D., from Western Psychiatric Institute and Clinic; and me, Anne Marie Albano, Ph.D., at Columbia University. With our colleague Joel Sherrill, Ph.D., at the NIMH, and our co-collaborators at our sites, we enrolled 488 children and adolescents ages seven to seventeen in a randomized controlled trial. The study was designed to answer some very important questions:

- Are CBT and medication safe and effective treatments for childhood anxiety disorders?
- Does the combination of CBT and medication offer greater benefit to youth suffering from anxiety than either treatment alone?

After twelve weeks of treatment, we found that among the participants receiving combination treatment, an astonishing 81 percent were significantly improved, and this treatment approach was superior to CBT alone, medication alone, or a placebo. That is, these children did much, much better than those who received only one kind of treatment and those receiving the placebo.

Good news, right? This shows us that the combination of treatments gives a child a very high chance of recovering from anxiety. And there's more good news. Sixty percent of the children who received CBT alone and 55 percent of those who received medication alone also were significantly better at week 12 as compared with the placebo. So there's not one, not two, but three effective options:

1. CBT
2. Medication
3. A combination of both

We also found that over the longer term, the children who had received the active treatments continued to do well six months later with monthly visits to their providers.

All this being said, I want to be crystal clear about one thing: Start with CBT alone. If you catch the anxiety early enough and get

CLINICAL TRIALS: A PRIMER

A randomized controlled trial (RCT): The RCT is the most well established procedure for testing the effectiveness of a treatment. After going through an evaluation process to determine eligibility, participants are randomly assigned to the active treatment condition (the experimental condition) or a control group (placebo or an accepted therapy). Similar to tossing a coin, participants have an equal chance of being assigned to conditions, thus preventing bias toward one treatment over another.

Blind study: The participants do not know whether they're taking medication or a placebo. In a double-blind study, neither the participants nor the treatment providers know if the treatment is a placebo.

Blind, independent evaluators: Trained expert evaluators who assess the individuals in the study and are kept blind to treatment condition by the study investigators.

to a quality CBT therapist if needed, your child should do well without medication. In chapter 12 I'll talk about when and why you might consider medication for children who are not responding to CBT only. But, and I can't make this clear enough, start with CBT alone.

The CAMS study was a double-blind, randomized control study where participants were assessed by independent, blind evaluators. While not perfect, we strove as best as we could get in scientific rigor while addressing these most common and debilitating anxiety conditions in children.

CBT: The Basic Principles

Now that I've shown you the evidence that CBT is helpful, let me explain in a bit more detail what it is.

Education: Knowledge is power, and CBT will teach your child about anxiety: what it is, where it comes from, how it keeps on happening. He will also learn how to identify what sets off his anxiety and how he reacts to these triggers. And your child will learn how each component of CBT is designed to provide new skills to manage the anxiety and become more and more competent and confident in approaching things that formerly paralyzed him.

Body awareness and management: Body awareness teaches the child to recognize the physical sensations and revving up associated with anxiety. Once he recognizes the feelings, CBT teaches the child age-appropriate relaxation techniques, such as deep breathing and progressive relaxation, to help counteract the escalating anxiety in the body.

Cognitive restructuring: The child learns how to pinpoint the negative, anxiety-provoking thoughts, images, and ideas that fuel his anxiety and avoidance, and to replace them with more realistic and coping-focused thinking. In other words, your child becomes armed with a plan to attack the anxiety, manage the situation, and rationally think through how to stick with each step of the way.

Exposure: You and your child will then put his newfound anxiety-coping skills into practice while gradually facing anxiety-provoking situations, using a procedure called "exposure," which involves exposing the child to feared situations in a step-by-step, gradual manner.

CBT is based on the idea that an individual is always interacting with the environment—with other people, in various situations, and with different things (dogs, taking tests, costume characters, the dark, staying with a sitter, etc.)—and that there's a back-and-forth interaction between the person and environment.

As your child gains experience, develops, and matures, his thoughts are shaped by these interactions—he may experience certain emotions in a situation that then become associated with that event. For example, if your child raises his hand in class and gives the wrong answer, children in the class may laugh, which could lead to his feeling embarrassed. Or, the teacher could respond with a gentle "That's not quite right, Billy, but good try," which may result in his feeling encouraged. Or perhaps the teacher gives hardly any attention at all to his wrong answer, simply saying, "Not quite. Who else thinks they know this?" and moving on, which results in Billy feeling neutral.

Over time, your child amasses dozens of these types of experiences and thus connects certain feelings with different situations, all of which then shape the way he thinks and feels and what he does next. In other words, if he worries that children will continue to chuckle at him in class, he may start thinking that raising his hand is only going to lead to humiliation. Then he'll begin to doubt his abilities, feel anxious inside, and not raise his hand anymore. He may even give up trying to do homework or to study altogether. This vicious cycle of thinking that bad things will happen in class (getting laughed at), feeling physically uncomfortable during school situations (stomach butterflies), and behaving in ways that avoid the situations (hides behind the child in front of him, doesn't look at the teacher, asks you if he can stay at home) starts to set in and only works to increase his anxiety.

I've oversimplified this because there are many, many influences on your child's thoughts, feelings, and behaviors. As we discussed in chapter 1, some are inborn and not readily identified and others come at him throughout the course of the day from many different avenues. The point is that from the start of a person's life, interacting with others and in situations sets up a process of learning to think, feel, and behave that can either work well or lead to difficulties. CBT addresses each of these separate components—the thoughts, feelings, and behaviors that are problematic for your child—and teaches him how to overcome the negative and focus on coping and adapting in more proactive ways.

CBT teaches skills to help the child learn to change the patterns of thinking, feeling, and behaving that keep her stuck in a spiral of fear and avoidance. By helping children become aware of their negative thinking, CBT allows them to look at challenging situations more realistically and, in turn, to respond to them more productively.

A key goal for CBT is to help the child learn how to tell the difference between real threats and ones that exist only in the child's mind. As a child avoids or escapes from situations that cause anxiety, she misses out on the chance to be in the situation and cope—and to find out exactly how scary or threatening the situation really is.

Think of it this way: Your child runs into your room every night because she's afraid of sleeping alone. "There may be something in my room that will get me!" or "What if I don't wake up in the morning?" Each time she is allowed to stay in your bed, she misses out on the chance to learn that her room is safe, nothing will hurt her, and she will wake up morning after morning just fine.

Instead of avoiding the situation that scares her, your child must gradually learn to stay in her room, which is the only way she's going to see for herself that sleeping there isn't dangerous at all. You play a crucial role in the success of therapy by rewarding your child's coping efforts, no matter how small they may seem to you, and not reinforcing any attempts to avoid the situation.

Remember how I told you that I had a fear of injections that amounted to a phobia when I was a child? Later, when I was seventeen and a senior in high school, I found myself in a situation where I could not run from the doctor anymore. Out of the blue, I had a fainting spell in school. At the time I was dating a classmate whose father just happened to be a family practitioner. My mom, knowing I would not go willingly to a doctor, conspired with my boyfriend and tricked me into going to his dad's office "to run an errand," at which point Dr. Froelich greeted me with, "Hello, Anne Marie, I understand you had a bit of a fainting spell. This was probably because of the Florida heat, but let's take a look at you."

I was frozen with fear, but if I ran out of his office, I would look like a fool! And so with trepidation I submitted to an exam, and then a blood test. I felt total panic, but I had to control it and just sit and let it happen.

Dr. Froelich spoke gently as he tied my arm with the tourniquet and inserted the needle. And then his secretary came in and said, "Dr. Froelich, you have an emergency call!" And so, with the needle in my arm, Dr. Froelich took the call! It felt like an hour, though I'm sure it was only a minute or two.

And something happened while I was sitting there. I began to relax. I did more than simply survive. I didn't run away, my arm didn't stiffen up, and I was fine. Without even realizing it, I had engaged in my first "therapeutic exposure," not as a therapist, but as a patient.

It would be several years before I was a psychology student and learned about this somewhat new process of treating anxiety and fear through behavior therapy, but Dr. Froelich was responsible for showing me how anxiety could be effectively treated and I was better for it. I still get a bit of anxiety when I have to get a shot, but I never again had the extreme fear, nor did I avoid again. I learned that exposure was the key and I will always have Dr. Froelich (and my mom and then-boyfriend) to thank for that.

Questions and Answers with Anne Marie

Q: My child seems anxious, but not to the point of having a disorder. Can CBT help my child?

A: The principles that guide CBT most certainly can. For example, paying attention and praising him when he's handling a difficult situation will make it more likely that he'll handle it well again. At the same time, dialing down your attempts to talk him out of anxiety and removing any attention that's given to his complaints will make these behaviors less likely to occur. Teaching your child to label his feelings and speak calmly about his concerns, and walking him through the steps to problem solving, are skills that will serve him well over the long term.

Q: I don't want to take my child to a therapist. Can I do these exercises on my own?

A: Possibly. Your child is better served by a therapist if his anxiety is moderate to extreme and he's suffering too much. Also, sometimes parents are not able to turn their child around because they're too close to the situation and bring their own biases into the mix. The therapist can look at the whole situation objectively and offer you and your child guidance in how to move forward and succeed.

Q: I have anxiety myself. Am I really the best person to help my child deal with her anxiety?

A: This is an honest and heartfelt question that I get from many parents. The short answer is that we need to understand how much anxiety you have and whether it gets in the way of your parenting. We then can figure out how best to coach you to help your child to overcome her anxiety. To help decide, ask yourself a few questions:

When I see my child struggling, do I feel panicky and think *I have to get him out of that uncomfortable situation?*

Am I often telling myself, *She'll grow out of this, I did, it's just a stage that will pass with time?*

Do I find myself making excuses for my child, because I know *exactly* how he feels?

If you answered yes to any of these questions, you are likely parenting based on your feelings and your history. Rather than filter this through the thinking, *Well, I did okay* or *I know how bad that can be*, you should try to focus on how things could be better for your child.

Q: My child is only four, but he seems to have major anxieties already. Is CBT the right type of therapy for him?

A: Absolutely. In fact, CBT is the only type of therapy for him. At this early age, do not start with medication, and don't go to an unfocused and open-ended talk therapy. Let me say this again: CBT is *the* therapy for anxiety in children and adolescents. Early childhood is the right time to get on top of these problems. You'll be able to learn age-appropriate strategies that you'll then be able to teach your child to help manage his fears and worries.

My colleagues Jonathan Comer, Ph.D., and Anthony Puliafico, Ph.D., with our colleagues at Columbia University and Boston University, have created a program called the CALM program (coaching approach behavior and leading through modeling), for children ages three to seven years, to address separation, fear, and worry. This program is based on the Parent-Child Interaction Therapy approach developed by Sheila Eyberg, Ph.D., and Cheryl McNeil, Ph.D., for young children with disruptive behavior disorders. In both programs, the therapist coaches you, the parent, in specific ways to reinforce your child and promote bravery and coping.

For example, let's say we have a child who is plagued with separation anxiety. The parent and child are told that when they hear a bell, the parent is going to walk out of the room for five minutes. The bell rings, and the parent begins to walk out. While observing through closed-circuit television, the therapist tells the parent through a Bluetooth headset, "Don't hug your child, even if he cries. Say simply, 'I'm going now and I'll be back in five minutes.'" If the child begins to cry, the therapist tells the parent, "Just ignore the crying and come outside quickly."

Hugging the child will reinforce the tears. Displaying confidence in leaving will convey to the child, "I know you can handle this!" This therapy helps parents, usually within twelve one-hour sessions, to change the struggles and negative behaviors that have been set up by anxiety and avoidance, and to foster healthy coping in their children.

Q: My child is fifteen and has had anxiety all his life. Nothing's helped so far. Is it hopeless?

A: Far from it. My favorite age group to work with is teenagers, because seeing them blossom as they confront long-term fears and watching their worlds open up to new experiences and emotional growth is the absolute best feeling for me, ever! Teenagers take to CBT very well, as it appeals to their maturing reasoning abilities, and each step provides them with more and more confidence and hope for a brighter future.

ONE OF THE IMPORTANT THINGS for you to learn is how to let go and allow your teenager to stumble, mess up, try again and again, and handle things as much on his own as possible. Much like our early childhood approach, you can coach your teen. But the goal is to help him find his own solutions, try them out, evaluate how things worked, and try again.

My advice to parents of teenagers is: Listen. Ask them about what they think, how they feel, and what they want to do. Pay attention to what they say and don't tell them how to think, feel, or behave. Ask questions to guide them and do not judge them. When you make it a habit of doing that, they'll come back to you for guidance and feel empowered by your permission to try for themselves, rather than feel embarrassed about their missteps.

I've now given you an in-depth understanding about what CBT is and why I believe in it so strongly. With CBT, your child will learn specific skills that will help her for the long term, you will be involved in setting goals and monitoring her progress, and, most important, your child will become empowered with understanding anxiety and how to manage it effectively as she takes on challenging situations. In the next chapter I will give you a step-by-step program on how you can use CBT to help your child manage her anxiety, regardless of what kind of anxiety it is.

4

Annihilate the Anxiety: Your Plan of Attack

Now that you've learned about cognitive behavioral therapy, which can help stop anxiety in its tracks, I'm going to give you a blueprint on how you're going to use it. And even though you may not have every detail about your child's specific anxiety, you can still start to execute the plan as soon as you read it.

All the advice in this chapter, and in the chapters that follow, comes from the fundamentals I've learned working in cognitive behavioral therapy (CBT) for the past twenty-five years. The techniques that I will show you here work for all the types of anxiety—separation anxiety, generalized anxiety, and social anxiety (all of which I will go into in more detail during the next few chapters), as well as for specific phobias and the less common types of anxiety, like obsessive-compulsive disorder (OCD) and panic disorder.

This blueprint will familiarize you with the steps and methods we use to teach children how to overcome their anxieties. You don't need to know right now which type of anxiety your child has in order to understand the blueprint. Later, when you've determined which type of anxiety your child has, you can plug in specific strategies to meet your child's needs, and I'll give you some examples for each type of anxiety.

This chapter and the chapters that follow will show you a step-by-step CBT action plan that you can use with your child to help her cope with her anxiety. While some children will need the help of a professional (and I'll talk more about that in chapter 11), many children can be helped with some simple strategies you can use with her yourself. Also, if you decide that going to a professional therapist with your child is the best option, you can use these techniques in conjunction with and through the guidance of the therapist, to match what the therapist is doing in the office.

In this chapter I'm going to give you the basic script. Then, in the chapters to come, I'll help you figure out which type of anxiety (or anxieties) your child suffers from, and I'll tailor your script to match the anxiety.

What to Expect

By its nature, excessive anxiety stalls a child's development by holding him back from doing the things children do. At the same time, anxiety has been working on you as well. You've been limiting your expectations for what your child can and should be doing for himself. Anxiety creates a vicious cycle: Your child shies away from a challenge, you step in and take over, and then you both develop the expectation that he can't handle the normal, everyday stuff of life that children are supposed to learn to handle.

So, up until now you've probably asked very little of your child. That's going to change, as we help teach your child the coping mechanisms she's never been taught before. From this day forward, I want you to have the same expectations for your child as you would of any other child. You should expect her to go to birthday parties, talk to adults, sleep though the night in her own bed. However, all these new expectations won't be fulfilled overnight, and your child may feel overwhelmed by what you're now asking of her. You can help by breaking down big hurdles into smaller, manageable steps that your child can pull off. For example, she can go to a party, but you agree that as long as she's talking to others, you'll stay with her for the first half hour. You'll tuck her in and stay near her bed for ten minutes, but then you'll leave and she'll spend the rest of the night in her room alone. Every time she takes charge of something that's difficult for her, she'll become more and more confident that she can handle the next challenge.

Help Your Child Cope with Worry

As I've explained in chapter 3, CBT is a proven treatment for anxiety disorders that is based on well-established principles. In actuality, these principles underlie the strategies used by effective parents, teachers, supervisors, bosses, and professors—even by well-run communities and societies. The basis of CBT is to teach your child to retrain how he thinks about a situation. Instead of sounding alarm bells in every instance, sending his body into a tailspin and running away, your child will look at what's truly in front of him and be able to behave appropriately.

Up until now, your first line of defense against worry has probably been to reassure your child that there's nothing to worry about. How's that been working for you? I'm going to bet you're thinking,

Not so well, and I'll tell you why. Reassuring your child may help in the short term, but in the long term it only backfires. When you give your child comfort again and again, it becomes the only way he knows to make himself feel better. So instead of finding it within himself, the only way he can calm down is to come to you. Again. And again. Even if you tell him there's nothing to worry about, that's not in his thought processes. His first response is to feel the fear. Essentially, his brain is tricking him into thinking that a normal, not-so-scary situation is something he should be nervous about, and he doesn't know what to do with those feelings.

You know that proverb: Give a man a fish and you feed him for a day; teach a man to fish and you feed him for a lifetime. In this book I'm going to help you teach your child how to fish. So instead of telling your child again and again that there's nothing to worry about, I'm going to help you to help her see the world more realistically, so she can dial down the worry all by herself.

Right now she's relying on her own crossed wires to tell her what to feel. And because of her psychological makeup, she's always on the lookout for proof to back up her worry beliefs. She's gotten very good at spinning her worry wheels, or constantly setting off her fight-or-flight response, which only serves to green-light her worry even more.

Her first instinct is to shrink from the source of the fear. And you, as a parent, will be tempted to help her retreat. But instead, what you must do is help her feel the fear and go toward it anyway. Once she sees that there's nothing to fear but fear itself—excuse the cliché—she'll build on her successes.

Cognitive Behavioral Therapy in Action

Let's begin with this notion: CBT is based on the idea that our emotions have three separate components: the cognitive (what you think), the somatic (what your body feels), and the behavioral (what you do). For instance:

Lauren gets an A on a test and is happy.

> *What she thinks:* I did great on this! I'm proud of myself!
> *What she feels:* Increased heart rate, warm all over
> *What she does:* Smiles, shows her test to her friend, runs home after school to show her mom

Matthew goes outside to ride his bike but finds it's been stolen and he is angry.

> *What he thinks:* Who took my bike? Mom is going to be so mad at me for leaving it here! I'm going to have to pay for a new one!
> *What he feels:* Muscle tension, stomach upset, racing heart, shallow breaths, flushing in his face
> *What he does:* Clenches his fists, kicks a wall, grunts and yells, finds his mother and stammers as he tries to explain what happened

Ashley sees her mother packing to send her to summer camp in the morning. She is nervous and scared about going away.

> *What she thinks:* I'm not going to know anyone! I'm going to miss my mom and dad. What if the counselors don't like me?

What she feels: Butterflies in her stomach, shaking through her body

What she does: Begs her mom to let her stay home, cries, attempts to take the clothes out of the duffel bag

CBT focuses on the interaction of these thoughts, feelings, and behaviors, and how they each influence the others in sometimes helpful and sometimes not-so-helpful ways. Any one of these can start an anxiety cycle—a thought (I'm going to camp in the morning), a feeling (butterflies in the stomach), or a behavior (helping her mom to pack the duffel). No matter how the cycle starts, the three components shape how the child thinks, feels, and behaves.

The Anxiety Cycle

These mechanisms can rev up an emotion and make it more intense, or they can wind down to make it more calm and grounded. A child with anxiety tends to think more along the lines of the nervous and negative. One of the goals of CBT is to help the child to recognize when his thinking may be unhelpful or distorted and to teach that child specific cognitive skills to help him think more rationally about what is actually happening in front of him. At the same time, the child learns to calm himself through body management skills. And, in a step-by-step fashion, the child learns that avoiding and escaping challenging situations only makes the negative thoughts and anxious feelings more intense.

The skills taught in CBT help the child learn to change the patterns of thinking, feeling, and behaving that keep her stuck in a cycle of fear and avoidance. By helping a child become aware of her negative thinking, CBT allows her to look at challenging situations more realistically and, in turn, to respond to them more productively.

You play a crucial role in the success of therapy by reinforcing your child's coping efforts, no matter how small they may seem to you, and not reinforcing any attempts to avoid the situation.

Unlike traditional talk therapy, CBT focuses on teaching the child practical skills. A child who's afraid of being in a social situation will learn step by step how to manage within a group—and even be the center of attention—while replacing thoughts like *"I'm embarrassed"* with, *"I may be nervous but I'm joining in here to meet new friends."* A child who sees danger lurking in every corner will learn how to see that the world isn't nearly as perilous as he once thought.

So, below, I'm going to explain to you the six basic steps of CBT. I've laid them out in order, though once you've moved on to step 2, that doesn't mean you'll never move back to step 1. Each gain you make may eventually take you backward again, so don't get frustrated if you go back and forth among the steps a bit.

Step 1: Spot the Signs

The first step in solving any problem is the ability to recognize it. Your child must be able to understand the range of emotions he's feeling and begin to see the differences in his own emotional states, what we term "feelings recognition." Once he's mastered this, he'll be able to notice the first twinge of anxiety and tap into his newfound coping skills. You can help your child develop this feelings recognition skill by

- Showing him pictures (from magazines, books, television shows) and asking him to identify how each person is feeling. Point out clues provided by facial expressions and body posture to help make subtle distinctions among feelings.
- Role-playing different feeling states with your child and taking turns guessing what emotion the other person is acting out, something we call "feelings charades." With older children and adolescents, present hypothetical situations and ask your child to identify the emotion someone might experience in that situation.
- Labeling your own emotions. For example, if you find yourself standing in a long checkout line at the grocery, try saying, "I get so bored when I have to wait in line."

If a friend of yours cancels a lunch date, let your child know, "I'm sad (or disappointed) that I won't be seeing my friend today." If your spouse is late in returning home after work you might say, "I'm a little impatient that Daddy is late for dinner and I'd like for us to eat." Labeling your own feelings, and expressing them in a collected and calm tone, can help your child learn that feelings can crop up without losing control. We'll look at following these labels with steps that model coping with the emotion later.

In addition to emotions, children need to be able to recognize physical reactions to anxiety, and they can use those physical changes as a cue to put a coping plan into effect. I'm not much for television viewing, but it can be useful as a tool to help in these exercises. Ask your child if she can recall a cartoon character in an anxiety-provoking situation. What comes to mind for me are the old-time cartoon characters, like Road Runner, Bugs Bunny, and Sylvester. These characters often show exaggerated reactions when they're frightened or nervous, such as hair standing on end, violent shaking, red faces, and so on. This will help your child to begin to think about physical responses to anxiety and will give you a place to start talking about the reactions she feels in her own body when she's caught by anxiety. Does her heart race? Stomach churn? Breath quicken? Does she sweat or her muscles tense? If your child is struggling with this concept in a calm state, gently start to point out the reactions you notice when you find she's in an anxious state down the road.

Step 2: Chill Out

Once your child learns to identify what he's feeling emotionally and physically when he's anxious, you can teach him strategies to decrease and even tolerate those feelings. Let him know that if he can get his body to calm down, he'll be able to think more clearly and cope better. Deep breathing, or "belly breathing," can be the first tool in his arsenal when trying to calm himself.

When anxious, people have a tendency to over-breathe. That is, they take in more shallow and quick breaths, which pumps oxygen more quickly through the body and helps to activate the fight-or-flight response. The same thing happens when you're exercising—you take more shallow breaths so that oxygen gets to your muscles and you can run or sustain an aerobic workout. In the anxious state, the quick breathing helps oxygen get to the large muscles, too, in case the person has to fight or run away from something that is threatening (the classic fight-or-flight response).

Whether the quick breathing comes from exercise or anxiety, sensations accompany it, including breathlessness, sweating, shaking, stomach upset, and light-headedness. This may be fine for an adult who's just finished a 5K, but for a child who's sitting doing homework, it can scream Discomfort! Anxiety!

Although the sensations seem awful when you're experiencing them, the fact is that they're harmless and will go away even if you do nothing. Think about the way that your body calms down after a workout. Your breathing gradually returns to normal and the sweating stops, your heart rate lowers, and any dryness in the mouth or throat clears up. The same return to baseline will happen after an episode of anxiety. The fight-or-flight response will dissipate as the body takes action to counter this response and return you to a steady, calm state.

If you've ever driven down a street and suddenly someone pulls out in front of you, causing you to slam on the brakes and swerve to avoid hitting their car, you've likely experienced these sensations: sudden breathlessness, muscle tension, shaking, and a pounding heart. And once the careless driver has pulled away, you notice yourself slowly calming down, each physical symptom lessening and then resolving fully within a few minutes. This is the fight-or-flight response doing what it is supposed to do for you—orienting you to the source of the danger (the other car) and having you react quickly (swerve and focus your attention on the threat), followed by a return to baseline.

The fight-or-flight process can be triggered by anything the child perceives to be an immediate threat—being called on in class (*Oh no, embarrassment!*), being put to sleep in a darkened room (*Yikes, is there someone under the bed?*), or waiting to be picked up and his mom is late (*Help me, my mom must be in an accident!*). These ideas are real and scary to your child. The fight-or-flight response kicks in and your child panics. However, if your child learns to keep his breathing easy, deep, and slow, the trigger for high anxiety and its symptoms will be more difficult to set off and your child will remain in greater control of his emotions.

To teach your child to maintain slow, deep breathing (or "belly breathing"), tell him:

- Imagine a tube running from the back of your throat down into your belly.
- At the end of the tube is a balloon in the color of your choice.
- Put your hand over your belly, with your pinky on your belly button.
- As you inhale slowly, feel how the balloon under your

hand fills up with air and poofs out your stomach. The inhale should be slow to the count of one (pause), two (pause), and three (pause).

• Then, slowly exhale to a slow, backward count of three (pause), two (pause), and one (pause) as the air leaves the balloon and you feel your tummy deflating.

• If your child has trouble breathing deeply, have him lie on the floor with a cup or toy on his belly that he can try to move up and down with each inhale and exhale.

We typically have the child do two of these practices daily for up to five minutes each at first, and then move to ten minutes at a time, to learn the technique. It's important to practice when the child is relaxed so that he will get the hang of it and learn to monitor his breathing. Often we make belly breathing a family activity so that everyone is learning a convenient and portable coping skill. Once he's got the hang of it, encourage him to practice in the grocery line, on the school bus, when waiting for someone who's late, or in situations that provoke almost any emotion.

Another good exercise is called progressive muscle relaxation (PMR), which can help teach your child the difference between tense and relaxed states in her body. PMR is helpful for relieving the muscle tension and state of physical stress that accompany worry. As your child practices and gets better and better at distinguishing the feelings, she can actually use the relaxation to ward off tension before it starts. Practice these exercises during a quiet time of the day, such as bedtime, particularly since this is also a good tool for children who have trouble sleeping due to separation anxiety, or if they're afraid they'll fall off the bed or they just can't fall asleep because their mind is consumed with worry.

- Have your child lie down in a comfortable place, arms lying straight by her side, letting her legs fall straight out, not bent at the knee. Start with some steady breathing—have her put her hand on her belly like you taught her above.

- Starting with her right foot: Tell her to focus on squeezing the muscles as hard as she can for about eight seconds by fanning out her toes and arching the foot, then relax them, letting the tension leave her body through that foot.

- Ask her, "Do you feel a little tingle in your foot? That's okay, because it means you're getting nice and cozy and relaxed."

- Have her move to her left foot, squeezing and fanning out the toes, and then relaxing, and as she relaxes the tension moves out of her body.

- Next she can focus on the calves—tense and relax—then her thighs. All the while she should be breathing steadily and calmly, in and out.

- Have your child move through all of her main muscles, tensing and relaxing her stomach (pulling it in and making it flat), chest (by holding a deep breath), shoulders (shrug them up to the ears), arms (make a muscle), and hands (squeeze into a fist).

- She should end up at her eyebrows, raising them really high, like she's very surprised, then relax again and feel all the tension leaving her face.

At the end of the exercise, tell her to notice how she's feeling—it should be pure relaxation from the top of her head to the bottom of her feet. This is the way you want her to feel at home, at school, and with friends and family.

Step 3: Match Fears with Reality Through "Detective Thinking"

Children with anxiety tend to see danger lurking in every corner. And very specific images come with these fears—the child imagines the scenario as if it is actually happening in that moment. Because the fear is so real to him, the fight-or-flight response kicks in and the physical sensations of anxiety become associated with these thoughts, deepening his conviction that the world is a dangerous and threatening place. This sets into motion a vicious cycle: These anxiety-provoking thoughts and beliefs link to the physical feelings of anxiety, and because they're so uncomfortable, they signal to the child that something's wrong. This in turn links to anxious behaviors.

So let's say your daughter suffers from separation anxiety. She's standing outside the school waiting for you to pick her up at 2:40. Once it's 2:41, the image of you in a car accident flashes through her head. That makes her heart race faster and her palms sweat, which makes her feel that something's truly wrong, which in turn makes the images worse. She's too young to think, *This is just me imagining this.* To her, the picture in her mind, and the feeling, is very real.

Challenging these types of unrealistic thoughts can help your child better control her anxious responses and behavior. So, while you were late picking up your daughter her thoughts ran immediately to "Something bad happened to Mom. She must be in an accident." To tell her to simply think positively and say, "Mom's okay, she's going to pick me up and we'll have fun," doesn't speak to her fear—that you were in an accident. The positive thoughts just kick the can down the road, leaving your child to keep repeating, "Mom's okay, Mom's okay, Mom's okay," until the feared image of you in a car wreck leaves her crying, "but she's been in an accident!" She needs very simple and clear facts to help her to cope with the realities of the situation. Something like, *"Mom is okay and is probably just stuck in traffic, because lots of parents are driving to schools now to pick up their kids. I will wait here and do some reading or talk to my friends until she arrives."*

To help your child swap the scary thoughts with realistic alternatives, he needs to first pinpoint his specific worries. You can help him tune in to his own anxious self-talk by illustrating the concept with comic strip thought bubbles. Show your child cartoon drawings of situations he fears—going to sleep by himself, going to school, staying home with a babysitter—and ask him to place thoughts into the characters' thought bubbles. Once you have a sense of what he fears, you can lead him through a process of challenging each thought, where your child plays the detective role, evaluating the evidence for his worried thoughts.

Let's go back to your daughter waiting at school. The character's thought bubble probably says, "My mom's been in an accident and she's never going to come pick me up."

- Ask your child, "How many times have I picked you up at school? And how many times have I been in an accident and not come at all?" She has no choice but to answer that you've picked her up dozens of times and always gotten there.
- Push the process even further by asking what else might have happened if you're late picking her up, and what has happened before when you've been a bit late. This

forces your child to think through the other, more realistic possibilities: You've hit traffic, you've run into a
friend and talked for a bit.

- The more she does this, the more she'll realize that many
  different neutral, everyday situations can and do happen,
  and that the image she's conjured up in her mind is, in
  fact, very unlikely.

- Eventually, without your prompting, your child will be
  able to challenge her own way of catastrophic thinking
  and, instead, come up with more realistic thoughts she
  can use to calm herself down and control the worry.

Banish These Words!

Brushing off your child's worry by saying things like "There's nothing to
worry about" doesn't help him fight the anxiety. What does help is the
child's ability to size up the situation himself, and then figure out how
to deal with it. When the child can look at what's in front of him, review
what proof he has for worry, then focus his thoughts on how to cope,
he can replace the improbable thoughts and beliefs with more sensible
ones. In other words, instead of pooh-poohing your child's worry, we
want him to ask himself, "How likely is it that this situation will happen" and then jump to, "Even if things don't go exactly as I'd like, what
can I do to handle the situation?"

Step 4: Develop a Deal-with-It Plan

Now that your child is getting a handle on his emotions and feelings, he can knuckle down on what he can do in an anxiety-

provoking situation. CBT therapists teach families a process called "problem solving," which involves identifying goals, brainstorming all sorts of solutions, evaluating the choices, and then choosing the best plan of action. To start problem solving, define in very clear terms the goal your child wants to achieve in an anxiety-provoking situation. Next, ask your child to come up with some things that will help him work through the concern, from the most serious to the most silly. Then go through them with him and choose the ones that will get him to his goal in the most reasonable way, weeding out the ones that will increase the anxiety. Make sure the list includes negative or unhelpful alternatives (e.g., I can cheat on the homework; I can act sick and stay home), as he will come to see why these won't work when he evaluates them. But be sure to help him list proactive and practical solutions so he will realize why these are better options. So, your twelve-year-old son with generalized anxiety breaks out into a cold sweat and feels stuck whenever his teacher gives an in-class assignment because he doesn't know how to get started. His goal is to complete the assignment within the allotted time. His deal-with-it plan choices include:

- Asking the teacher for extra time
- Taking a few deep breaths and time to focus his mind on the task
- Running out of the room
- Going through the assignment and first doing the things he knows how to do easily
- Calling his mom to pick him up
- Challenging his anxious thoughts
- Writing down anything on the paper and not worrying if it makes sense

When you go through the list, you throw out asking the teacher for extra time, running out of the room, and calling Mom to pick him up, since none of those will benefit him in the long run. He also can see that just writing anything isn't going to achieve his goal. But all of the other choices are great and will move him toward his goal.

Step 5: Bounty for Bravery

Anxious children tend to be hard on themselves—they often don't reward themselves for their efforts, only for absolute successes. When your child is making an effort to overcome her anxiety, praise her for her attempt. Tell your child that you are proud of her for confronting her fears; she needs reinforcement for small steps in the right direction, not just huge leaps. Encourage your child to pat herself on the back or to engage in a favorite activity. When you say what you liked about her behavior in coping, you are helping her to value her efforts.

MAKE REWARDS WORK FOR YOU

Some parents are loath to offer rewards for things that their child should naturally be doing. "No one gave me a special treat for going to school each day!" "What? He's going to expect a gift every time he sleeps in his own bed? No way!" However, small and reasonable rewards are great to help shape appropriate and coping-focused behavior when they are used strategically and systematically. Rewards should be:

- chosen by the child (with some input from you)

- kept simple

- something the child doesn't have access to, so you can control it

- something your child actually wants

- contingent on behavior

- given as immediately as possible

Step 6: Ready, Set, Go

Once your child is armed with coping skills, he can begin to meet situations that give him the shakes head-on through the process of exposure. Ease into it: Start with the things that are the least anxiety-provoking and move up gradually. Think of this as climbing a fear or worry staircase. I actually have children and parents draw a picture for themselves. At the bottom, the first step, is something that the child is a little bit worried about or a bit afraid to do.

Let's take the example of a child who has generalized anxiety and she's always worried about her family's safety. In her mind, the house could blow up, burglars could break in, and someone could steal the family's identities via the Internet (yes, these were the worries of a ten-year-old patient of mine). Your child's first step could be leaving the family computer on all day long, which the child thinks is an invitation to hacking. The next step should be something she fears a bit more. This could involve leaving the house for a family outing and purposely not turning on the alarm. The next step should be something the child fears a bit more, let's say it's hearing sirens for fear there's a burglar in the neighborhood. In this case you can have her sit with her eyes closed and listen to sirens on a recording (or via the Internet).

As you can see, each step as you go up the staircase is something she fears more and more. The top step is something she's absolutely petrified of, or petrified to do, such as going to sleep without checking that the doors and windows are all locked. At the very top of the staircase, draw your child in a celebratory state.

Work with your child to come up with a list of difficult anxiety-provoking experiences to put on the staircase. You can always adjust them later, if your child finds that one task is simply too difficult and she'd like to try another one instead. Then, have your child choose which item to work on on the bottom step. If it's leaving the house without putting on the alarm, have her do that, using the coping skills you've taught her. Remember, practice this with her once, then let her do the practice without your guidance two more times. When she's able to leave the house without checking the alarm, give her a sticker to put on the step to signify she's conquered that fear.

The Exposure Staircase

Let your child move up the staircase at her own pace, gently encouraging her to keep moving rather than getting stuck at any one point. With an older child we might not draw a staircase and use stickers (for fear of her walking out on us), but rather, we'll list her worrisome situations on index cards and then have the teen sort those from the most difficult to the least. Starting with the easier tasks, we'll make a deal for the teen to attempt the task (using her breathing and cognitive skills) and, once achieved, she is taught to give some self-reinforcement for her efforts—your daughter might treat herself to a new iTunes download or have some friends over for pizza. The point is for her to feel good about attempting the challenge and to progress through this deck of cards.

Confronting her lesser fears first will give her a sense of mastery and accomplishment, which in turn will help her be better able to tackle the bigger ones. When she gets to the top, she can get a large reinforcer that she chooses herself.

An Important Idea to Grasp

Anxiety stems from the fear of not being able to predict when bad things will happen, coupled with the need to have total control over a situation. In the real world, we know that every situation includes aspects that are out of our control. We like to be under the illusion that we're always in the driver's seat but, in reality, control only goes to a point—it can rain on the day of your child's birthday picnic, a trip is canceled because your partner is given a mega deadline to meet at work, your child's favorite teacher goes on maternity leave right before state testing begins. Control is really a limited reality.

Your child needs to learn to let go of the notion of having to predict things accurately and control situations to his utmost satisfaction. He's got to learn to deal with things as they come—to go with the flow. He needs to experience situations that vary widely from one time to the next (today the teacher is in a good mood; tomorrow he might be a bit gruff) and to adapt to the ever-changing world. And this is also what you must do for your anxious child: Model flexibility, problem solving, and going with the flow!

Creating a Fear Staircase

To help create a fear staircase, use this work sheet to determine which fears can be at the bottom and which should be at the top. If your child can come up with the situations he fears most himself, he'll have a better chance of confronting them. If he refuses to sit down with you and work on the staircase, come up with some of the steps for him.

FEAR FEELINGS SCALE

0	Piece of cake
1–2	Makes me a little anxious, but I can muscle through it
3–4	Makes me anxious and I try to avoid it sometimes
5–7	Definitely makes me anxious and I do my best to get out of it
8–9	Makes me scared and I avoid it like the plague
10	Get me out of here!!!!

FEAR STAIRCASE (TO BE FILLED IN BY PARENT AND CHILD)

0	
1–2	
3–4	
5–7	
8–9	
10	

In this chapter I've helped draw a map of how to teach your child ways to recognize what's going on in her body that's amping up her anxiety. You've learned some relaxation techniques to help her calm down and ways she can home in on the negative, anxiety-provoking thoughts, images, and ideas that fuel her anxiety and avoidance, and how she can replace them with more realistic and coping-focused thinking.

Now that you've got a handle on how you're going to deal with your child's anxiety in a general way, I'm going to tell you about some common specific anxieties and anxiety disorders that children suffer from. Keep in mind, of course, that some children have multiple anxieties, so your child may show signs of more than one kind. I'm going to show you how to take what you've learned in this chapter and apply it to the specific anxiety that your child suffers from. And you'll be amazed at how a whole new—and calm—world will open up for all of you.

5

The Classic Clinger: Understanding Separation Anxiety

When I first started in this field in the 1980s, nobody—not even most experts—took separation anxiety very seriously. "Don't worry, it's no big deal," "It's just a phase," and "He'll grow out of it" were common phrases heard by moms and dads. But if you have a child with separation anxiety, I don't have to tell you, it *is* a big deal. And, as you also already know, it's not just a phase and many *don't* grow out of it.

Parents of children with separation anxiety experience a wide range of emotions, and many of those feelings often conflict. Of course, we all love our children and we want them to love us back. We cherish the time we spend with them and delight in the fact that they want to spend time with us. But there's a point at which it becomes too much. When your child is stuck to you day and night, when you can't leave the house without fielding an onslaught of questions ("Where are you going?" "When will you be back?"), when you can't even get a full night's sleep with your spouse without another body in the bed (your child's!), it's natural to harbor resentment—and you may feel enormous guilt about feeling that way.

I understand all those feelings. I hear about them day after day in my office. In this chapter as well as the next, I'm going to give you an in-depth understanding of what separation anxiety looks like, explaining

- how it comes from a natural, evolutionary process that sometimes goes awry
- how to spot it in your child
- how it affects you and your child

I'll also show you how some of the things you're doing in the hopes of easing your child's anxiety may, in part, actually be feeding into it. While you may have the best of intentions, instead of helping your child alleviate his difficulties, you may very well be perpetuating them.

QUIZ: COULD YOUR CHILD HAVE SEPARATION ANXIETY DISORDER?

Answer yes or no to the following questions.

- Does your child make excuses to stay home from things that other children seem to be doing, like parties and sleepovers? Yes/No

- Does your child have difficulties going to school or staying in school for the full day? Yes/No

- Does your child have trouble falling asleep without you there or trouble sleeping through the night alone? Yes/No

- When you leave your child at home, either with a sitter or, if she's older, alone for a brief period, does she constantly call or text you? Yes/No

- Does your child follow you around the house, always keeping you in sight? Yes/No

- Does your child complain of physical symptoms—headaches, stom-achaches, or nausea—when you talk about leaving her somewhere? Yes/No

- Does your child argue with you or throw a tantrum whenever the issue of separation comes up? Yes/No

- Does your child seem to be worried that something will happen to you or your spouse when you're away from her? Yes/No

- Does your child talk about being kidnapped or getting lost when she's away from you? Yes/No

- If you're late picking up your child from a party, does she panic? Yes/No

- Does your child have nightmares about being separated from you or that something bad is happening to you? Yes/No

- Are your child's grades or friendships being affected by her anxiety? Yes/No

If you answered yes to any of these questions, your child might have an issue with separation anxiety, which affects 3 percent to 5 percent of children and adolescents, usually affecting more girls than boys. Al-though mild separation anxiety is normal and expected in infants and toddlers, children should move out of this stage by the end of toddler-hood and become comfortable staying with loving relatives, meeting their preschool teachers and sitters, and interacting with other children without their parents close at hand. Separation anxiety disorder (SAD) is typically diagnosed between the ages of seven and nine, though it can occur any time before age eighteen.

Sandy's Story

In my clinic I've seen hundreds of children suffering with separation anxiety, but my first encounter with one particular patient stands out in my mind. Eleven-year-old Sandy and her parents, Todd and Sue, were scheduled for their first appointment at 4:00 p.m. By 4:10 nobody had arrived. I was just reaching for my phone book when I heard a frantic knock at my office door. "Dr. Albano! Help! Dr. Albano!" As I opened the door I found a woman, stammering, "Help, help us, please!" She grabbed my hand and pulled me toward the front door, through the hallway, and into the parking lot. All the while I was thinking, *Who in the world is this person?*

Through the lot full of cars, I saw a man standing by a minivan with the back door open, gesturing for us to hurry. That's when I first saw Sandy. She lay prone in the backseat shaking. Her eyes were closed, her breath was fast and shallow, and her hands hung straight down at her sides. "She's having a seizure!" cried her father. "Please do something!" I must admit that my initial thoughts ran along the lines of *Seizure? These people need an emergency room, not an anxiety clinic!* But fairly quickly, I realized that this was my new patient, Sandy, who seemed to be having a panic reaction.

I slipped into the back of the van and put one of my fingers underneath her hand. "Squeeze my finger twice if you can hear me." When I felt the two squeezes, I was able to relax; if she was following instructions, this was indeed a panic attack. For the next forty minutes, I talked Sandy into slowing her breath, opening her eyes, and sitting up in her seat. We spent time getting to know each other and, more than anything, for her to begin to trust me and to tell me her story.

Because I met Sandy in the car that first time, she was able to trust me enough during the next visit to walk into the clinic with her parents. Her mother came into the room for half of our session, and Sandy allowed her to sit in the waiting area after settling in and exploring my office.

Over the next few weeks I learned about Sandy's lifelong struggle with anxiety. From not being able to be held by anyone but her parents as a baby, to sleeping in her parents' room until just the prior year, Sandy was intensely afraid of being separated. Initially she would only agree to go to class if Sue sat in the back of the kindergarten room. During the early grades, Sue volunteered in the library and cafeteria to be in the school building. However, instead of feeling settled, Sandy made frequent requests to visit her mother and check that she was still there.

School policy changed when Sandy was in fourth grade: Parents were now forbidden to be inside the building during the school day. Sue tried to calm Sandy by telling her she'd wait in the car all day long (and she did do this!), but more and more frequently Sandy refused to go to school.

Todd and Sue had long since given up trying to have a night out alone—they'd tried dozens of times over the years to leave Sandy with various babysitters, but each time they simply could not leave. Sandy would scream and cry, and Sue, horrified at her daughter's shrieking, could not walk out the door. Although Todd tried to put his foot down, Sue would always overrule him. "She's our daughter, we can't leave her hysterical like this," was Sue's familiar refrain. As you might expect, this didn't sit well with Todd, and strain between the two parents grew at a steady pace.

On a home visit, I was astonished to find incredibly elaborate (and expensive) playground equipment and a pint-size motorized car crowding the backyard. In the family room, every type of electronic game, several huge television screens, a potter's wheel, and easels for painting sat in full view. Todd sheepishly explained that this expansive collection was used to bribe Sandy in exchange for her going to school. Though initially each toy had worked—Sandy kept her promise and went to school for a few days—her anxiety quickly overshadowed the excitement of her new toy.

At the time of referral, Sandy had missed three straight months of her sixth-grade year and her parents were at a loss as to what to do to help their daughter. Sandy was suffering from some of the most severe separation anxiety I'd seen, but I knew that if she and her family were willing to put in the work, they could overcome this problem. Sandy was in dire need of practical, effective, and age-appropriate skills to help her manage anxiety and master the situations that provoked her fears and worries. In addition to individual therapy for Sandy, her parents needed to learn about the vicious cycle of overprotection that had ensnarled them and, contrary to their best intentions, had perpetuated their child's difficulties.

What Is Separation Anxiety?

Separation anxiety is normal. It develops in all children and has interesting and complex evolutionary roots. It begins at around nine months, roughly the same time a child is learning how to crawl and then to walk. While the toddler begins to scoot away from Mom, he realizes how terrifying independence can be. That instinctual feeling of needing to be near his mother keeps him going back to safety before venturing out too far. He crawls to the kitchen, checks out the new tile floor, he's not sure if he can navigate it safely, he looks back to see that Mom's still sitting in the living room, then he crawls a little farther. He toddles over to chase a dog, the dog barks, and he runs right back to Mom's loving (and safe) arms. The baby practices this push-pull—away and back—over and over, and eventually the push away becomes more and more comfortable.

Developmentally, separation anxiety starts just about the time when a baby starts to understand object permanence—just because a child can't see the people she loves doesn't mean they don't exist. Early on, if you hide a baby's toy behind your back, she acts as if the toy is gone forever. However, over time she begins to understand that things don't simply disappear. When you're hiding her toy behind your back, it's still there, though she can't see it.

You know how a baby loves to play the "dropsy" game? He drops his toy over the side of the crib, or his Cheerios over the side of his high chair, fully expecting Mommy to give it back to him. And when she does, he drops it again and again with delight. No matter how many times he drops that little O, it comes right back to him. By doing this over and over, he learns that although it's out of sight for the moment, the cereal never really disappears. Thus, he is practicing and mastering this exciting new concept: object permanence.

Just as the toy behind your back or the Cheerios on the floor are out of sight but still exist, you, too, still exist, even when your baby can't see you. This type of understanding helps the child to develop a true attachment to you, as well as to the adults who are most often around her. Whether you're in the room next door or on another planet, it's all the same to her—you exist, but you've disappeared. And since babies don't understand the concept of time, they don't know if or when you'll come back, which leads to a sense of anxiety: separation anxiety. When you leave the room, your baby will feel anxious and look around for you. And each time she finds you, she realizes that while you're gone for the moment, you always come back, and her separation anxiety lessens.

The infant's sense of safety in his relationship with his primary caregiver begins during his first year. He cries, his mom responds with a hug, and the baby feels confident that she'll be there when he needs her, leading to a secure attachment. Studies show that young children who experience a major change in a primary caregiver may be less able to develop that secure attachment and are more likely to develop SAD.

Other aspects of your child's cognitive development contribute to the emergence of this anxiety as well. At first, your newborn can't tell the difference between people he knows and perfect strangers, and he's utterly content being passed around from grandparents to aunts and uncles. But as his eyesight sharpens and his brain develops, he begins to recognize his caregivers and will fuss when he is handed over to people he doesn't know. In time he gets used to it—in fact, studies show that when an infant has several different people caring for him, he's less likely to protest when going to new people. He'll come to know and trust Grandma, Aunt Mary, Cousin Tony, his babysitter, and your closest friends. And this pays off in the long run. The more experience an infant has separating from his caregiver, the less likely he is to display separation anxiety later.

A Normal and Manageable Fear

Around twelve to twenty-four months, separation anxiety peaks, though it varies from child to child. It's not, say, abnormal for a three-year-old to feel some concern when her parent leaves the room. She may be slow to warm up, but the key is that the child can be distracted from those feelings. With practice she becomes more comfortable on her own, and she doesn't obsess about who's not with her. Even an older child may be sad, or even cry when left at day care or elementary school the first few times, though the crying will subside when the child warms up to her new surroundings, usually within a few days to a few weeks. For the non-anxious child, the enjoyment and reinforcement she finds—playing with her friends, enjoying new games, attention from teachers and classroom aides—overshadows her concern about being away from you. And as she sees her mom smile with pride when she shows off her artwork, she gains more and more of a sense of accomplishment and happiness for doing things on her own.

A Faulty Progression, a Paralyzing Fear

For some children, something stops short in the process. No matter how much practice the child has with the push-pull, the disappearing and reappearing, the separation and reuniting, he doesn't get used to it. Instead of learning that his mother (or father) will always be there when he comes home from school, he wants—and *needs*—to know where she is at all times, tracking her every move. He gets extremely homesick whenever he's away from home and he becomes consumed with the fear that something horrible will happen to Mom or Dad when they're away from him. Thoughts like *Mom might get into a car accident and die* and *What if someone kidnaps me?* fill his head when his parents aren't with him. Nothing else matters. All he can do is focus on how to get back to them. Until he does, his breathing gets faster, his heart races, his muscles twitch, he feels light-headed. He's worked himself into a complete state of panic.

These children have difficulty separating from their parents for any length of time. Forget school—they can't even be left alone in their own bedrooms. To them, good night means good-bye forever. They have trouble going to sleep in their own bed, often insisting that a parent sleep next to them, and even their sleep is filled with nightmares about separation. Their school and social lives suffer tremendously, and they refuse to participate in the activities that make childhood fun—playing at friends' houses, going on sleepovers, and attending summer camps.

Although problematic separation anxiety may subside as a child grows older, sometimes it still remains, hidden underneath. Carrie had mild separation anxiety for her entire childhood. She slept in her parents' bed more nights than not until second grade, at which point her parents celebrated (to themselves) the continuous nights they enjoyed once she stayed put in her room. By middle school, Carrie still refused to sleep at other children's homes, but she had an active social life, having friends play at her house. During her first year of high school the class went on an overnight trip; Carrie stayed behind, complaining of a stomachache. But she was independent, her parents thought. She took public transportation to school by herself and stayed home alone in the evenings when her parents were out. So by the time Carrie reached her senior year of high school, there was no real concern about her taking the next big step: heading off to college. With good grades, a record of service and extracurricular activities, and fantastic letters of recommendation from teachers, Carrie had her pick of several schools that accepted her, and they chose a good liberal arts college in the Midwest.

Two weeks before leaving for school, Carrie complained of intense stomach upset, but her doctor found nothing wrong with her. Then came complaints of headaches. And then muscle aches and pains. And then her stomach problems returned, but now with nausea and vomiting. For the last week before college was supposed to start, Carrie was curled up in her bed, crying and refusing to see relatives who came to say good-bye. Panicked by this downturn, Carrie's parents got Carrie a medical deferral for one semester.

Within the hour Carrie was out of bed, showered, and talking to a friend on the phone. Her mother overheard her laughing and wishing her friend the best at school, sounding *relieved* that she'd be going later in the year. That night, she ate a full meal, something she hadn't done in weeks. Her physical complaints went away as mysteriously as they had come.

Her case typifies what we often see in an older adolescent: Safe separations, like getting to school and maybe even spending a few overnights at relatives' houses, can get them through the teenage years, but when the time comes to be truly independent, separation anxiety can flare back up and stop them from making the next step in development, stalling the transition to young adulthood.

What Can Set Off an Episode of SAD?

- First night sleeping in a big-kid bed

- First time going to preschool or day care

- A new babysitter

- Starting kindergarten

- Mondays

- First day back to school after an illness, vacation, or summer break

- First day of middle school

- Parents going on a kid-free vacation

To be diagnosed with SAD the anxiety must

- be beyond what's expected for the child's developmental level,

❖ be persistent,

❖ begin before age eighteen, and

❖ cause significant distress.

As we've discussed before, like any anxiety disorder, experts believe that the cause of SAD is most likely a combination of biological factors (such as genetics, family history of anxiety, and the infant temperament) and the environment. Children with a family history of anxiety disorders are at higher risk, as are children who exhibit an inhibited temperament (an overall level of fearfulness, lack of exploring their environment, and anxious attachment to the caregiver when a new person enters the same room) and who lack the ability to soothe themselves at an early age. If left untreated, children with SAD have a higher risk of depression and other anxiety disorders as adolescents and adults.

Life with Separation Anxiety

As heartbreaking as it is to see the children in my office who suffer from separation anxiety, it's just as devastating to watch the struggles of their parents. Parenting a child with separation anxiety is a full-time job—with no overtime or vacation pay. Their children cling to them 24/7, often shadowing them around the house, winding up right under their feet. Parents have told me how they've literally stepped on their children when getting out of bed or tripped over them while standing up from the dining-room table because their son or daughter has slipped next to them, unnoticed.

Parents of older children with SAD wait and wait and wait for their child to accept a sleepover at a friend's house, but the day never seems to come. Their teenager may sulk about how her friends now choose going to the mall rather than hanging out at her house. Parents may be torn: On the one hand, they have the rare teenager who actually wants to stick by her parents. On the other, they wonder if the child will ever move along and get out into the world.

Parents of children with SAD also worry endlessly when their children complain of stomachaches, nausea, and headaches, only to realize the child hasn't caught a bug—they're literally getting sick because a separation is looming. And there are only so many temper tantrums one can contend with without becoming downright irritated.

I hear stories of parents who are exasperated, not to mention embarrassed, having to constantly field phone calls from their anxious children. What type of excuse do you make to slip away unobtrusively from a business bargaining table, a get-together with an old friend, or a long-overdue medical exam when your child is on the other end of the line hammering you with questions: *Where are you? How long will you be gone? How much longer? Why do you have to leave me? When will you come home? Why not now when I need you?* My heart goes out to parents who confess their conflicting emotions. While their heart aches listening to their child's panic-stricken voice, they also can't help gritting their teeth a bit because they simply cannot get a moment's peace.

Today's technology only adds to the problem. Years ago a parent could get a break, at the very least while on a train, in a car, or just taking a walk outside. These days, with laptops, cell phones, and texting, they are on call for their child around the clock.

The Road to Separation Anxiety

Consider the early developmental paths of two children. First, we have Erin, who was easy to manage from the onset of her little life.

As an infant, when her parents heard her fussing from her crib, there was always a very specific reason: a wet diaper, the pacifier was out of reach, or it was feeding time. Her parents used their intuition and the tone of her cries to guide whether the distress was real or something transient that would pass without their involvement. Indeed, she loved to be cuddled, but she just as easily was put in a crib or bouncy seat, with her eyes following a mobile or looking about the room while she gurgled to herself or sucked on her pacifier.

Initially she slept in a bassinet next to her parents' bed, but she was moved into her own room after a month. By six months, she could be heard cooing in her crib at the break of dawn, but her parents let her be and she'd fall back asleep within a few minutes. By age two, she fussed a little bit on the first night that her parents were away for a couple's vacation, leaving her with an aunt. But she played and laughed, and slept soundly during the four nights that they were away, and she ran to them with delight upon their return.

As she progressed through elementary school, Erin had the occasional fear—hesitancy at seeing the dentist or getting a shot at the doctor's office, some tears at separating for her first sleepaway camp session. But at each, her parents remained calm and reassuring, and they redirected the focus toward the good—Erin would meet new friends at camp and she'd feel better after a doctor's intervention.

Toward middle school, when friendships become more complicated and peer acceptance and rejection were felt strongly, Erin had the occasional spat with friends. Her mother listened and asked questions: "What happened?" "What did you do?" "Is there anything you would want to do differently next time something like this happens?" "How do *you* want to handle this?" This led Erin to arrive at her own solutions, with some parental input, and feel empowered in managing her relationships and in solving problems.

Compare this to Sandy, whom we saw in the beginning of the

chapter. It seemed, almost from birth, that the only place Sandy was content was on her mother's lap. At first Sue was elated that her daughter always wanted to be near, and she hugged Sandy close when watching a movie, playing with toys, or even eating her breakfast. In time, however, claustrophobia began to set in and Sue tried to have her sit by herself, but Sandy would throw a tantrum until Sue scooped her up. Although she didn't get much time for herself, Sue figured that Sandy would only be young once and she should enjoy this time with her as much as she could.

As Sandy grew, she got easily frustrated and Sue could not stand to see her so upset. So she did her best to shield her. "Swing me higher!" she'd say on the playground, and although other children her age were able to swing themselves, Sue pushed Sandy. When Sandy was in elementary school and complained that piano was too hard, Sue told the instructor not to come anymore. If Sandy got stumped on a math problem on her high school homework, Sue took the pencil out of her hand and worked it out for her.

Different Parenting Styles, Different Outcomes

The comparison of Erin and Sandy illustrates two different parenting styles interacting with different child temperaments. A vicious cycle seemed to take hold in Sandy's case. She cried, her parents ran to her side, which only increased her cries, and so on. Unfortunately, when a parent tries to alleviate her child's discomfort, she often exacerbates the anxiety. What began as an effort by a concerned mom to soothe her crying young child who was afraid of going to school eventually developed into a pattern of continuous rescue and reassurance. At the first sign of a complaint, the parents swooped in, shielding their anxiety-ridden child from any potential assault. Sandy didn't want to go to school unless her mother waited outside? Sue obliged. Sandy was nervous to go to a friend's house? Sue bought a house full of toys to get Sandy's friends to come to them.

It's easy to fall into these kinds of traps. When a child tells a parent he's scared that something bad will happen, a parent's natural reaction is to reassure. "Mommy's fine, nothing bad is going to happen to me." Although this sounds helpful, it can actually serve to increase the child's anxiety. While the reassurance will make your child feel better for the moment, the feeling will soon wear off, and a child who has never learned how to soothe himself will only know one place to go to fix his worry—to you, his parent. Rescuing your child at every anxiety-provoking situation also doesn't help. When you pick your child up every time he complains that he wants to leave a playdate or birthday party, you're doing two very complicating things. First, you're sending him the message that he doesn't have the ability to cope with the situation on his own. And you're robbing him of the opportunity to master the situation himself. In other words, rescuing the child with separation anxiety will only serve to increase his anxiety over the long run and solidify the idea that "I can't do this without Mom or Dad."

Permitting or even encouraging avoidant behavior, such as keeping your child out of camp because he's too afraid to go or letting your child refuse playdates, does something else as well: It cheats your child of the opportunity to conclude that the situation is probably not as awful as he thought and, in fact, it may be fun. Once he powers through the butterflies and steps onto the camp bus, he'll realize that the great time he's having playing baseball is overshadowing his feelings that something might happen to his parents. In fact, he's not even thinking about them anymore because he's so busy having fun with his new friends. In addition, being able to work through the butterflies will give him a triumphant feeling of success, which will boost his feelings of self-worth.

Helicopter Parenting: Detrimental for Anxious Children

Parents of anxious children sometimes fall into the trap of trying to control the situation for them. Under the guise of not wanting to see their child fail or suffer again, parents take over and become master planners. Rather than allow the children to make decisions and generate their own ideas of what to do and how to do things, parents of many anxious children are overly involved and intrude upon plans and projects. Eight-year-old Jason is invited to an after-school playdate by David, a classroom friend. David's mother offers to pick the boys up, have them play at her home, and bring Jason home by 5:00 p.m. Although Jason had been reluctant to go on playdates in the past, he is genuinely excited for this get-together and eagerly packs his backpack with some favorite toys to share with David.

All the while, his mother questions him. "What will you two do at the playdate?" she says to her son. "What do you think you'll need to bring? Are you going to go outside? Did you pack a sweatshirt just in case it gets chilly?" Jason doesn't know the answers to any of these questions. He hasn't thought that much about the playdate before—only that he and his friend would play the afternoon away.

But now he's starting to worry. *Will he have a good time at David's house without his mom there? Will he be okay? What if he needs something that he forgot to bring?* Surprisingly, when school lets out Jason's mom is there, bearing bags of goodies for the boys and chocolate for the moms. She's also brought a bathing suit, a change of clothes, and a baseball glove for Jason, "just in case" he needs any of them for the afternoon.

David's mother doesn't quite know what to do, so she shrugs her shoulders and allows her uninvited guest to join, feeling a bit irritated that instead of folding the load of laundry sitting in the dryer while the boys are busy playing, she's forced to entertain Jason's mother.

What a lost opportunity! Jason was willing to try something that had been scaring him, but his mother snatched the chance away from him. Guided by her fear that he would be uncomfortable and unprepared, she jumped in to save him before he needed to be rescued. There was no hint of anxiety or a problem, but by taking the control out of Jason's hands, his mother only contributed to his feelings of being lost and out of control.

While it's difficult to see your child manage ambiguous and less than clearly defined situations, that's the only way she's going to learn to problem solve and be flexible in her thinking. In fact, one study found that when parents took over tasks that children could perform on their own, children were more likely to have symptoms of separation anxiety. Stepping over these bounds limits the child's development of a sense of mastery, fosters excessive dependence on caregivers, and ultimately maintains symptoms of SAD or even makes them worse.

The Vicious Cycle of Separation Anxiety

Just as parents influence a child's anxiety, the reverse is also true. The more anxious the child becomes, the further parents often go in their efforts to relieve the distress. Before long, the child's anxiety starts taking over the parents' lives as well. While I'll have an entire chapter dealing with this issue later in the book, I'd like to touch on

QUIZ: ARE YOU HELPING OR HURTING?

Answer yes or no to the following questions.

- When your toddler cries in the middle of the night, do you run immediately to quiet him down? Yes/No

- When your six-year-old has trouble falling asleep in his room, do you let him fall asleep in your bed and transfer him to his own bed in the middle of the night? Yes/No

- When your eight-year-old is invited to his first sleepover and says he wants to try it, do you think he can't handle it and do your best to dissuade him? Yes/No

- When you were five years old, your father left the family home. Do you make sure to tell your daughter at least once—often twice—a day that you and her father will never abandon her so she'll feel safe and secure? Yes/No

- Your twelve-year-old son was invited to a boy/girl party. He says he doesn't want to go. Even though you've called to make sure there will be adult supervision and you know most of the children who were invited, are you delighted he doesn't want to go and tell him he's made a good choice? Yes/No

If you answered yes to any of these questions, you may be contributing to—and even exacerbating—your child's separation anxiety. As much as you think you're helping, you actually may be making things much worse.

it a bit here, since separation anxiety is one disorder in particular that truly sends ripples through a family.

Consider Brian and Rosemary. The couple met in graduate school and each went on to work for established financial firms. Their lives kept sailing along smoothly after the birth of their first child. But after their second child, Jon, was born, the family hit choppy waters.

As an infant, Jon was difficult to soothe, and babysitters came and went in rapid succession. By age three, Brian and Rosemary's first child had entered day care happily, but Jon clung to his parents when being dropped off and was inconsolable when they left. So Brian and Rosemary took turns cutting back their work hours to be home with him.

As Jon was starting kindergarten, Rosemary cut back her work hours even more and eventually stopped working altogether. Yet Jon's anxiety was spiraling out of control. Rosemary resented leaving the job she loved. She was angry at Brian and Jon about it—and guilty for feeling this way. Brian missed the loss of intimacy with his wife. Their older child seemed to be raising herself because of Jon's monopoly on his parents' time. And yet, despite these sacrifices, Jon's anxiety just grew more and more excruciating as time went on.

When one child in a family has an anxiety disorder, everyone in the household feels the effects. Day after day, I see parents whose other relationships, including those with their spouse and other children, have been put on hold while they focus on the anxious child. Work, hobbies, friendships, and even sex have frequently fallen by the wayside. Whether it's a single or two-parent household, the amount of energy that must be spent comforting, reassuring, and trying to soothe the anxious child is all-consuming, and every other relationship in the household will suffer.

Because the child takes up so much energy, parents are all too quick to cave and cancel their plans or let their child sleep in their bed. But that doesn't help the situation resolve itself. It only makes things worse. The parents, siblings, and even sometimes the extended family begin to revolve around the child with separation anxiety, trying to manipulate situations so the anxious child doesn't have to be without them. But the more they reassure, the more their child clutches in desperation.

IN THIS CHAPTER YOU'VE gotten a snapshot of what separation anxiety looks like and how and why it develops. In the next chapter, I'm going to give you some concrete ways to help you and your child. I know it seems out of reach right now, but I promise—with a little work on both of your parts, your child *can* and *will* learn to separate.

6

Parenting a Child with
Separation Anxiety

As I explained in the previous chapter, whether your child is six or sixteen, parenting a child with separation anxiety can be extremely frustrating. Before you gave birth to your child, you probably dreamed of him playing at a friend's house, having fun at kindergarten, going to summer camp, and dropping him off at college. You might also have pictured some tears. Of course, the tears you pictured were yours as your child ran off into the kindergarten class or unpacked his clothes in his dorm room without even a look back at you.

But for your child, the reality probably looks quite different. Your child would rather stay home and hang out with you—and you're worried that means he's missing out on the fun of being a child. At the same time, you find yourself living a claustrophobic existence, unable to unglue this child from your side. But it doesn't have to be that way. In this chapter I will teach you specific strategies to help your child to feel comfortable on his own. He'll be able to see the world more realistically and not use you as a crutch in his day-to-day existence.

How to Break Up with Your Child

In chapters 3 and 4 you read about the form of therapy that is about to make profound changes in your life and the life of your child. Cognitive behavioral therapy (CBT) can work wonders for most children with separation anxiety disorder (SAD). CBT for SAD helps children recognize how they're feeling when they're forced to separate from their parents (full-scale panic!) and helps teach them how to calm down (deep breaths!), problem solve, and develop a coping plan when they're feeling anxious. It also helps them take a good look at themselves and what they're doing (clinging to Mom and Dad!) and creates a reward system of their choosing. Children are then taught to put their newfound coping skills into practice while gradually making the move away from their parents.

I've already shown you the general script to use when implementing CBT with your child. Now let's bring it to life for the child with SAD.

Step 1: Spot the Signs

You want your child to be able to recognize what she's feeling and when the feelings occur related to separations. From the previous chapter you've familiarized her with the "feelings recognition" skill by showing her pictures and asking her to identify how each person is feeling, and talking about television characters and their physical reactions to their wide range of emotions. Now you can start talking about what happens in her own body when she's away from you. Does her heart race? Stomach churn? Breath quicken? Does she sweat or her muscles tense?

Another way to help a young child learn to recognize the physical feelings he's having when separated from you is using the game of hide-and-seek.

- Get a large piece of butcher paper and roll it out on the floor.
- Have your child lie down on it and, with a marker, draw an outline of your child's body.
- Next, have your child draw and color in key body parts—the heart, the stomach, the eyes, nose, and mouth, the forehead, hands and feet, and lungs.
- Explain to your child that you're going to work with her to identify which body parts get "active" when you and she are separated.
- With your child in one room, explain that you're going to move to another room and stay there until your child finds you. But your child has to wait for certain lengths of time before she can come and seek you—you set this up for one minute, three minutes, five minutes, and so on.
- Once she finds you, lead your child back to the paper and have her take a marker and put a circle around any body part that had funny sensations while you were out of sight.
- Discuss what happened with each body part that was marked (e.g., "I had butterflies in my tummy," "I started to breathe fast"). In this way, you're teaching your child to pay attention to these feelings as they start to occur.

Step 2: Chill Out

Now that he's able to spot the emotional and physical feelings associated with his anxiety, you can teach your child strategies to decrease and even tolerate those feelings. Remember the belly breathing we learned in chapter 4? Let him know that when he's away from you and feeling anxious, he should turn to his breath to try to help calm himself.

For the child with separation anxiety, it's important to practice "mini" belly breathing exercises, a shorter form of the ten-minute breathing exercises you learned in chapter 4, in places where she most often worries about being separated from you. Encourage your child to do brief, one- or two-minute deep and slow breathing practices, while riding the bus, waiting in line at school, and whenever she finds herself away from you. For young children, find a special set of stickers that you and your child agree are the "belly reminders." Older children can use index cards that read "Breathe" or "Belly Breathe." Then place these stickers or cards on things that she's likely to be using when she's not with you (e.g., on the inside of her school organizer or pencil case; somewhere on her bedside table where she can see it; on the mirror in the bathroom where she looks at herself when brushing her teeth; on her backpack. Whenever she sees a belly reminder, she practices her deep breathing. By having her do this in situations where you are not right there with her, you're helping her to make the connection between calm breathing and being on her own.

Yoga is another terrific tool, particularly for older children, to help them learn more breath awareness. Take a yoga class with your child, and afterward ask him, "How does your body feel now?" Then ask him to try to think about your going out for the night and leaving him home alone—how does his body feel then? Encourage him to do the deep breathing he's learned in class whenever he's feeling anxious. In this way, he can get his body under control and then can think more logically. *Okay, my parents are going out for the night. What am I worried about? I'm old enough to handle this, I'll come up with some things to do while they are out.*

Step 3: Train in "Detective Thinking"

As we have discussed, children with SAD worry incessantly that when they're separated, something awful will happen to them or to their parents. I've heard very young children describe fantastic worries: that perhaps their parents will fall ill with an unknown disease or have a car accident on the way to work, or that they themselves will be kidnapped or get lost.

Your child is picturing the scenario as if it is actually happening in that moment and he's setting off the fight-or-flight response of panicking. So, for example, your son is at a party and you're supposed to pick him up at 9:00 p.m. When the clock strikes 9:01, he begins to literally make himself sick, imagining all the horrible things that could have befallen you: you're in an accident or somehow are lost and can't find your way to his friend's house, or maybe you've been arrested by mistake and are being led away. And he may also be picturing himself alone, without you, and thinking that you'll never come back.

Instead of sitting there and concocting all these scenarios in his head, he needs to ask himself, "How likely is it that something actually happened to my mom?" And, "Okay, she's a little late. What can I do to handle the situation?" To help your child, you can question him, as the following illustrates:

BOBBY: Why were you so late? Don't ever do that again, I was so worried!

MOM: Bobby, what time did I say that I'd pick you up?

BOBBY: You said nine o'clock and now it's already almost nine thirty! I thought something bad happened to you!

MOM: So, Bobby, can you please tell me what might have made me be late tonight?

BOBBY: I don't know, maybe you forgot to leave on time.

MOM: No, I didn't forget anything. What else?

BOBBY: Maybe you could've had an accident!

MOM: No, there wasn't an accident. What else?

BOBBY: Maybe you were on the phone and got caught up?

MOM: Okay, and what else can you think of?

BOBBY: Well, you might have been having fun out to dinner with Dad.

MOM: And what else?

BOBBY: You might have ordered dessert. Or, maybe you saw some friends while you were out and started talking to them.

MOM: Well, you're right about some things. I did go out to eat with Dad and it did take the waiter a while to take our order, and we had a very good dinner and dessert. And I had a lot of fun, too. But, now, tell me, what was so bad that happened?

BOBBY: Well, I got nervous that you weren't ever going to pick me up.

MOM: And how many times have I ever not picked you up?

BOBBY: Never. You always get me.

MOM: Bingo. And now what have you figured out tonight?

BOBBY: When you aren't right on time, you are having fun and nothing is wrong.

This process will help your child to challenge his own way of catastrophic thinking. Instead, he'll come up with more realistic thoughts that he can use to calm himself down and control the worry.

Step 4: Develop a Deal-with-It Plan

So now that she knows how she's feeling during separation, your child can work on how to handle those feelings. Children with SAD only see one solution: Cling to the parent for dear life! Give her a list of other responses, so she doesn't have to be so clingy. Come up with some things that will help her work through the anxiety, then go through them with her and weed out the ones that will increase the anxiety. For example, keeping a picture of the family with her or playing her favorite board game with the sitter when you're gone, or having a video chat with some school friends can be helpful. Having her call you several times during the separation or having you come home within a certain amount of time, not so much. Keep the list in plain sight to remind your child what she can do while you're gone.

Step 5: Bounty for Bravery

As noted in chapter 4, it's important for your child to learn to feel good about his accomplishments in separating from you and managing his anxiety. I work with a super team of clinical psychologists who are creative and very in tune with the likes and dislikes of children and adolescents. And they are attuned to the fact that these likes and dislikes can change very quickly: One day it's Pokémon cards. The next day that child is over those cards and on to Power Rangers action figures. First it's cell phones to text, then it's BlackBerrys to BBM (BlackBerry Messenger). And so our team came up with

"Bravery Bucks" that a child can earn for coping with difficult situations.

You and your child can assign denominations to different challenges, such as one Buck for playing alone in her room for a half hour, two Bucks for not calling you while she stays with a sitter and you run an errand to the store, and five Bucks for going to sleep while you are out for the evening. We teach the child to put the Bravery Buck into a jar himself, to promote his understanding of self-reinforcement. At the end of a week, he can turn in the Bravery Bucks for special reinforcers, such as extra time on a computer game, having a special playdate, or, yes, even getting a new bicycle if he saves long enough. The point is for your child to feel good about his separation accomplishments and to learn how to self-reinforce with enjoyable activity, a change from being caught in feeling upset and anxious over separation.

TO MAKE BRAVERY BUCKS

Cut some green paper the size of a dollar and have your child decorate different denominations of these Bravery Bucks—one-, two-, and five-Buck levels. If you have a photo printer or copier, you can put a head-shot of your child on the bill, just like having a George Washington one-dollar bill!

Step 6: Ready, Set, Go

We learned about the fear staircase in chapter 4. Each step on the staircase is a task or situation that your child fears, the bottom stair being the least feared; as the staircase goes up, the tasks gradually get more and more difficult, the top stair being the worst situation your child could think of. To create the staircase, give each separation situation a rating from 0 to 10 for how much the situation causes worry or anxiety, that is, how much it bothers your child right now. You will then rank the order, from the least bothersome (0, 1, 2) through to the most bothersome situations (8, 9, 10), so the more bothersome situations are on the top steps of the staircase.

As we build the staircase for separation anxiety, start with relatively easy situations that your child is likely to accomplish. At the bottom of the staircase could be:

- staying alone in the living room for five minutes while Mom's in the dining room
- playing alone for ten minutes while Mom's cooking dinner
- not calling while Mom's running an errand for twenty minutes

As your child moves up the staircase and masters each step, you can work to build more challenging situations into the mix:

- your child goes to a friend's house and stays for an hour without Mom there
- your child stays with a sitter for two hours
- your teenager stays alone in the house for a few hours

Remember to have photos or drawings of each step as your child moves up the staircase, and put these either on a poster or have her keep a journal of successes. Add photos of the special reinforcers that she earns at the end of each week.

Work with your child to come up with a list of difficult separation experiences and choose which ones to work on first. Let your child move up the ladder at his own pace, gently encouraging him to keep moving rather than getting stuck at any one point. Confronting his lesser fears will give him a sense of mastery and accomplishment, which in turn will help him be better able to tackle the bigger ones. Reinforce him for his efforts to ensure that he'll continue this path of brave behavior.

Creating a Fear Staircase

To help create a fear staircase, use this work sheet to determine which fears can be at the bottom and which should be at the top. As we noted in chapter 2, one of the most essential tools to overcoming anxiety is learning that you don't need to have total control of the situation. If you and your child can come up with a range of situations that could go wrong—you're late picking him up, you go out and leave your cell phone at home where he can see it, and you (oh my . . .) leave the house to run an errand without his knowing that you're gone, he'll have a better chance of confronting the variety of situations that pop up in everyday life. It may be difficult for him to think through all the possibilities of what could trip his anxiety switch, so use your imagination to drum up different scenarios.

ANXIETY FEELINGS SCALE

0	Piece of cake
1–2	Makes me a little anxious, but I can muscle through it
3–4	Makes me anxious and I try to avoid it sometimes
5–7	Definitely makes me anxious and I do my best to get out of it
8–9	Makes me scared and I avoid it like the plague
10	Mommy!!!!

EXAMPLES OF SEPARATION ANXIETY SITUATIONS

0	Sitting with Mom and watching TV
1–2	Mom is on the phone in her room and I'm alone in the living room
3–4	Staying alone in my bedroom to play for a half hour without Mom
5–7	Mom goes out to run an errand for thirty minutes and doesn't tell me where she's going
8–9	Waiting for Mom at school and I know she'll be late but don't know how late she's going to be!
10	My parents leave me with a sitter and I don't know where they went or what time they are coming back!

FEAR STAIRCASE (TO BE FILLED IN BY PARENT AND CHILD)

0	
1–2	
3–4	
5–7	
8–9	
10	

Parental Prescriptions

Now that you've got some guidelines to help your child relax, problem solve, and develop a coping plan, I want to give you some general rules to follow to help your child with separation anxiety.

First, always model brave behavior! Anxiety tends to run in families and, as we know, children tend to learn behavior by observing their parents. Take advantage of this by acting as a coping model for

A Note About Older Children

Although the majority of children will overcome a high degree of separation anxiety by the time they're in high school, sometimes, despite the parents' best attempts, children still will not separate. If you have a child approaching fourth or fifth grade with separation anxiety, I will tell you the same thing I tell parents of older children all the time: The older your children get, the more the window of opportunity will close to help them learn that they can manage separating from you. I'm not saying this to scare you. I'm telling you so that now, while your child is still at home, you can help your child move past this. You want your child to go to college and be able to live a full life without you. And that's not going to suddenly happen by itself. As he gets older, he may get less demonstrative in his tantrums, but if your child is staying around the house, you can bet his world is shrinking more and more compared to his friends' worlds. Your job is to help him open it up and move around more comfortably in it.

In addition to the CBT steps I've already outlined

- ❖ Encourage your teen to go on outings with friends

- ❖ Send your teen for overnight sleepovers at friends' houses

- ❖ Don't let your child avoid overnight school trips and don't volunteer to chaperone, even if your teen asks

- ❖ Persuade your teen to take a trip on a train or a plane to visit a relative

your child. I'm not telling you to confess all the ins and outs of your own angst. But you can let your child in on what you were afraid of when you were a child—and what you still fear—and how you handle it.

Always encourage your child's brave behavior. Separation experiences will come up every day. Your child will be challenged to go to school without you, to be on a different floor in the house, to put herself to sleep alone, and so on. Catch him being brave, even if just a little. Praise her using the specific behavior you want to see; for example, you might say, "Josh, you're doing an excellent job going up to your room by yourself!" Some parents are afraid to pay attention to non-anxious behavior because they think they'll jinx it. On the contrary, the more you notice the behavior you want to encourage, the more likely your child will be to repeat it.

On the flip side, ignore behaviors you want to discourage, like crying, whining, and clinging. Remember, attention from you is a very powerful reinforcer! Provide your child with small items (stickers, small toys) or things he likes to do (spending extra time playing outside, having a friend over for an extra playdate, or extra time on the computer) when he makes an effort to separate. When he whines, simply look away and engage in another activity without him, until the whining stops. If you give attention to the behavior ("Johnny, please stop whining. Mommy will only be gone for an hour. C'mon, please be a brave boy for Mommy."), you are reinforcing the whining. Plus you'll be missing an opportunity to praise him when he acts appropriately ("I like how you are now doing your homework. Nice job!").

Always be on the lookout for opportunities where your child can practice her newfound separation skills. Schedule playdates away from you and your home, have her go to the store and run errands for you if she's old enough. Give positive attention to any efforts you see at coping effectively with these challenges.

Do your best to discourage avoidance. While it's difficult to see your child upset, as I've said before, allowing your child to dodge the situations that cause him anxiety will only bolster the behavior. Instead of letting him avoid his fears, help him face them, so he can come to the realization that the situation is not as awful as he feared and he has the skills to deal with it. When your child tries to sidestep situations, encourage him to use the coping skills we've discussed. And remember, while helping him is good, feeding him all the answers is not. Your job is to scaffold and support, not do it for him.

Don't reassure excessively. While that will decrease your child's anxiety temporarily, the feeling will soon wear off and she'll return to you for even more reassurance. And let your child fend for herself sometimes. Continually rescuing her sends a message that she doesn't have the ability to deal with the situation on her own and robs her of the opportunity to master the situation herself.

Don't allow your child to avoid situations he's afraid of. It doesn't give him the chance to see that the situation is probably not as dire as he thought and, in fact, it may be fun. And don't be overly controlling. Becoming a master planner for your child doesn't give him the chance to come up with his own ideas of what to do and how to do things.

DO'S AND DON'TS FOR PARENTING THE CHILD WITH SEPARATION ANXIETY

Do's

- Model brave behavior.
- Praise and reward efforts at coping.
- Ignore whining and crying behavior.
- Help your child face his fears in steplike fashion; start with the easy things first.
- Discourage avoidance of anxiety-provoking situations.
- Be empathic; validate emotions, but not necessarily behavior.

- Prepare your child for anxiety-provoking situations in advance—develop a coping plan so that he feels prepared to confront the fearful situation.

Don'ts

- Excessively reassure your child by telling him that "nothing bad is going to happen," "everything will be fine," or "there is nothing to worry about."
- Rescue your child from anxiety-provoking situations (e.g., picking him up from school early, staying with him at birthday parties, staying home rather than going out at night).
- Permit or encourage avoidant behavior (e.g., keeping your child out of camp because it is too stressful, letting your child refuse playdates outside of the home, permitting the child to sleep in bed with you).
- Model anxiety by talking excessively about your own fears and worries and avoiding situations that make you anxious.
- Be overly involved—some parents will respond to a child's anxiety by taking over and attempting to direct the situation, rather than encouraging the child to cope with the situation.

Common Challenges

Your child will be facing new situations every day. Here's some advice on how to cope with some of the most common separation fears.

What About Me?

If you're like Sandy's mom, Sue, or Jon's mother, Rosemary, you may have given up much in the last couple of years to placate your anxious child. You've turned down invitations to parties and dinners and any one-on-one time with your spouse because you couldn't bear your child's suffering at being without you. You're used to having your child by your side 24/7, and after the initial rush of having him gain his independence, you may be finding yourself feeling some loss because, to some degree, it was comforting and reassuring to be taking care of your child. And you always had your buddy with you, so you could share in lots of his day-to-day moments.

But now you need to help him move along a bit—and that may be an uncomfortable feeling for both of you. Push through it. Don't revert to old habits. If you're out to dinner with friends and you realize you haven't heard from your son in hours—don't pick up the phone yourself! Don't continue the habits that have sustained the anxiety for both of you. And make sure to nurture yourself. Think about all the things you did before your child's anxiety spun out of control. Join a gym again, go bowling with friends again, plan a trip with your spouse.

Walking into a Crowded Group

Whether it's a party where you and your child know everyone, or a group of complete strangers, crowds can be overwhelming for anyone, but particularly scary for the child with separation anxiety when you're distracted and not paying attention to her. Before you leave for the party, speak to your child about who is going to be there. If you can, show her a few pictures. Do this in a matter-of-fact way ("And my cousin Tommy will be there with his son, Joey, and he's your age") to take the pressure off.

At the party, model confidence. When you see someone he knows, gently encourage him. "Hey, there's your friend Jimmy over there playing knock hockey. Go say hello to him." The first few times you do this, stay within his sight but don't give him too much attention. Gradually, move yourself farther away from him and mix with the crowd. Use positive praise for coping and having fun and ignore any whining and complaints that may come along the way. Avoid labeling your child as "shy" to the other adults, which can become a self-fulfilling prophecy.

Bedtime

One of the most common questions I get from parents of children with SAD is about the family bed. Some families love the closeness they feel when the entire family cuddles together at night. But for the child with anxiety, this practice only strengthens separation anxiety and creates confusion about why everyone can't be together during the daytime as well. For parents who value the closeness of a family bed and are reluctant to change, I compare it to valuing certain foods but having to change how you cook if a family member develops diabetes.

Take the following example. Diane and Max had two children, Sammy, age eight, and Tricia, age four. Max was an airline pilot and traveled on overnight trips to Europe, where he was gone for several nights in a row. Early on, having the children in her room, and often in the bed, made managing a young child and a baby easier for Diane. Over time, this developed into both children being in bed with their mom, who struggled to get them out of the bed and into their own rooms when their father returned from a trip.

By the time Sammy entered kindergarten, he decided he preferred to sleep in his own room and would put himself to sleep. But Tricia loved being with her mommy and cuddled in her parents' bed whenever her dad was away. More and more, she resisted going into her own bed. When Max returned from a trip, it often took nearly a week to move Tricia to her own room, and they were lucky if she stayed there the full night—she usually crawled back in during the night and was nestled next to her mother by morning. Then another trip would come and Tricia was back in Mom and Dad's bed for the full night. And so the cycle repeated itself. Max had enough of this and was growing more resentful of the child and angry at his wife, whom he blamed for perpetuating the problem.

They sought help at our clinic to move their daughter out of their bed once and for all. In our first session, Max begged his daughter to go to sleep in her room and blurted out, "If you sleep in your own bed this week, I'll buy you a playhouse for the backyard!" I was taken aback at the promise, which I knew this father would keep but which I also knew would change the child's behavior for maybe one week, but not much more. First, it was too big a payoff. There's no need to go for broke on what should be a natural and normal behavior. Next, the child was not involved in choosing the reinforcer, so there was very little buy-in on her part. Did she even *want* a playhouse in the backyard? Third, the father had lost sight that this was a child's behavior that warranted both parents cooperating and engaging their daughter in a unified and optimistic front. Together, they needed to give the message "We know you can do this" rather than "I'll buy this from you for the moment."

I quickly redirected this child away from the big prize and on to a more reasoned and long-lasting approach to changing her behavior. In chapter 4, I talked about using positive reinforcers to help shape behavior. Here's an example of how I used it in my office.

DR. A: Tricia, is there anything that you would like to have for breakfast that you don't get in your house?

TRICIA: Yes! Fruity Pebbles! We're not allowed to eat those!

DR. A: So, let me see here, what do you have for breakfast now?

TRICIA: Momma makes me eggs or we eat waffles, and sometimes we have oatmeal.

DR. A: Okay, so it's important to have a good breakfast, isn't it?

TRICIA: Yes!

With this, I took out a very small Dixie cup that I keep stashed away for just this type of situation.

DR. A: Suppose you were to sleep in your bed all night long, then get up and eat all the breakfast that your mom or dad makes for you. You eat up the whole thing. Would you then like to have a cup of Fruity Pebbles as an extra special treat?

TRICIA: Yes! I love Fruity Pebbles!

Although her parents were stunned and taken aback by this, I continued on with Tricia and was quite concrete and simple in my discussion.

DR. A: Okay, so here's what we're doing. Every time that you stay in your bed all night long and then eat all of your breakfast the next morning, you're going to be able to have a cup full of Fruity Pebbles. Okay?

TRICIA: Yeah! Yes!

DR. A: Okay, and I'd like you to put a sticker on this chart for each day that you get the Fruity Pebbles, and then bring this back to me so I can see how you're doing!

As I then explained to the parents, finding a valued motivator for the child to work toward, in this case the Fruity Pebbles, is more effective than promising big rewards that are pulled from the air, no matter how attractive they may seem. Also, Tricia doesn't have 24/7 access to the cereal. She only gets to eat it when she has slept alone in her room. The small reinforcer is given after the meal, so it doesn't interfere with her breakfast and overall healthy eating habits, and she gets only a small amount—enough to satisfy her. On the sticker chart, Diane found a picture of a Fruity Pebbles box that she cut out and pasted on the form, and each morning when Tricia slept in her bed and earned her treat, she got a star. Each week they'd bring me the form so that I could "high-five" and celebrate Tricia's success with her.

It took only three days of not getting the treat to align Tricia's behavior and have her sleeping in her own bed. Of note: After several weeks of steady sleeping in her own room, Tricia arrived at the clinic for a follow-up and announced quite loudly in the waiting area, "Dr. Albano! My mom wanted me to sleep with her and I said, 'No! I want my Fruity Pebbles so I am not sleeping with you!'" Out of the mouths of babes come words of wisdom: to keep consistent on the program so that old habits don't revert back. We certainly shared a lot of high fives that day.

If your child fusses and frets at bedtime, possibly even needs you to fall asleep with him, but he stays in his bed all night by himself, develop a bedtime ritual that signals sleep time is approaching. A warm bath, a massage with lotion, some deep breathing exercises, and a few books are all great choices to soothe his body and mind. At first, do these rituals with him; as he gets older, move for him to do them alone. For younger children, play very soft music that will turn off after ten minutes. If your child whimpers or even cries, don't rush back to comfort him. For older children, place photos of you and your spouse in his sight line. When it's time to say good night, give him a quick kiss and leave the room before he falls asleep.

Babysitter or Day Care

Ask a new Saturday-night sitter to come early. With a new full-time nanny or day care provider, try to take a half day off from work so everyone can get comfortable with one another while you're there to facilitate. It may be tempting to dash out the door the minute your child turns his head, but that will heighten clinginess even more if he never knows when you might sneak away. Instead, play together with the sitter or day care provider, then slowly back up and let her take over.

When everyone seems happy, say your good-byes. Don't linger! That shows you're just as nervous as he is. Even if you're dying inside, paint a big ole grin on your face and give a cheerful wave as you walk out the door. And once you're gone, stay gone, even if he's crying. If you intermittently give in, that's a jackpot. He'll know if he cries long enough, eventually you'll come back.

The First Day of School

Whether it's the first day of kindergarten or the first day of middle school, after a long summer break with you and being at home, children with separation anxiety have trouble getting back to the routine of school. If this will be your child's first foray into school, "play" school with her beforehand. See if you can find out the class-room routine (circle time, weather chart, wash hands, snack, etc.) and act out what she'll be doing so she can get a feel for it.

If he's been to school before, go visit the classroom so he can become familiar with the new space. If you can, have your child meet the teacher. It's great if you can take pictures of him with the new teacher, at his desk and cubby, and in front of the school. Mount the pictures on a poster board at home. Take photos of your child and his new friends as you come to know them and build a scrap-book of school experiences. And put a picture of you or a special toy in his backpack that he can keep in his cubby if he needs comfort-ing. When dropping him off, give him a kiss and leave without lingering.

Going to Sleepaway Camp

By the time children are nine or ten years of age, many are going to summer sleepaway camp and coming home with grand stories of canoeing and singing campfire songs, covered with lanyards that they made and swapped with new friends. The child with separation anxiety often feels conflicted—left out of these activities because she's too scared to try. But I have good news: I've had many suc-cesses helping children with early separation anxiety go off to camp and turn their fears into successes. I know that might be difficult for you to believe, but it's true.

To prepare him, start with sleepover practices. Have him stay overnight at a friend's house or with a relative, and gradually move this to staying two nights in a row. Build on these overnight expe-riences by having them happen several times during the winter and spring—I've had children sleep over some four or five times at friends' houses.

Next, browse the Web with your child for the camps you've heard about, and look at all the photos and information about the camp and its activities, focusing particularly on the activities she likes best (especially things she can't do at home, like waterskiing and lake swimming). Attend any orientations with your child in your local area, and make shopping for new clothes and picking out camp gear a fun experience for both of you. Make sure she knows you'll write to her every day, and make it easy for her to write to you by packing pre-addressed, stamped envelopes for her to mail to you and others, such as grandparents and friends.

Don't over-reassure—repeatedly saying "You'll be fine" causes the child with anxiety to look for ways to discredit you. Practice scenarios he'll find in camp. Help him come up with strategies on how he'll meet new friends, decide which activities to do, and so on. Speak to the counselors before camp starts to let them know your child is anxious about being away and may become homesick. Believe me, yours is not the first anxious child the camp has seen. Develop a plan detailing when your child can make phone calls home. Perhaps in addition to his regularly scheduled calls, the camp can give him some extra calls if he practices positive coping skills. Of course, make sure to work this out with the camp before making your child any promises. And speak to your child, and the camp, about the rules of phone calls. You will only speak to your child if he's not crying.

Make a deal with your child that he stays for a pre-specified period of time. It may be only one week to start, or perhaps two. If you can prearrange with the camp that he can stay longer if he wants, great. This gives your child a sense of control. Also, if you call the shots ("We want you to stay one week"), then he won't be feeling as though he's escaping if he decides to come home after the week. Instead, you will celebrate his successful week of summer camp.

When you do talk to her on the phone, focus on all the fun she's having—don't let her cry and beg to come home. If she does, gently end the call and ask her to call back again when she's calmed down. (A counselor should be with her to help make this possible.) Remember, many times the crying will only occur if *you* are overly anxious ("Honey, are you *really* okay?") or concerned with the separation ("I miss you so, so much, we've never been away from you before!"), so be upbeat and positive yourself. And keep the call brief—shorter is better with a child who has separation anxiety.

WHILE MOST CHILDREN GO through periods of separation anxiety at some point in their lives, for some children this anxiety remains constant and affects friendships, school, and even their health. But as you've seen in this chapter, SAD doesn't have to take hold forever. Your child can learn to calm himself, think rationally and clearly, and overcome his separation anxiety through the step-by-step practice of handling scary situations that we have discussed. Getting control over SAD is important for helping your child to learn effective ways of solving problems and managing his feelings, and the skills learned in managing SAD will serve him over the long term as he takes on new challenges throughout his life.

7

The World-Class Worrywart: Understanding Generalized Anxiety

I t's 11:00 p.m. and everyone in the Rivera house is asleep—everyone, that is, except nine-year-old Maya. When the lights go off and the house is hushed, Maya's angst-ridden thoughts power up to turbocharged. Maya agonizes over everything: her parents' health, her friends' health, her own health, her parents' financial situation, school, friends, earthquakes, fires, clowns, car crashes, the dark, the sun, global warming, robbers—her fears run the gamut from the obvious to the obscure.

Blame Maya's constant hand-wringing on the most common anxiety disorder in children and adolescents: generalized anxiety disorder (GAD). Sure, all children lose sleep over worry on occasion. But children with GAD worry a lot, and their worries are intense and debilitating.

The parents of these worrywarts are dog-tired mentally. Their children are constantly catapulting questions at them: "What if I oversleep on the morning of a big test?" "What if someone gets hurt while we're camping?" "What if Mom or Dad gets laid off and there's not enough money?" And whatever answer their parents give, it's never good enough. There is always—always—a follow-up question. And then another, and another after that.

It's as if you always have to be one step ahead of the worry when you have a child with GAD. Every move you make becomes cause for an inquisition. Dad comes home from work an hour early: "Did you get fired?" Mom brings a pile of mail inside the house: "Do we have enough money to pay all those bills?" So your life becomes a duck-and-cover operation. You look over your shoulder to make sure nobody's reading your mail. Every phone conversation is concealed behind a closed door. Even if the call is completely insignificant, your child will find something in it to fret about, which will make your life completely and utterly miserable.

If you're feeling worn down by the relentless questioning and maneuvering, these next two chapters are for you. I'll help you gain an in-depth understanding of

- what generalized anxiety is all about
- how it develops
- how to spot it in your child
- how you can help your child overcome it

Lauren's Story

Lauren's story is fairly typical of a child with GAD. I first met her when she was in the eighth grade. She sat on the edge of the chair, folded her hands in her lap, and leaned in toward me as we started

QUIZ: COULD YOUR CHILD HAVE GAD?

Answer yes or no to the following questions.

- Does your child eavesdrop on your conversations and ask you whom you were talking to and why? Yes/No

- Does your eight-year-old have trouble sleeping and often complain of stomachaches and headaches? Yes/No

- Does your daughter get a paper cut and then tell you she saw a television show where a finger with a paper cut developed gangrene and had to be amputated? Yes/No

- When you mention that a neighbor has been sick, does your child begin to obsess over your health, asking you how you feel for weeks afterward? Yes/No

- After your child's friend calls to cancel their playdate, is your child inconsolable and does he insist that everybody in school hates him, even though his friend had a valid reason for canceling? Yes/No

- When you and your husband have an argument, does your daughter claim you're going to get a divorce, even after you've told her you're not? Yes/No

- Does your thirteen-year-old bring home a 90 on a test and cry that she'll never get into a good college? Yes/No

- Does your son take everything you say literally? Yes/No

- Do most of your child's questions begin with "what if"? Does she ask what can go wrong next? Yes/No

- Is your child bossy with her friends, insisting that they follow the rules of every game "just right"; otherwise they're not allowed to play? Yes/No

If you answered yes to any of these questions, your child could have a problem with GAD.

our conversation. Red outlined her beautiful blue eyes and she often yawned while I talked. I didn't take that as disinterest, though—this girl was genuinely tired.

Lauren took every question I asked very seriously, staring at me while she revised her answers again and again. After every response she asked, "Does that sound right?" even though I told her several times that there were no right or wrong answers.

Lauren's parents told me about her constant questions, which started very soon after she began to talk. "Will I choke on this?" "What if I don't make any friends in day care?" "What if the plane crashes?" "What if you and Daddy get a divorce?" As she got older, her questions got more complicated. "Where does lightning come from?" "Do dogs always bark before they bite someone?" "Will germs get on me if I sit next to someone sick at school?" By the second grade she began repeating the same questions again and again, often followed by "Why?" and "Are you sure?" and "How do you know that?"

Lauren brought home good grades, yet she berated herself for being stupid and not knowing exactly what the teacher was going to ask on a test. Homework was always a struggle. Lauren's mother helped and even hired expensive tutors at one point, but it was the same story night after night: She'd start something, cry that it wasn't good enough, tear it to shreds, and start over again.

With her peers, Lauren was bossy and controlling. She hated working in groups; when forced to, she struggled for control and turned other children off. Lauren felt there was a "right" way or a better way to do things, and she didn't trust that her peers knew what to do. And they, in return, saw her as overbearing and controlling. For one group project in seventh grade, the other students begged the teacher to take Lauren off their team, because every time the group agreed on the work during the day, Lauren took the project home and changed it. By the middle of eighth grade, Lauren was isolated, anxious, irritable, and sorely in need of help.

Lauren's parents called me after her class was given a short writing assignment to complete over the weekend about what they looked forward to in high school. As usual, Lauren's questions began: "Will high school lead me to a good college?" "Mom, I don't know what I want to do when I grow up!" "Maybe they will make me go to a different school." "Is this some sort of test? Are they trying to trick me?" She couldn't sleep Friday night, and by Saturday night she was shaking uncontrollably. Frightened by the intensity of Lauren's anxiety, her parents called the pediatrician in the middle of the night. He prescribed an antianxiety medication to help Lauren through the next few days and made a very pointed recommendation to get her into cognitive behavioral therapy (CBT) immediately.

While Lauren's story might seem extreme, I've heard dozens of stories just like hers in my years of practice. And I've heard these children's frustrated parents, who can't seem to ease their children's anxieties, no matter how hard they try.

Wired for Worry

Worry isn't all bad. As we learned in chapter 1, children are actually preprogrammed to cultivate a healthy amount of worry, which helps to motivate them and protect them from danger. As your child's nervous system is developing, she begins to crawl and then toddle around the house, exploring and engaging with the environment. You are there providing encouragement, support, and usually some warning ("No, no, Sasha, don't touch that, it's hot, hot!") when something can be dangerous. Over time, your child develops more independence, and on occasion you may even hear a crash followed by an "Uh-oh!" as your ever swifter child knocks your favorite ceramic bowl off a table. All the while, she is learning to associate her actions with certain feelings, ideas, and outcomes.

Somewhere between the ages of two and four, children develop the ability to predict the immediate future. You throw a ball to the ground; it will bounce back up. The doorbell rings; Mom will leave to go answer it. By elementary school, a more advanced imagination helps children come up with all sorts of outcomes. Some are good. *If I cross the street here I may get to the other side just fine. I may see a friend on the other side of the street and we may go out for ice cream later.* Others, not so much. *If I cross the street here I may trip and fall, I may get hit by a car. My mother may get hit by a car.* This ability to accurately predict the dangerousness of certain situations keeps us safe.

Children with GAD differ in very distinct ways from what's typical. Wendy Silverman, Ph.D., an expert in childhood anxiety disorders, and her colleagues at Florida International University found that the children who came in for treatment for GAD at her clinic worried about the same kinds of things as every other child: school, health issues, harm befalling themselves or others, and safety. The difference was the *intensity* of their worry.

Children with generalized anxiety have great difficulty seeing the positive or even the neutral. It's as if they're preprogrammed to eternally see life's lemons. As they make their way into the world, their danger meter becomes set on high and all roads lead to Dreadful Avenue. Instead of helping to avoid danger, the danger meter paralyzes them. The unknown is viewed as perilous and unbearable, and even if the odds are stacked against anything going wrong, they're putting all their chips on the worst-case scenario. These fraidy-cats can find fear in even the happiest times. A trip to Disney World, pure bliss for most children, is cause for a four-alarm fire.

What if we miss our flight? What if our plane crashes? Will we have to wait in long lines for the rides? Will I be safe on the rides? What if I get nauseous? Will our hotel be close to the park? What if the pool water is not clean?

Not only will the worst happen, but the child with GAD has no faith in himself. He's sure that he's completely inept and incompetent and won't be able to handle what's thrown at him. A typical child wonders about getting sick and figures if it happens (as it likely will), he'll stay home for a few days, get better, then make up the work he's missed at school. The child with GAD wonders whether or not he'll get sick, and then his worry wheels start spinning: *If the doctor gives me medicine, it might not work and then I'll miss a lot of school. What if I'm out of school when the teacher gives the most important information for our next math test? Then I'll fail the math test and I'll never be able to make up the work and I'll have to repeat the grade.* So he's hit with a double whammy—his world goes to pot, and he lacks the wherewithal to handle it.

Forecasting the Future for the Non-anxious Child

Can't predict everything about the future? No problem for the typical child. She understands that life can spin up, down, sideways, and backward, and while we can do our best to nudge our future forward the way we want it, there's only so far we can steer it. This skill of dealing successfully with uncertainty develops over time, and the more practice she has with uncertainty, the better she gets at managing it. You know that saying, "#$% happens"? Most children understand that and realize that while a bad ending is possible, it's just one of any number of ways a situation can shake out. That is, anything is possible, but the probability of something happening is another matter. It's possible to win the lottery, but the realistic probability may be one in twenty million. In general, non-anxious children tend to be optimistic, or, at least, they tend not to dwell on the negative.

The child's inner voice—what he says to himself in response to his own fears and worries—talks him out of anxiety and helps him remain calm. It's not that typical children don't worry, it's that they're able to move their focus away from the worrisome thoughts and more toward the neutral or even pleasant ideas. They can refocus their attention on other things and put the worry aside.

Barry, a typical eleven-year-old child, worries that he's not going to do well on his math test. Certain things are within his control. He can bump up his studying time. He can use flash cards and have his mother quiz him on the material. Other things he has no control over. The classroom may be stuffy and hot, making it difficult for him to concentrate. The teacher may ask questions he didn't realize were going to be on the test. The teacher may grade on a curve; the teacher may be a tough grader; the teacher may be in a bad mood on test day; Barry may be in a bad mood on test day. Dozens of internal and external factors come into play, and Barry realizes that although he can do as much as he can to get a good grade, he can't guarantee that all things will go perfectly.

As a child matures, she gets even better at steering the future as her problem-solving skills improve. Two teenagers, Rob and Lou, want to run for student council. Anxiety gives them both pause. Rob, a typical teenager, uses his problem-solving skills to power through it. He evaluates the situation and comes up with various ways to achieve his goal. First, he goes through all the things that he might do in order to win. He thinks to himself:

- *I can put up campaign posters.*
- *I can talk to as many kids as I can.*
- *I can pay my friends to vote for me.*
- *I can put up a Facebook page.*
- *I can have my parents buy a billboard.*
- *I can run a negative campaign about my opponents.*

Then he assesses the ideas that are realistic (putting up posters, talking to classmates, doing a Facebook page) and the ones that might not bode well for him in the long run (running a negative campaign, paying friends for votes) and the ones that are just plain silly (having his parents buy a billboard). Rob weighs each option and comes up with a plan that may involve one or more of the proposals. Then he puts the plan into place. Whether or not he gets elected, he can look back and evaluate what he did well and what he might do differently to increase his chances of winning in the future.

Lou is a teen with GAD. When he thinks about running for election, the anxiety stalls his problem-solving power. The thoughts that run through his head are more along the following lines:

- *Who would vote for me?*
- *I can't make an election speech!*
- *What if I lose and then I won't have anything on my college application to talk about?*
- *What if I win? Then I'll have so much more work to do!*

At each step of the process he doubts himself. He may buy some poster board but he doesn't know the perfect slogan to write on it. If he does write something, it's not going to be as good as what his opponent comes up with. If he does actually win, he attributes it not to his own abilities but to luck, or a mistake (they must not have meant to vote for me). He doesn't enjoy the process and looks at it as a chore that he'll fail or will burden him in some way if he wins. He's damned if he does and damned if he doesn't.

Braced for Disaster

As I've shown you, children with generalized anxiety can't handle the fact that they have limited control over everyday life and that they can't accurately predict every outcome. And they bet that every situation will end badly, they exaggerate what they think will happen to a catastrophic degree, and they underestimate their own abilities to cope.

For this reason, a child with excessive worry is typically in what psychologists call a "future-oriented mood state," where he is always preparing for something bad to happen. Take, for example, eight-year-old Teddy. When he and his family took a beach vacation, he was glued to the Weather Channel to make sure no hurricanes, tidal waves, or flash floods were expected in the area. He made sure his mother, Maxine, packed a first-aid kit, and when they got to the hotel he checked and rechecked that their room locked properly. At the beach his siblings jumped in the waves and splashed around merrily with their parents, but Teddy stood paralyzed on the shore, attacking the lifeguards with questions: "Are there sharks out there?" "What happens if someone gets bit?" "Do you have a shark-bite kit?" "Do you know how to rescue people?" "What if you get a cramp?" Maxine finally had to take him away because he was distracting the lifeguards from their job.

Like all children with GAD, Teddy was anticipating almost every bad thing that could happen and was trying to find a way to stop the disaster before it occurred. But, unlike knowing that winning the lottery is a long shot, Teddy believed that as soon as his toes hit the surf, a shark would be waiting to nip at him. He was almost as sure of this as he was that the sun would rise each morning.

His nonstop questions were meant to cover all the bases. But no matter what the answers were, he dismissed them because they didn't fit with his ideas of doom and gloom. Instead, he quoted ad nauseam the one story he found on the Internet that showed a series of shark attacks to prove that "it could happen here, too, and it could happen this very day when we're at the beach!" This kind of negative thinking can only result in a heightened state of anxiety—danger lurks under each and every wave.

I had the good fortune to study with one of the world's leading authorities on anxiety, David H. Barlow, Ph.D. He describes the experience of worry as a state of "anxious apprehension" where the person thinks, "That terrible event could happen (again), and I might not be able to deal with it, but I've got to be ready to try." The child remains in a state of anxious apprehension, on edge and ready to react, always thinking the worst-case scenario is right around the corner. *"The doctor will miss something and Mom will die." "The burglar will eventually find a way into the house." "There's a better way to do these homework assignments but I'm not smart enough to figure that out."*

Worried Sick . . . Literally

These ideas keep the child in an ever-ready state of preparedness. They're always on high alert, poised for the worst. Remember the fight-or-flight response I talked about in chapter 1? This response is focused on an immediate threat—similar to a car that pulls out in front of you. SLAM, there it is! You hit the brakes as your brain sees the danger before you've even processed it, automatically responding to avert the careless driver. The child with GAD is in a chronic state of future-oriented worry. It's as if you're driving down the road and never know when a car might pull out, but you're clenching the steering wheel, scanning the street and straining to see what's coming from all sides, and driving ever so carefully because you just . . . never . . . know . . . when . . . that . . . car . . . will . . . pull . . . out!

For the child with GAD, his brain is perpetually firing signals to the central nervous system, overworking the adrenal glands to send out scads of stress hormones. His muscles are tense and ready to react, he's breathing more quickly, and he might seem distracted because he's not able to keep his focus. And this nonstop igniting of his stress hormones leads to headaches, muscle aches, irritability, stomach distress, and sleeplessness.

Although sometimes the child's worry focuses on something she can pinpoint, at other times nothing in particular has her in a sweat. The focus of her worry may shift, but the inability to control it remains. Because they're often consumed with worry, children with GAD may have a difficult time concentrating, processing information, and successfully engaging in various activities. Because of their constant need for reassurance, they may have difficulty making and keeping friends.

Children with generalized anxiety are often quite hard on themselves and on others, to the point of being overly conforming about rules—right versus wrong, good versus bad. Their standards are high for themselves and they can be almost tyrannical with their friends, making sure everyone always does everything the "right" way. Maddie follows the rules of Monopoly to the letter, but if her friend wants to trade properties, which isn't in the rules, Maddie breaks down and throws the board. Children with GAD are also perfectionists, and they're brutal in their self-reproach if they fail to meet the high standards they set for themselves. Jonah gets so frustrated with a homework assignment that he snaps at his mother, then he's filled with remorse for failing her as a son.

They insist on performing tasks over and over again so they can get them perfect. And even if they do perform well, they continue to berate themselves. One study found that children and adolescents with GAD who received As on homework and tests continued to worry about failing the next test.

GAD has been identified in children as young as four years old, though it's more likely to appear a bit later—various studies have found the onset to be in the range of about eleven to thirteen years of age. Studies have found that it affects anywhere from 3 percent to 11 percent of children and adolescents.

As with all the anxiety disorders, a combination of biology, family, and environmental factors is likely involved.

- **Temperament:** Inhibited babies and babies who are slow to warm up to new situations are more likely to suffer from GAD later in life.
- **Family history:** Blame nature as well as nurture. Parents who suffer from anxiety themselves tend to pass on their fears to their children, as do parents who are depressed. Their own distorted view of the world may result in setting strict limits on their children, which bolsters the idea that the world is a scary place.
- **Pushy parents:** Parents who set the bar too high tend to have children who are perfectionists and are insecure. Because they're terrified of losing out on opportunities, these children avoid any situations where they might do poorly.
- **Early traumas and stressful events:** Children who were rejected, neglected, or abandoned by their parents

may end up feeling insecure, which can raise the risk of developing GAD.

- **Brain chemistry:** As I explained in chapter 1, children with GAD appear to be short on gamma-aminobutyric acid (GABA), the neurotransmitter that helps calm the limbic system (the brain's emotion hub) and manages the action of the stress hormones epinephrine, norepinephrine, and dopamine.

Investigators Carl Weems, Ph.D., Wendy Silverman, Ph.D., and Annette La Greca, Ph.D., found the top fears among children with generalized anxiety were about

- tests and grades
- natural disasters
- being attacked
- future school performance
- being bullied or scapegoated by their peers

QUIZ: ARE YOU HELPING OR HURTING?

Answer yes or no to the following questions.

- When your child has an essay due, do you find yourself editing draft after draft by yourself? Yes/No

- If your child complains of a stomachache and wants to go to the doctor, do you take her right away? Yes/No

- Do you spend hours endlessly answering your child's questions, never saying, "I've answered the question. It's enough"? Yes/No

- Do you often write notes to your child's teacher, saying that the work is too difficult? Yes/No

- Do you continually tell your child that things are going to be okay? Yes/No

- Do you avoid anything in particular because you feel it's too dangerous for your child? Yes/No

- Do you allow your child to skip things she's too nervous to do? Yes/No

If you answered yes to any of these questions, you may be contributing to your child's GAD. And you may even be making it worse.

Life in the Underground

Like the parents we saw in the previous chapters who have children with separation anxiety disorder (SAD), parents of children with GAD do everything they can to make things easier on their children, even to the point where their lives become a series of cover-ups and covert operations. Anything they share with their children becomes fodder for a week's worth of worry. A neighbor has cancer becomes "Is it contagious? Can you get it? Can I? What if you get it and die? What will happen to me?" I've had parents who wouldn't bring newspapers and magazines into the house and they put parental controls on the television and computers so their children couldn't see the news. But keeping things from their children doesn't necessarily help. And, in fact, it could potentially make things worse.

Take the story of twelve-year-old Amanda. While she was at sleepaway camp her father had to have an emergency appendectomy. Because Amanda was a worrier, her mother, Rhonda, made the family promise that nobody would tell her. What Amanda didn't know wouldn't hurt her, Rhonda thought. When Amanda returned home her father had nearly recovered but still needed to stay home for a few more days. The questions began right away: "Why are you home? What's wrong? Did you get fired? You're never home from work!" Her parents tried to convince her that he was just taking a few days off to spend with the family, but Amanda was skeptical.

Things blew up when Amanda accidentally saw her dad's bandage. "What is that!?! I knew something was wrong!" she shrieked, until her parents told her the truth. Amanda screamed that she didn't believe it was only an appendectomy. "He's going to die! Daddy's going to die!" she insisted over and over. When her parents finally calmed her down, she told them she was never going back to camp.

While keeping things from children with GAD may work temporarily, there's only so far you can take that. Eventually the truth will come out—the child will catch something on television while walking past a store, a cousin won't know that an aunt's illness was supposed to be a secret, and when the child finds out that his parents have kept something from him he'll be wary of trusting anything they say to him in the future. It's better to swallow hard and tell the truth now rather than pay for it later.

Endless Questions: From Cute to Crazy-making

As I mentioned at the beginning of the chapter, one of the most eye-rolling aspects of having a child with GAD is the eternal string of questions. One parent told me she felt like a human Google. "My daughter is constantly asking me questions and I have to answer, answer again, and answer yet again," she said. Even if you have an

M.D., Ph.D., and a J.D., your child always needs proof that what you said is legit.

While at first parents may be overjoyed at the precociousness of their child, they soon tire of the need for constant comfort. When children are very young, they'll take their parents' answers at face value. Remember Lauren and her constant questions? When she was two and asked her mom where she was going, "the store" was just fine as an answer. But as children age and their cognitive abilities mature, they learn that dangers abound in the world. "Don't touch the stove," "Hold my hand when we cross the street," "Don't eat too quickly, you'll choke."

As their imaginations mature they can concoct more and more dangers. See the dialogue below: As Lauren's parents found out, no matter what reassurances they gave her, she'd imagine dangers lurking everywhere and fire back another question.

LAUREN: What if you or Daddy gets sick and then dies?

MOM: We're healthy, sweetie, but if anyone gets sick, we will call our doctor.

LAUREN: But what if we don't have a good doctor, or he doesn't know what kind of medicine you would need?

MOM: Nothing bad will happen and doctors are all trained to take care of everything, so there's nothing to worry about.

LAUREN: But what if there's something making you sick that you don't know you have, and it looks like a cold but maybe it's the start of cancer, and the doctor doesn't know that it's there? I mean, can they *see* cancer when they look in our throats? If they can't see what's inside you, then you will get worse and worse.

MOM: Honey, the doctor will do tests if something is bad, but we are fine and there's no need to worry.

LAUREN: Yeah, but sometimes the doctors miss something, right? Molly's mom died because she had something wrong and the doctor couldn't do anything about it, right? I don't want you to die!

As the questions become more sophisticated, parents of an anxious child tend to increase their involvement to comfort and reassure. As with SAD, this sets up a vicious cycle. Parents provide more and more reassurance but the child is less and less apt to believe them. If the child isn't forced to see the situation herself, she returns again and again to her parents for help. That sends parents into a tailspin—they don't want their child to suffer, so they try to minimize her exposure to upsetting situations and ideas.

Remember when Lauren was so stressed and upset and sure she would fail every class at school that her parents hired expensive tutors and they made sure to do her homework with her every night? This is an all-too-familiar scenario for many of the parents with whom I've worked over the years. Lauren was already thinking, *I'm not smart enough to do this.* Then, her parents stepped in and hired pricey tutors and helped her with homework. *I knew it!* Lauren thinks. *I knew I wasn't smart enough! If I were, Mom wouldn't have to help me!*

These scenarios play over and over again across the anxiety disorders—when parents become overly involved in allaying the child's concerns, it deprives the child of the opportunity to struggle with the situation and learn how to adapt or to move on by himself. He will always need Mommy or Daddy to help. And it forces the parents to do more and more. They become secretaries, research assistants, schedulers . . . they take over the to-do lists of the child's life because they want everything to go perfectly to minimize their child's worries. One parent told me that when she called a teacher to tell him she didn't understand the homework her daughter had been given, the teacher said, "It's not your place to understand." While the parent was furious and reported the teacher to the principal, I told her that the teacher was absolutely right. She was forgetting that the homework was given to her child, not to her. And no amount of intervention on her part was going to change that.

I'll discuss this much more in the next chapter, but I just want to plant this seed in your mind: The best thing you can do for your child goes against the nature of parenting. While you want to comfort, reassure, and protect, when it comes to worry and anxiety, you need to pull back some . . . and then some more. Instead of rushing in to give the child the answer and to calm and comfort him, your child is better served by you asking him about his thoughts and guiding him toward discovering the alternatives.

IN THIS CHAPTER you've gotten a taste of what GAD is, where it comes from, and how you may be contributing unwittingly to your child's anxiety. In the next chapter I'm going to show you how you can help your child see the world a bit more realistically. Even though right now your child may be seeing danger lurking in every corner, there are ways to help him focus on the safe places and to realize that even if the worst does happen, he's got the goods to face it.

8

Parenting a Child with Generalized Anxiety

In twenty-five years of treating anxious youngsters, I've heard countless excuses for escaping and avoiding situations that provoke anxiety, and I've learned to recognize the excuses for what they are. If you're new to this, however, you may not be able to so easily distinguish a bona fide excuse from a bluff.

Let's say your child has a big book report due. Lots of students worry about finishing on time or getting a good grade, but most manage to control the worry and do the report anyway—and, in the process, they notice that their uncomfortable feelings subside as they make progress on the report.

Not the case for the child with generalized anxiety. That child makes excuses, stalls, fusses, and frets, and sometimes he even manages to avoid the report altogether. Sadly, by the time you recognize what's really going on, the anxiety has taken hold, and your child may have convinced even himself that the excuses are more true than not. That's what this chapter can help you with: clueing you in sooner, so the anxiety doesn't have to get the best of your child. And here's the good news: Since generalized anxiety disorder (GAD) tends to be chronic—starting in early childhood and continuing into adolescence, usually getting worse as your child gets older— your best chance of conquering it is to get control over it as early as possible. In other words, jump on it this minute.

Tweak the Circuitry

In the last chapter you learned about GAD, how it develops, and how you may be unwittingly contributing to your child's anxiety. This chapter will show you how you can help your child see the world a bit more rationally and give him the confidence that he can handle setbacks when they do happen.

Children with GAD automatically go to *What's the worst thing that can happen in this situation?* Your job is to help retrain her brain to take that a step further, to help her get to *What's the most likely thing that can happen in this situation?* By doing this, you make every situation more realistic and more solvable. When you recognize how your child's mind is playing tricks on her, she can learn how to dial down the worry and turn up the volume on more levelheaded thinking.

How do we do this? Remember cognitive behavioral therapy (CBT), which I introduced you to in chapter 3? It's very effective for children with GAD. It helps them identify what they're thinking and feeling during bouts of anxiety (wide-scale terror!) and teaches them how to calm down, problem solve, and develop a coping plan when they're feeling worried. It also helps them take a cold, hard look at themselves and what they're doing and creates a reward system of their choosing. Children are then taught to put their new-found coping skills into practice on a day-to-day level so they can get through the day without abject terror 24/7. In chapter 4, I showed you the general script to use when implementing CBT with your child. Now let's put it into practice for the child with GAD.

Step 1: Spot the Signs

The child with GAD always feels as though she's cornered, not knowing which way to turn, but she's poised and ready because something wicked is about to happen. The physical feelings of GAD are akin to standing on the edge of a gangplank, with a pirate poking his sword into your back, and there are big-mouthed sharks snapping at you from the water below—you're ready to jump into the water to escape from the sword but afraid to leap into the mouths of those fish. In other words, your child is always on edge and waiting for the right signal to jump and avoid a disaster. Tension is the name of the game with GAD. With this scenario in mind, ask your child to tell you where she feels the tension in her body. Which muscles seize up? Where are the aches and pains? Can she relax if she wishes or is she always on the edge of the gangplank?

Step 2: Chill Out

Now that your child able is to spot the emotional and physical feelings associated with his anxiety, you can teach him strategies to decrease and even tolerate those feelings. Remember the belly breathing we learned in chapter 4? Let him know that when he's feeling anxious, he should turn to his breath to try to help calm himself.

To address the muscle tension and other physical symptoms associated specifically with GAD, I like to use progressive muscle relaxation (PMR), which you learned about in chapter 4. This technique was first developed by a Harvard Medical School professor, Herbert Benson, M.D., and published in his 1975 book, *The Relax-*

ation Response. Dr. Benson has spent his career studying the states of deep relaxation in the body that can be achieved through the systematic tensing and relaxing of the different muscle groups and also through meditation.

By teaching your child the difference between when his muscles are tense and when they're relaxed, he can actually learn to bring on the relaxing feelings on cue—at the first sign that he's tightening up and entering a worry episode. Make PMR a daily family activity. You'll help your anxious child practice and not feel like he's the only one in the family doing it. And who knows? It may help you as well.

Seriously, try it yourself when you recognize tightness or stiffness in your neck or shoulders at times of high stress and challenge. PMR has been found to be effective in reducing blood pressure, decreasing pain associated with tension and migraine headaches, and even reducing the stress and upset experienced in irritable bowel syndrome.

Step 3: Train in "Detective Thinking"

As we discussed in chapter 7, children with GAD worry about anything and everything, and they do so without pause. You can help your child fine-tune his thinking process, so it doesn't always go to disaster, through the Socratic method of questioning. For example:

MOM: Tell me what you're worried about.

ASHLEY: I saw in your magazine that kids have to start preparing for college really early, and I'm behind everyone already.

MOM: Ashley, you're in the eighth grade. You've got plenty of time to prep for college.

ASHLEY: No, you don't understand. Kids my age are taking the SATs and getting into special summer programs at the big colleges.

MOM: Hmm, well, there certainly are kids who do these types of things. But tell me, how have you been doing in school?

ASHLEY: I do okay. I get good grades and I'm on the student council. You have to do some volunteer stuff—the colleges like that.

MOM: Yes, you get very good grades and are an honor roll student, so doesn't that mean you're pretty well prepared for high school?

ASHLEY: Well, yes, but what if I don't get into the best AP classes in high school?

MOM: Wait a minute. Let's take one step at a time. You're an honor student, you've gotten very good grades all along, and your teachers think you're doing great. What makes you think that you're not going to get into the advanced courses and do well?

ASHLEY: Well, I don't know. I just feel like I need to do more because it seems other kids are doing these things.

MOM: Fine, but focus on what you've done. Tell me about you and what you know about yourself.

ASHLEY: I do well in school. And I like to read and I'm great in math.

MOM: What else?

ASHLEY: I'm going to a good high school next year and I bet I'll get into the AP courses that I want because my teachers think I'm a good student.

MOM: That's right. So what do you think about some of these stories of kids your age taking the SATs?

ASHLEY: Well, I guess that's what they want to do with their summers. I'd rather still go to my camp and volunteer at the nursery school program that Aunt Rosie runs. I bet that's a good community service project for my college applications.

MOM: That's right. But those applications aren't due for several years, so let's focus on what you're doing now and your plans for the next few months.

ASHLEY: I need to have fun with my friends because we're going to different high schools soon, and we won't all be seeing each other next year.

MOM: That's right. And what do you think about that?

ASHLEY: Maybe I can have a class party to say good-bye to everyone at the end of the year.

This process will help your child to challenge her own way of catastrophic thinking and instead come up with more realistic thoughts that she can use to calm herself down and control the worry.

Step 4: Develop a Deal-with-It Plan

So now that your child has identified how his anxiety affects him, he can work on how to handle those feelings. Children with GAD tend to avoid and evade. Come up with a list of other approaches to help him work through the anxiety, then go through them to figure out if they're really going to help. Ask him, "If you did X, do you think that would make you feel better?" You might even want to rate them on a scale of 1 to 10 to help him choose which strategy would be most beneficial.

Let's look at Tommy and how his dad helps him come up with strategies to help him. Tommy storms into the house yelling, "I can't take it anymore! I hate school!" Dad goes to his room and asks him what's going on. Tommy's overwhelmed—his baseball team is traveling for an away game on Tuesday, a social studies test is scheduled for Wednesday, and he has a math test on Thursday. He also has an outline due for a group project in biology on Friday, but he hasn't yet met with his group. "How am I going to get this all done?" Tommy cries.

So now we know the problem—it's not that he hates school; he's overwhelmed. To help him come up with a strategy that will work, Dad first asks him to define the goal, asking, "How would you like the week to turn out?" Tommy replies, "I want to get things done and do things as best as I can." Since Tommy's goal is reasonable, Dad asks him to throw out as many solutions as he can think of.

- I can use a calendar and schedule in times to study and work on the group project.
- I can break things up each day and do a little bit at a time.
- I can call in sick for one of the tests.
- I can cheat.
- I can put more time into my worst subject and less into the things I do well.
- I can start working on the group project by e-mail and get that going.
- I can see if the coach will give us an excuse to not come in on Wednesday.
- I can skip on going out both tonight and tomorrow with friends and study one of these nights.

After the brainstorm, Tommy and Dad look at each of his proposed plans and Dad asks him what seems reasonable and makes the most sense in getting to his goal. Tommy decides on a series of these steps—he'd stay in tonight, contact the group via e-mail before going out tomorrow night to get that going, make a study plan for giving more time to social studies and less to math, and chip away at his studying and schoolwork in doable pieces rather than putting things off.

Now Tommy's got a concrete plan in place, and he feels prepared to take on his work.

Step 5: Bounty for Bravery

One of the things we see in Tommy's plan is the night out with friends. He's come to the end of the school week and has a big one coming up, but with a reasonable plan for study and work, a night out to relax can reinforce his coping plan and give him a sense of balance. Social reinforcement—seeing friends, chatting on the Internet, going out with family for pizza, baking cookies with some friends—are great reinforcers for adolescents. For younger children, building in positive activity with family members and engaging in things the children enjoy are also good bounty for coping and talking back to worry. Special time with a parent or relative, choosing a favorite game to play, or an outing to the zoo or a local fun spot are activities that reinforce the child's coping behavior.

Step 6: Ready, Set, Go

As we build the staircase for general anxiety, the top step should be your child's ultimate goal. For example, let's suppose your daughter

GRANDMA'S RULE

What do David Premack, Ph.D., Robert De Niro, and most grandmothers have in common? The answer is that they encourage using reinforcers only after something challenging is finished. Dr. Premack found that if you devote time to something that you have to do (but don't necessarily want to), like, say, doing math homework, and you follow that with something that you really want and like to do, like shooting hoops with Dad, the act of doing homework is reinforced. In the film *A Bronx Tale*, Robert De Niro plays a father who drives a city bus and is struggling to keep his son from falling under the spell of local mobsters. In one scene, the boy is accompanying his father as the bus pulls into its last stop on City Island, a place where there is a favored ice cream shop. As his father parks the bus, the boy exclaims, "Dad, can I have an ice cream?" to which De Niro replies, "We do our job first [clean up the bus] and then I'll get you an ice cream." And, as my grandmother would say, "First you finish your pasta, then you can have your dessert." This is a very simple and powerful tenet to learn and to teach your children. Work, then reinforce yourself!

is so anxious about doing well in school that she takes control of school assignments that are supposed to be completed as a group. As I've explained earlier, children with GAD think there's a "right" way to do things, and they often strive for perfectionism that they feel the other kids don't get. She spends too much time on the work, she's cutting out the other kids (who roll their eyes at her), and ultimately she gets overwhelmed and breaks down in tears. Set a new goal with her: to share the work on class projects. Each step of her staircase will lead to the top—to reach her goal. We'll start with relatively easy situations that she's likely to accomplish, then work our way up to the tougher stuff.

Step 1: I will ask the other kids what they want to do for the project and listen to their choices.

Step 2: I'm going to remind myself that we all have different strengths and everyone needs a chance to show off their work.

Step 3: I'm going to choose the two things I'd most like to do and ask the kids if it's okay.

Step 4: I will only send a reminder to other group members if they are a day late with their work.

Step 5: I will hold myself back from doing other people's work.

Step 6: I will share the editing tasks with the other kids and we'll hand the project in together as a team!

Remember to have photos or drawings of each step as your child moves up the staircase, and copies of projects or other school assignments that she hands in, and either put these on a poster (for younger kids) or have her keep a journal (for older kids) of successes. And add in photos of the special reinforcers that she earns at the end of each week.

Work with your child to come up with a list of difficult experiences and choose which ones to work on first. Let your child move up the ladder at his own pace, gently encouraging him to keep moving rather than getting stuck at any one point. Confronting his lesser fears will give him a sense of mastery and accomplishment, which in turn will help him be better able to tackle the bigger ones.

Creating a Fear Staircase

As with separation anxiety, you'll want to create a staircase of situations for your child to climb and conquer. Another approach to making these staircases with our clients is to brainstorm all the situations and put each situation on a separate index card. After the situations are on the cards, have your child go through and put a rating from 0 to 10 for how much the situation causes worry or anxiety and how much it bothers your child right now. He will then rank order, from the least bothersome (0, 1, 2) through to the most bothersome situations (8, 9, 10), so the higher situations are on the top steps of the staircase.

Try to frame each step in a positive or neutral way, and not in a negative tone. So, instead of saying, "I won't keep asking my mom if she's getting sick," the step would read: "I can ask my mom once per day how she is feeling."

FEAR FEELINGS SCALE

0	Piece of cake
1–2	Makes me a little anxious, but I can muscle through it
3–4	Makes me anxious and I try to avoid it sometimes
5–7	Definitely makes me anxious and I do my best to get out of it
8–9	Makes me scared and I avoid it like the plague
10	Get me out of here!!!!

SAMPLE FEAR STAIRCASE OF AN ANXIOUS TEENAGE BOY

2	Overhearing my mom make a doctor's appointment for herself
3	Seeing my parents' bills on the table
4	Messing up on a homework problem
4	Watching TV news about crime
5	Taking a timed test

6	Overhearing my parents having an argument
6	Being late to school or a meeting
7	Not having all my papers and books to do my homework
8	Leaving my homework at home
10	Getting only a B+ or an A on a test

FEAR STAIRCASE (TO BE FILLED IN BY PARENT AND CHILD)

0	
1–2	
3–4	
5–7	
8–9	
10	

With the staircase in place, encourage your child to start at the bottom and work on each situation, one at a time. Ask him to use his cognitive coping skills, relaxation techniques, and breathing. Instead of his usual avoiding, he should use his brand-new problem-solving skills to tackle each step one at a time. Once he masters one step and feels in control of that situation (it no longer causes worry), then he can move to the next. At each step, use your Socratic questioning to help him think through the following:

- What's the worst that can happen?
- How likely is this to happen?
- What can I do to cope with this?
- What is my goal in this situation?

Encourage your child to respond to these questions with realistic ideas and to examine the evidence to support her ideas. And be sure to let your child know that every effort makes you happy for her. Every bit of encouragement helps!

Parental Prescriptions

Now that you've gotten some steps on how to deal head-on with your child's chronic worry, let's look at some other, broader advice to help your child fret less.

Look at Your Child's Diet

As I've mentioned in chapter 7, children with GAD tend to be on high alert all the time. Their neurons are setting off a series of re-actions that activate the circuitry that releases stress hormones, and you don't want them eating or drinking anything that's going to make them even more jittery. Cut out all caffeine (it can be in choc-olate, soda, and other drinks) and cut down on sugar and simple carbs, which can send your child's blood sugar on a roller-coaster ride. Choose snacks high in complex carbs, protein, and a bit of healthy fat. Some good choices: plain yogurt with a sprinkle of al-monds, whole-wheat crackers with some low-fat cheese, or carrot sticks with hummus. And make sure your child eats at steady inter-vals and doesn't skip meals; skipping meals can send blood sugar plummeting.

Get Your Child Moving

Exercise is one of the best ways to relieve stress and get the stress hormones under control. When your child exercises, her body releases a set of chemicals known as endorphins. Experts call these the "feel good" chemicals because they trigger a positive feeling throughout the body. Ever heard of the runner's high? Credit endorphins for the feeling, which can last long after your child's feet stop moving.

Exercise also helps calm your child's mind—a walk or bike ride, a few laps around the track, or a dip in the pool can help him hush the anxious overdrive activity going on in his mind as he's focusing on his body's movements. Regular exercise can also help increase his self-confidence, so he'll be more assured that he can indeed handle what life throws at him. What's more, exercise helps improve sleep, which is often restless for children with GAD.

No, your child doesn't have to go to the gym every day to get the benefits of exercise. Try activities like walking, gymnastics, karate, dance, and sports. Shoot some baskets with him, throw a ball around with her, and go for a bike ride as a family. Even household chores, like raking leaves, doing dishes, and vacuuming, count (bonus!). Make sure your child gets a minimum of thirty minutes of physical activity every day.

Make Sure Your Child Gets a Good Night's Sleep

Children with GAD often spend much of the night tossing and turning. Not only does this keep your child's immune system down, it makes her even more anxious during the day because she's tired and cranky and can't concentrate. To help your child snooze better:

- Make sure she goes to sleep and wakes up at the same time every day—and keep to this schedule as much as possible on weekends and during vacations.
- Exercise should be done earlier in the day and not within a few hours before bed.
- Create a nightly wind-down ritual. For young children it can be a warm bath, a story, and a song. Older children can do a crossword puzzle or read a book by themselves before bed.
- Shut off all electronics (television, video games, computer) thirty to sixty minutes before bed.
- Keep your child's room cool, dark, and quiet.
- Banish electronics (that includes TV) from your child's bedroom.

Introduce Your Child to Mindfulness and Yoga

Many CBT therapists incorporate mindfulness meditation practices and yoga to help their clients stay present and in the moment rather than run ahead of themselves with anxious predictions and ideas. I've found in my work that adolescents often take very well to these techniques, and many high schools are even offering these activities as part of the physical education programs. Search out some good DVDs or a local yoga studio and encourage your child to try these practices to relax his mind and body.

Common Challenges

Your child will be facing new situations every day. Here's how to cope with some of the most common fears your child may be focusing on.

Test Anxiety

Children with GAD are forever doubting their abilities, particularly when it comes to schoolwork, something that's ever present in a child's life. Tests can be particularly difficult to manage. The child with GAD can spend hours and hours studying for a test, trying to make sure he covers every single word that the teacher ever spoke, often trying to cover more than that. Help your child organize by creating a chart listing all the upcoming tests. He can update the chart each week. Set a reasonable study time each night (one hour, okay; four hours, not okay). Use a timer to keep him truthful. When he hears the buzzer go off, he closes the books.

Speak to her about addressing the what-if questions in her mind. Much of the anxiety that's building comes from her negative self-talk: *What if I get in the classroom and forget everything I've learned? What if the teacher asks me a question I haven't studied? What if I fail the test?* "What if" questions are answered with facts. Teach your child to tell herself what she knows about her efforts: *I studied for several hours. I know a lot of this material. I paid attention in class.* And, having a good plan also challenges the anxiety of the "what if": *I will go through and answer the questions that I know first, and then do the more challenging ones; I will jot an outline quickly to organize my essay response.* Facts and a plan will give your child a good sense of control over the anxiety.

If your child is superstressed the night before a big test, make sure he knocks off early and does something fun. Take him to an early movie (yes, on a school night!), watch a basketball game on TV, or send him out with Dad to play tennis to get his mind off the test.

Worries About Friends

Children with GAD worry about their friends incessantly. I'll talk more in the next chapter about children with social anxiety, who also worry about friends, but their worries are more along the lines of *Nobody likes me, nobody's going to pick me for the team in gym class.* The worries for children with GAD sound more like *I've said the wrong thing and now Jimmy will hate me,* and *Oh my gosh, I'm playing on this baseball team and what if the catcher gets into a fight with the batter on the other team and then it'll ruin the way we play and we'll lose.* With social anxiety, the fears are about being liked. With GAD it's about having a certain standard—they must follow the rules to a tee, they must give everything they have to every school project, and so on.

Children with GAD also tend to be quite controlling, so they turn friends off by scolding them for not following the rules exactly right. Your challenge is to help your child learn that everyone brings certain strengths to the table, and even mistakes are okay in the scheme of things. You might say something like, *"Mary may not write as much as you think she should on her portion of the project, but what she does write is great and that's important."* Or *"Harrison may not throw as hard as you think he should, but he's still an important part of your baseball team."*

One of my favorite ways to stretch this muscle is doing a family cookie-baking night. First Dad reads a bit of the recipe and puts in his ingredients, then Mom does her share, then Suzy does a bit. Every once in a while, put in something totally wrong—like baking soda instead of baking powder—to show Suzy that mistakes happen, and you can all laugh it off.

Worries About Money

These days it's hard for anyone not to worry about money. We all know people who have lost their jobs, and everyone's cutting back in response to the economy. It's hard not to argue that the economy has hit everyone hard, but that doesn't mean that your family is going to be out on the street anytime soon. Give your child a realistic picture of what's going on, in a matter-of-fact way. "Yes, things are difficult with the economy, but this is how it affects us." Then tell him ways you're saving—maybe you're not going out for dinners as much as you used to, or the car you're driving isn't quite as fancy. But by making these kinds of changes, your family is taking steps to manage during difficult times. The important thing is not to just say, "We'll be fine," because that leaves a lot to his imagination, such as, "But what if we won't be!"

Letting your child help you save money for some of his own personal expenses is also a good way to ease an anxious mind. So, while you might be tightening the belt on household and larger family expenses, the time is right for Joey to learn the value of some work and earning to save for desirable (but not essential) items— you'll still pay for clothes, school fees, and health care. Maybe your son can shovel some neighbors' driveways to make some money to buy the things he wants and maybe give a little to the household if he wishes. He'll learn how to earn, to save, and to allocate money for things he wants. And he'll learn to delay gratification by saving up for some of the more expensive things that children enjoy, such as concert tickets or video games. The more children with anxiety can recognize that there are ways to manage the situation, the better they'll feel.

SOME DO'S AND DON'TS OF PARENTING CHILDREN WITH GAD

Do's

- Model coping behavior for your child: Find some reasonable challenges of your own, and talk out loud about how you will manage the situation.
- Give positive feedback whenever you catch your child coping. If you see her quietly doing homework, for example, a gentle pat on her shoulder can signal that you're happy with how she's handling things.
- Walk away when the whining begins, to let your child calm down.
- Use the fear cards and staircase method to organize a plan for your child.
- Encourage your child to take on anxiety-provoking situations.
- Let your child know that you understand, but also that you know she can learn to cope.
- Use Socratic questions to help your child come up with a good coping plan.

Don'ts

- Take over and handle the situation for your child.
- Make excuses for your child or allow him to escape situations.
- Jump to rearrange things to make them easier for your child or to minimize an age-appropriate challenge.
- Focus on what's gone wrong in your life.

9

The More-Than-Shy Child: Understanding Social Phobia

The film *Napoleon Dynamite* is focused on an overly awkward adolescent who doesn't quite know (or care) that he's the odd man out and the epitome of the social outcast. But look beyond Napoleon and we see Deb, a highly socially anxious teenager who is ever in touch with her fear and constantly seeing herself through the eyes of those around her. We first meet Deb when Napoleon answers the door and finds her offering 75 percent off of "Glamour Shots," as well as boondoggle key chains. We watch as Deb stumbles and the anxiety within her builds, then freezes her. Then it gets so bad that she flees, leaving behind her sales kit.

Tina Majorino, the actress who plays Deb, very skillfully portrays the mounting fight-or-flight response that's happening within Deb. Quite frankly, you can't help but feel great sympathy for Deb and get a sense of the emotional pain she's experiencing.

I've watched this film with many teenagers who laugh wholeheartedly at Napoleon but cringe when they meet Deb and often tell me, "I'd never be able to look someone in the eye again if that was me." Well, in Deb, I see on the big screen what goes on for all children with social phobia. They feel caught in the limelight, not knowing what to do next, and they forever want to do what Deb did in the scene: run for the hills.

It's disheartening to see your child so paralyzed and isolated by fear. But by learning more about social phobia, you can help your child break free of it—and help yourself feel more encouraged about what lies ahead for both of you.

In this chapter, as well as the next, you'll gain an in-depth understanding of

- what social anxiety is
- how it develops
- how to spot it in your child
- how you can help your child overcome it

QUIZ: COULD YOUR CHILD HAVE SOCIAL ANXIETY DISORDER?

Answer yes or no to the following questions.

- Does your child seem deathly afraid of looking silly or incompetent, or being embarrassed? Is he always concerned about looking "just right"? Yes/No

- Does your child refuse to speak to anyone except to you, and she won't speak outside of your house? Yes/No

- Does your child ask to stay home from school, or ask you to ask the teacher if he can be excused from oral presentations? Yes/No

- Is your child already a teenager, but you still have to order for her in a restaurant? Yes/No

- Does your child's teacher tell you he never raises his hand or answers questions in class? Yes/No

- Does your child have only one or two close friends, and refuses to go places where there will be more than just a few children gathering? Yes/No

- Within a few minutes of dropping your child off at a party or school event, does she call to be picked up? Yes/No

- Does your child refuse to eat at school, but chows down at home? Yes/No

- Does your daughter love playing the piano, but refuses to participate in the piano recital? Yes/No

- Does your son turn down invitations to most playdates, parties, and sleepovers? Yes/No

If you answered yes to any of these questions, your child could have a problem with social anxiety disorder (SAD), which affects about 9 percent of youth in the United States at some point in their lifetime. The disorder is usually diagnosed between four and seventeen years of age, though most commonly right around puberty, in the preteen years.

Dan's Story

In all my time working with children, I cannot think of a single one who hasn't touched my heart. But Dan, a sixteen-year-old junior in high school, stands out among the rest. Freud talked about the "countertransference reaction," where something about the patient taps into the therapist's own history and development, triggering a strong emotional response. For me, that patient was Dan.

I met Dan when I was a new psychologist in training at Dr. Barlow's clinic, eager to help my clients and to please my supervisors. During our first meeting, Dan's voice shook as he described his typical school day. He'd wake up with an immediate sense of dread, the tension and nausea increasing with each step toward the school. Dan always timed his arrival to coincide precisely with the first bell, so he could avoid making conversation with his peers. He chose a seat near the back of the room and described how he made himself "small" by hiding behind the person in front of him and avoiding eye contact with the teacher.

He was acutely aware of the clock ticking and willed it to move quickly through each hour. Most striking to me was the way Dan described his lunch period, as I had never heard anything like it before. Rather than going into the cafeteria, he ate alone in a bathroom stall. Every day his mother would pack him a sandwich and a pudding cup, but not a spoon. And every day Dan ate only the sandwich. The thought of going to the cafeteria to get a spoon was too much for him. Nor could he bear the thought of disappointing his mother or bringing any attention to his fears, so he never told her that he couldn't eat his pudding. Not go to the cafeteria? This is the scene where friends gather and make plans, compare notes, chatter about peers and parties. Not for Dan. This scene was petrifying to him and reminded him of what he was powerless in the face of—socializing comfortably with others.

Dan was depressed and felt hopeless about anything ever changing. At the end of our interview, in my naive way, I followed what I had learned during my training. "So, Dan," I asked, "where do you see yourself in five years?"

Tears welled in his eyes as he looked straight into mine and said,

"Dr. Albano, if these are supposed to be the best years of my life, I don't see myself alive in five years." That moment is etched in my mind for eternity. Imagine, a sixteen-year-old boy in such distress that he can't see himself living until his twenty-first birthday. To this day I feel the lump in my throat that swelled at his words.

In some ways, Dan's story reminded me of my own high school experience. It began with intense social anxiety as my family moved us from New York to Florida. I knew no one at my new school and was immediately teased for my "New Yawk" accent. But my version soon diverges from Dan's. Within a few weeks I had settled in and made new friends. High school went on to be filled with dating and football games and many after-school activities. I cannot recall a single day thinking that this wasn't the best of times.

When I met Dan's parents, Margie and John, they described Dan as their "shy child" as compared to his outgoing older brother. Dan was slow to warm up, even to family members, and never spontaneously spoke to anyone. Although he would go to school, Dan always seemed on edge from Sunday night through Friday afternoon. He preferred to play by himself or with his brother, and rarely wanted to go outside with the neighborhood children. Margie and John encouraged Dan to play T-ball and soccer, but he cried and complained so much that they let him quit by age ten. Margie dreaded parent-teacher conferences, where each year she'd hear the same thing: "Oh, yes, Dan. What a quiet boy, I don't even know that he's in my classroom."

John expressed his frustration about his son's behavior, telling me how he stopped ordering for him in restaurants and would not let Margie do it either, in order to force Dan to speak to waiters; otherwise he'd go hungry. But this was the only situation where Dan would ask for anything. Margie felt enormous guilt, her eyes wet with tears as she told me, "Dan made things easy for us by not doing any of the typical after-school activities, so I never had to chauffeur him around like I did my other son. We didn't understand what was really going on until it was too late. How do you force a child to engage with others? He shakes so badly, you'd think he was being asked to walk off the plank!"

All the World's a Stage

When you hear the term *social anxiety,* or *social phobia,* as it's also referred to, you think of someone who's deathly afraid to be in a social situation. But social phobia is more than just the fear of being around other people. It's an intense, debilitating fear of looking foolish in front of others. While most children, indeed, most people, aren't thrilled with the idea of being the center of attention, children with social anxiety think that all the world's a stage with a spotlight aiming squarely at them 24/7. All eyes are on them—or so they think. Every move they make is examined—or so they feel. And so, these children withdraw from any type of social situation because they're petrified they're going to say or do the wrong thing and then they'll never be able to face the world again.

Ironically, because they do their best to skirt all social situations, they wind up not knowing how to interact with their peers. This only makes them *more* uneasy being in a group. Because they're so anxious and unpracticed, they experience uncomfortable physical sensations—blushing, shaking, sweating, speaking unsteadily—which only serves to magnify their problems and make them feel as though they look even more peculiar than everyone else.

The physical components of all three disorders (separation anxiety disorder [SAD], generalized anxiety disorder [GAD], and social anxiety) can often look very much the same. The main difference is *when* the physical symptoms occur—whether it's at times of separation, times of general worry, or times of social interaction. (See page 184 for a chart on the focuses of the fears that distinguish the three anxiety disorders.)

Almost all children, with social anxiety or not, will turn red or tremble a bit when giving an oral report. But when most children continue to talk and focus their attention on what they're saying, they forget about what's going on in their bodies and their symptoms ease up. Not so for the child with social phobia. In her mind, she is the only child in the class who shakes and sweats. She pictures herself as being in a close-up of a film, where all eyes are on her and her every move is exaggerated and on display to see and to judge. In essence, she is Deb from the *Napoleon Dynamite* film. But, there's no standing ovation at the end of this performance, only feelings of humiliation and shame.

The thought of being embarrassed can be so intense that it actually induces a full-scale panic attack. Children with social phobia may cry, throw a tantrum, or freeze up with new people. Some children will outright refuse to speak, a condition known as selective mutism, which is an extreme form of social anxiety. (See page 188.) Adolescents often experience stomach distress, they may vomit, and they can become angry if forced to mingle. These children are tormented at the thought of that spotlight, and they're consumed with terror as they envision being the center of attention. They do their best to avoid social situations altogether, and when forced to endure them, they focus on what they think is going wrong rather than what is going right. When the torturous situation is over, they resolve never to do it again. The instant replay in their mind is focused solely on how badly it went, how terrible they looked or sounded, and how miserable the situation felt.

Invisible Children

The less these children interact, the more anxious they feel about interacting, which makes them avoid more and makes the anxiety worse. In other words, they set up a vicious cycle of avoidance and heightened anxiety that spirals on and on. And, in fact, in trying so hard to fade into the woodwork, these children actually succeed in becoming invisible to peers.

In psychology we speak about three types of social status in youth: the peer accepted, the peer rejected, and the peer neglected. Indulge me for a moment and think back to when you were in eighth grade. Are you there? Okay, now imagine that your parents are throwing you a birthday party and you can invite anyone you wish. Quickly, make your list. Here's what happens: The children you invite are the "peer accepted." Those are the children who are naturally fun to be around, the children whose company you enjoy. These are the children who are your friends, and the ones you hope will be your friends because everyone likes them.

Next, think about the children you don't want on your list. These are the "peer rejected" children. These children are the ones who ruin the party with upsetting and disruptive antics—spilling the soda, bumping into things, and running around wildly. Finally, think about your two lists (those you want at your party and those you don't) and compare it to the list of all the children you were with in eighth grade. Who didn't make it onto either list? These are the "peer neglected" children. Like Dan, these children disappeared during recess and lunch. They stayed in the classroom and cleaned the boards and erasers while you were having fun—not because they got in trouble, but because they chose to stay behind.

These children didn't show up to the school dances or the big sports games, and were practically invisible to their peers.

GOING UNNOTICED

Researchers who study inclusion and exclusion in youth use a similar method to the birthday list. They present a list of all the children in a class to students, along with a series of questions such as: "Who do you like to work with in a group?" "Who is a good friend?" "Who acts silly for no reason?" "Who is happy?" "Who seems angry often?" "Who always raises their hand?" "Who often gets in trouble?" The children also complete self-report questionnaires, which researchers use to measure their levels of social anxiety, depression, and other emotions.

Studies have consistently shown that children with high levels of social anxiety receive the lowest number of "nominations." That is, they are not associated with any of the questions that indicate acceptance/popularity or rejection. When they are nominated, it's for items such as "Who plays alone?" or "Who is shy?"

DOES YOUR CHILD HAVE SOCIAL ANXIETY DISORDER OR IS HE JUST SHY?

A SHY CHILD	A CHILD WITH SOCIAL ANXIETY
Makes and keeps friends	Has only a few, if any, friends
May be reluctant to enter social situations, but won't avoid them	Avoids social situations
Is uncomfortable in social situations	Experiences gut-wrenching distress in social situations
Is able to do the things children do	Has a daily life affected by fear
May get better as the child gets older	May get worse as the child gets older

What's Wrong with Being Shy?

Some people say that we're taking a normal personality trait—shyness—and turning it into a disorder. I could not disagree more. There is, without a doubt, a difference between shyness and social phobia, and nobody is trying to stamp shyness out of our culture. Shyness is a personality trait. The esteemed psychologist Philip G. Zimbardo, Ph.D., of Stanford University has spent his career studying shyness, placing it on a continuum nestled between occasional social awkwardness on the one end and disabling social phobia on the other. His work has shown that shyness is common, and roughly 40 percent of adults in the United States describe themselves as such. Shy people are uncomfortable in social situations where they may be the focus of attention, they think less of themselves than their non-shy counterparts, and they worry about looking foolish and not being welcomed by others.

But there's a line—I'll admit, sometimes it's blurry—but there is undoubtedly a line that gets crossed when the negative self-focus becomes so painful that the child refuses to go to school, says no to every party, and won't even eat a meal in front of a friend. This is not shyness (a shy child doesn't miss out on the things that children do—parties, movies, playmates). This is social phobia, a clinical disorder that warrants more intensive therapeutic intervention.

Where Does It Come From?

Nobody's sure why some children sail through oral reports and others cringe at the mere thought of one, but as with other anxiety disorders in children, it's most likely a mix of several factors. The child may have a genetic predisposition to it, temperament plays a role, and studies have shown a link between the inhibited infant personality type and the development of social phobia. But these biological factors are not enough to account for social phobia. The environment and the child's developing sense of self also contribute.

Overcontrolling and overprotective parenting styles, which I talked about in chapter 1, may come into play as well. Or it's possible that it's the other way around—the social anxiety of the child shapes the way the parents behave. It's the age-old chicken and egg conundrum. My guess is it's a little of both. Other environmental factors probably come into play as well—Sophie gets teased in school, some children don't want to play with her, perhaps an aunt tells her she's too quiet—which shape her developing self-talk, her inner dialogue of who she is and how competent she feels in different situations. Sophie's inner talk develops along the lines of "I don't fit in, no one likes me, I'm a loser" rather than "Let's see who is fun to hang out with here" and sets her up for the vicious cycle of negative thoughts, feelings, and avoidance in social situations.

With social anxiety, as the child grows it's easy to overlook that there's anything awry. When the child is young, it's perfectly natural for his parents to prompt him with new people and in new situations. "Look at Uncle Joe," "Say Hello to Great-Grandma Sue." As a typical child grows older, he no longer needs that coaching. But the child with social anxiety never stops needing it, and the parents continue to coax. And the more they do it, the more the child relies on it and the more the parents continue to do it.

William, ten, comes home from school and sees an invitation to a drop-off birthday party at the movies. William tells his mom he doesn't want to go. His mom, Karen, doesn't understand why.

"These are your friends. You should want to be with them." But William doesn't see it this way. He does not talk to many of these children at school because he thinks they will laugh at him. He sees the invitation as something the other child's mother made him send to William, not that he was invited because he was, well, wanted there by the child. He pictures himself stumbling around and not knowing what to say to the other guys. Maybe if his mother would come and get the nicer children to talk to him, well, maybe then it might be okay.

So, Karen coaxes and cajoles William until he agrees to go to the party, but only if Karen goes with him, which she does. After all, she's been going with him all this time. What's one more party? She walks him around, talking with the other children and bringing one after the other over to William to talk together. And as the party invitations continue to come, Karen continues to go with William to the parties. She walks around the room with him, introduces him to children, and does much of the talking while William stays by her side and looks at the ground. She's trying to help him—after all, she thinks, he just needs a little prompting. While on the outside this could look like separation anxiety, the distinction is that William isn't clinging to Karen for company—he's using her as a crutch to speak for him. In fact, he'd be fine sitting at home—with or without her—just as long as he doesn't have to be with other children.

As he gets older, the invitations begin to dwindle, until, by the time William is fourteen, they stop completely. William is quietly thrilled, while Karen wonders what could have happened. It's only then that she may turn around and realize there's a problem.

What distinguishes these three anxiety disorders? Mostly, the focus of their fears.

PRIMARY SYMPTOMS OF ANXIETY	SAD	SOCIAL ANXIETY	GAD
Physical	Headaches, stomachaches, trembling and shaking upon separation, panic attacks at times of separation	Blushing, sweating, shaking, stomach distress, panic attacks at times of social or evaluative challenges	Muscle aches, tension, gastrointestinal distress, sleep disturbances, concentration difficulties, headaches, and panic attacks prompted by worry
Behavioral	Avoidance of separating from parents or home	Avoidance of other people, including peers, or any evaluative situation or being the focus of attention	Avoidance of situations where the child is exposed to his worry triggers
Cognitive	The fear that something terrible will happen that will separate the child from his parents or loved ones	The fear of being humiliated, rejected, embarrassed, or thought badly of by others	Worry that some unwelcome, negative event will occur that the child can't predict or control

Under the Radar

Parents tell me that at first they were pleased to hear the excuses their children gave as to why they avoided social situations: "I really need time to do homework." "All the kids at school do drugs, so I don't want to go to their parties." "I'm more mature than my friends, so I don't like to hang out with them anymore." What parent wouldn't want to be raising such a mature, industrious, antidrug child? In some respects, having a child with social anxiety makes life easier on the parent. There's no surly teen tying up the phone line, and the parents don't have to stay up all night worrying about when their child is going to call for a ride home from the latest party. Yet, soon enough, they realized that the explanations were hiding the true problem.

Kim and Len come to mind when I think about the insidious course of social anxiety and how parents can so easily miss the disorder. Susan, the second-born of their four daughters, was a sweet and cuddly baby, much like her older sister. "She was no trouble at all!" Kim and Len told me in my office.

As the two little ones came along, Susan became the perfect mother's helper. The girls all started school without difficulty and were good students. Len interjected, "We heard from early on that Susan was the best student, the most well-behaved, the most helpful to the teacher." However, it wasn't until Susan was in the seventh grade that her gracious and overly helpful behavior began to take on a different meaning for her parents. "In teacher conferences, she was the shining star. But what we started to realize was that she was always with the teachers. She helped water the plants during recess, and she volunteered in the after-school program to tutor the first-graders." Susan's excuse was always that she "loved school" and wanted to be "just like Ms. Betty" or "Ms. Alice" or whoever her teacher was that year.

As she progressed through middle school her parents' concern increased. Party invitations came, but Susan always had excuses: "She's not a nice girl and I don't like her friends." "I want to stay and play with my sisters." "Can't I go to visit Grandma this weekend instead?" Things came to a head one Saturday night. "I had driven our two youngest daughters to different friends' houses for sleepovers, and Len had just dropped our oldest at a slumber party," Kim told me. "We both got home at the same time and were about to celebrate that we had a night alone together when we realized, there's Susan. There's always Susan."

"There she was, quietly sitting in the living room, playing on her laptop, with a big smile when we walked in the door. And she asked, 'What are we going to do tonight?' My stomach pitched. We were her entire social life."

Kim and Len are typical when it comes to parents of children with social anxiety disorder. At first, children with social anxiety disorder can be a breath of fresh air for overwrought, overscheduled parents. These children don't ask much. In fact, they often ask for nothing. They're happy just hanging out in their rooms, listening to music or watching television. They're not clamoring for new clothing to wear to the school dance or begging to be chauffeured from soccer to dance class.

Many parents blame themselves for not seeing it sooner, but I tell them this: This disorder is very hard to spot. In fact, it tricks you into thinking you have the child everyone else wants. These children are courteous, gentle, sweet—all the things you die for as a parent. How could you have seen any trouble? It's only by the time they're in high school, when children are supposed to be more independent, that the signs are more apparent.

As easy as it is to overlook as a problem, having a child with social anxiety can create frustration as well. It's embarrassing when your fourteen-year-old son won't shake your boss's hand at an office party. When you're elbow-deep in Thanksgiving turkey and the phone rings but your twelve-year-old won't answer it, it's annoying. When you thought you'd have some more alone time with your spouse as your child gets older, and yet, your child's always there, it's frustrating. When your straight-A student comes home with a C on a test and she says that she didn't speak up when she noticed her teacher made a mistake in grading, it's irritating.

Social Anxiety Triggers

What sparks social anxiety? Any or all of the following:

- Meeting new people
- Speaking in front of a group
- Starting a conversation
- Being called on in class
- Feeling flushed or having butterflies in the tummy
- Being the center of attention
- Going to a party
- Performing onstage or in sports
- Asking a teacher a question
- Joining a group of children
- Situations with unfamiliar people
- Going on a date
- Making a phone call
- Eating or drinking in public

From Sweeping to Specific

While separation anxiety is episodic in nature (children will experience it within a distinct period of time) and generalized anxiety is chronic (children experience it constantly), social anxiety takes two forms. When it's more generalized, children with social phobia are anxious in the majority of social situations they encounter. They have trouble starting and keeping up conversations with both children their own age and adults, they avoid contact with other children at all costs, and they refuse to participate in group activities like sports and parties. They may be nervous to speak to authority figures like teachers and avoid many different types of social situations, from taking tests to ordering pizza, from asking a teacher for help to calling up a friend to get together.

Social anxiety can also be more specific and limited to only certain situations, though it's not as common in children as it is in adults. Common nail-biters include speaking in class, performing in a group or in sports, using the public restroom, or even talking on the telephone. This is your classic child with test anxiety or the child who can't give a speech in class.

Experts think this non-generalized social phobia is less common in children because they have little choice in what to choose or avoid in their daily lives. In other words, they're almost forced into the spotlight daily, mandated to do the things they're afraid of. For example, a typical school day may involve test taking, reading aloud or giving an oral report, performing in gym or music class, interacting with peers in the lunchroom, asking for help from a teacher, writing on the blackboard, and many, many other situations. For the most part the child is going to have to endure these situations, albeit with great distress. And so, we have Dan sitting in a bathroom stall to avoid the cafeteria and Susan volunteering with young children to avoid mixing with friends in a club or after school. That's why it's crucial that you get to the crux of the problem as soon as you can, so the avoidance behavior doesn't become permanent.

Selective Mutism: The Silent Treatment

At 3:00 p.m. I quietly opened my office door to see my next appointment, five-year-old Erica, playing with dolls in the waiting room. She and her mother were brushing the dolls' hair, pretending they were in a beauty salon. I made a motion to Erica's mother, Lisa, not to say anything as I pretended to take no notice of Erica, who continued to talk quite animatedly. After a few minutes I began to gradually increase my attention toward Erica, first glancing occasionally toward her, then moving my chair slowly in her direction. The closer I got, the tenser Erica looked. And the minute I made a comment about Erica's doll, she clammed up.

In my office, Lisa gave me Erica's history: She met all her developmental milestones on time, including every one for speech. Yet, when she started preschool at three and a half, the teachers reported that Erica never uttered a word. They had a speech evaluation, which turned up nothing. Yet for the entire year, Erica never made a peep in school. Lisa and her husband, Ray, thought perhaps it was the school's fault, so the next year they enrolled her in a different school, and although she participated in group activities, she still didn't speak at all. The teachers begged, pleaded, and even tried to bribe Erica to speak, but still, nothing. At home with classmates she chatted up a storm, but at school, at birthday parties, and at other people's houses, she was tight-lipped. Lisa convinced Erica to join a T-ball team, and although she had fun at practices she did so silently.

Lisa had been to two different psychotherapists with Erica who both said she must have been traumatized sometime during her childhood, but Lisa could not recall anything that had happened to bring this on. "She's always been this way," Lisa told me with a sigh.

I eventually diagnosed Erica with selective mutism, an early and extreme form of social anxiety. Children with selective mutism are fully able to speak in one or more settings (usually at home with family) but stay mum in other social situations (at school and/or in public places, for example). Although these children have the physical and cognitive ability to speak, anxiety robs them of the ability to use their voice in particular places. Older children with social anxiety are usually able to avoid situations in which they'll be the center of attention. That's not the case with younger children, who have much less say in where they go and what they do. Their only recourse? To keep their lips sealed and stay quiet.

As the silent treatment continues the child becomes known as "the child who doesn't talk." Classmates begin to "read" signals from the child and actually speak for him. "Miss Smith, Teddy has to use the bathroom!"

Other diagnoses must be ruled out first with selective mutism, so speech, hearing, and language evaluations must be done. If they show nothing, to be diagnosed with selective mutism:

- The child regularly fails to speak in social situations
- The child shows impairment in daily functioning (typically in school, and by skipping social functions due to a fear of speaking)
- The silence lasts at least one month (beyond the first month of school)
- The silence is not due to a communication disorder (for example, stuttering)

ARE YOU HELPING OR HURTING?

Answer yes or no to the following questions.

- Your child has been working on an oral presentation for her English class all week. The morning of the presentation she complains of a stomachache. Do you let her stay home? Yes/No

- Your twelve-year-old daughter was invited to her first girl/boy party. She tells you she doesn't want to be at a party where there will be boys. Are you glad? Yes/No

- Your fifteen-year-old is invited to a study group, but tells you she prefers to study alone. Do you take her answer at face value? Yes/No

- When your child clams up in a social situation, do you find yourself saying, "He's just shy"? Yes/No

- When someone asks your child a question, do you often answer for him? Yes/No

- You answer the phone and a friend is calling for your son. He whispers to you, "Tell him I'm not here." Do you do what he asked? Yes/No

- Your daughter only wants to apply to colleges where there is no interview required. Do you think that's okay? Yes/No

If you answered yes to one or more of the questions, it's time to think about what you may be doing to allow your child's social anxiety to persist.

UP UNTIL NOW YOU'RE probably used to being the center of your child's social life. In the next chapter I'm going to give you some tools to help you help your child to expand his social world. You may think that's a daunting task, but with the right strategies, the world will open up for all of you.

10

Parenting a Child
with Social Phobia

Social phobia isn't the kind of disorder that announces itself loudly. On the contrary, time after time I see it sneak up on parents, who usually don't realize anything is amiss until the condition is well entrenched in their and their child's lives. Then one day it dawns on them: They're the ones who talk to the teacher when there's an issue, they're the ones who speak up with salesclerks, waiters, or neighbors, and they, not their children's peers, are the center of their children's social lives.

Once you notice the problem, you may be beset by concerns: Will my child ever make friends? Speak up for herself? Go on a date? Get a job? The answer is a resounding yes. You can help your child turn off the negative internal monologue and refocus her thoughts on more realistic, positive ones. And by empowering your child to confront and conquer social phobia, you can reduce your own anxiety as well.

Make Him Shine in the Limelight

In chapters 3 and 4 I introduced you to the form of therapy that is going to make significant changes in your life, and in the life of your child. Cognitive behavioral therapy (CBT) for social phobia helps children recognize how they're feeling when they're in social situations (panic!) and helps teach them how to calm down (breathe in, breathe out), problem-solve, and develop a coping plan when they're feeling in the spotlight. It also helps them take a good look at themselves and what they're doing and creates an internal reward system to help them feel more confident and satisfied. Children are then taught to put their newfound coping skills into practice while gradually making the move toward social situations.

I've already shown you the general script to use when using CBT with your child. Now let's focus in on it for the child with social anxiety.

Step 1: Spot the Signs

You want your child to be able to recognize what he's feeling and when the feelings occur related to social situations. Practice the "feelings recognition" skill with him by showing him pictures and asking him to identify how each person is feeling in challenging social situations. Be sure to choose pictures or scenes from TV or films that depict children who are the focus of attention for some reason—getting up to bat, being called on in class, walking up to a group of children—and make sure to choose scenes that depict embarrassing situations. Doing that will give you a place to start talking about the reactions your child feels in his own body when he's feeling center stage.

When most children walk past another group of children, they think nothing of it. But for the child with social anxiety, who feels like those children are pointing and laughing at her the minute she's out of earshot, her heart may be racing, her stomach may be churning, and her breath may be quickening. Does her face flush red and hot? Do her hands get clammy or does she sweat? What is your child experiencing?

Here's a very important thing to teach your child: Not everyone is looking at him at every moment. In fact, most children are more concerned with how they themselves look, rather than how other children look. And feeling nervous in situations where you are actually the focus of attention, and getting that stomach-feels-like-it's-in-your-throat feeling is normal. Yep, everyone feels butterflies when they begin an oral report. Almost every guy's voice will shake and his stomach will do a flip-flop or two the first few times asking a girl on a date. Many have sweaty hands when meeting someone new or going on interviews. And feeling your heart beat fast when you sit down to take an important exam is not unusual.

Letting your child know that these feelings are common, not to mention perfectly normal, is important. Your child might think the captain of the football team runs his first play without a second thought, the student council president gets up in front of the class with confidence, and the child picked to run an errand to the principal's office does it with no nerves. But that's simply not the case. Those children feel shaky and nervous at first just like your child. But where the children diverge lies in what they do after these feelings start. The other children take a deep breath, muscle through it, and find themselves at the other end of it with a winning touchdown, a round of applause, or some thanks from the principal. Your child stops cold in his tracks.

Step 2: Chill Out

Now that your child is able to spot the emotional and physical feelings associated with his anxiety, you can teach him strategies to decrease and even tolerate those feelings. Remember the belly breathing we learned in chapter 4? Let him know that when he's feeling anxious, he can always turn to his breath to try to help calm himself.

That being said, belly breathing is not the be-all and end-all for children with social anxiety. As I've just discussed, all children feel a rush of physical anxiety when they feel put in the spotlight. That's a natural reaction for anyone, anxious or otherwise. So we don't expect our children with social anxiety to completely get rid of these physical sensations with deep breathing or relaxation training. Instead, we want to help them tolerate the initial "uh-oh" sensation, which all children feel, and then learn to turn their attention away from the sensation and onto the task at hand—the oral report, the girl or guy on the date, the exam, the new children they are meeting, the college or job interviewer.

So while the breathing and relaxation will help, your child needs to know that the butterfly feelings will pass on their own. What he needs to do is turn his attention away from the feeling and instead concentrate on what he's doing. We want your child to use the initial sensations as a signal to start thinking about the situation and how he's going to handle it. He has to get up and make a speech in front of the class? The butterflies begin, and he takes a deep breath, lets the physical sensations be there, and focuses instead on the words on the page. He has to order his own dinner in a restaurant? He feels his throat tightening, he does some belly breathing, and he looks at the menu, decides what he wants, and puts his finger on the words so he can refer to them when the waiter comes around.

The sensations will go away as he participates and powers through the situation.

Step 3: Train in "Detective Thinking"

Here's where the work of managing social anxiety really steps up. As we discussed in the previous chapter, children with social anxiety always think they're squarely in the spotlight, the worst is going to happen when they're there, and they won't be able to handle the situation. They will look foolish, everyone will know they're a dismal failure, and their life will be in ruins.

Whatever your child is worrying about, she's picturing the scenario as if it is actually happening in that moment: She's setting off the fight-or-flight response of panicking and, more than ever, she's turning on her heels to run away. So, for example, it's the weekend before summer day camp starts, and your daughter is walking around with a long face, whimpering and whining about the start of camp. She's turning up the heat for you to let her stay home.

She may have even had a good time last year (after weeks of complaints and tears about going), but now, in her mind, she's going to be the odd girl out and she's conjuring up stories about the mishaps and misery that lie ahead. She's picturing herself being dropped off and discovering that she knows no one. All the campers who were nice to her last year have been replaced by the most popular, most athletic, most artistic children from the local schools, none of whom wants anything to do with her. She's imagining herself being shunned and ignored, while the other children are making new friends, exchanging lanyards, and being picked as captains of the color war teams.

Instead of concocting all these scenarios in her head, she needs to ask herself, *How likely is it that it would actually happen that way?* And, *Okay, so I'm going back to day camp. How can I meet kids and have a good time?*

To help your child, consider the following scenario:

MARA: I don't want to go back to camp! Why can't I stay at home this summer and just relax? School was so hard this year and I need a break! Camp is no fun.

MOM: Why do you think it won't be fun? What do you think will happen?

MARA: No one is going to hang out with me, I'll be all alone. I don't know anyone and it's not going to be fun.

MOM: Hmm, well, do you know if any of the kids that you met last year are going to be there?

MARA: My friend Cassie said that she's going to sleepaway camp, so she won't be there. I don't know about the other kids that I met.

MOM: What about other kids from your school? Is anyone going?

MARA: I'm not sure. Maybe Donna, but I don't know. I won't have any friends there.

MOM: Did you know anyone last year when you started camp?

MARA: No, I didn't.

MOM: Okay, but didn't you make some friends, like Cassie and some others?

MARA: Well, yes, but I just told you that Cassie won't be there.

MOM: Okay, but how did you meet Cassie? What did you do to make friends with Cassie?

MARA: Well, the counselors met us on the first day and set us up in groups. And then they played games with us to learn about one another. I met Cassie playing one of those games.

MOM: So, it's probably going to be similar this year. The counselors will introduce you kids to one another and help you a bit, right? What else is there to do to meet kids?

MARA: Well, we're assigned to two groups, actually. One is our cabana group, and that's where I met Cassie. But then I was put in a different activities group, and that's where I met other kids, like Laura and Stacy.

MOM: Oh, so there's more than one place to meet some kids. What do you think you can do yourself when you're in cabana and activities groups to meet friends?

MARA: I don't know. I suppose I can say hi to someone.

MOM: Yes, that's a good start. What tells you that another child might be friendly and wanting to become friends?

MARA: Well, I suppose if they smile at me and act friendly. I can see if there's a place to sit next to some girls who look friendly when we get there.

MOM: That sounds like a great start. Being friendly, smiling, and sitting close to the other kids will help you to make friends. And you're not sure that there won't be some kids that you know there, from last year or from your school?

MARA: I don't know really. I guess if someone is there that I know, then I can start out by saying hi to them.

MOM: Good idea! What do you say to trying this for a few days and seeing how it works?

MARA: Hmm. I guess I can do that. Maybe I'll even make another new friend this year.

This process will help your child to challenge her own way of catastrophic thinking and instead come up with more realistic thoughts that she can use to calm herself down and control the social anxiety. Rather than think the worst—*No one will be my friend!*—she now has a plan for what to do to maximize the chance of meeting some new children.

CHALLENGE YOUR CHILD'S THINKING

Children with anxiety always go to the worst-case scenario. See if your child can come up with another option by contesting his thinking. Have your child ask himself:

- Am I 100 percent sure that _____ will happen?

- Do I have evidence that _____ will happen?

- How many times has _____ happened before?

- Is _____ really so important that my whole future depends on its outcome?

- What is the likelihood that _____ ?

- Does _____'s opinion reflect that of everyone else?

- Do I have a crystal ball?

- What is the worst that could happen?

- What can I do to cope with or handle this situation?

Step 4: Develop a Deal-with-It Plan

As you can see from Mara's conversation with her mom, together the two strategized about things for Mara to do to meet friends: smile, be nice, and sit with the other children. Mara also added that she'll look for some familiar face in the crowd. You can help your child to brainstorm a host of possible solutions that will help him work through the anxiety, then go through them with him and weed out the ones that will increase the anxiety. Remember, brainstorming means putting in all types of potential solutions, helpful, unhelpful, and even silly ones. So, for example:

Meeting new kids: *I can* . . .

- Buy them something so they sit and talk to me (a silly option)
- Smile and say hello (this lets people know I'm friendly)
- Move closer to them to sit or hang out so I'm seen (this can lead to someone seeing me and saying hello)

Giving an oral report: *I can* . . .

- Practice in front of my family (rehearsing makes good sense)
- Ask if I can do a written report instead (this is avoiding)
- Talk as fast as I can to get it over with (this won't lead to a good performance)

Asking the teacher to recheck my paper: *I can* . . .

- Have my mom do it for me (I need to try this myself)
- Wait until after class and ask if we can meet about

the paper (this is a good plan that doesn't interfere with class time)

- Send the teacher an e-mail about this (this is okay, but if I ask in person, then I'm being more assertive)

Going on an interview for a summer internship, college, or part-time job: *I can . . .*

- Practice with some adults asking and answering questions before I go (good idea)
- Think about other things so I don't get nervous (this will leave me unprepared)
- Rehearse in the mirror the things I want to say (this is a good way to prepare ahead of time)

Step 5: Bounty for Bravery

As noted in chapter 4, it's important for your child to learn to feel good about his accomplishments in managing his anxiety and putting himself into social situations.

Remember the Bravery Bucks? You and your child can assign denominations to different challenges such as one Buck for raising her hand in class, two Bucks for going to a party, and five Bucks for giving an oral report. The trick with social anxiety is to use the Bravery Bucks to earn higher-level social and pleasant rewards that your child wants to do. For example, has your son been nagging you to take him to an amusement park? And does he want a night at home where he is king of the computer games, with no interference from little sister or brother? Great! Asking some friends to go with him to the amusement park earns him ten Bravery Bucks and gives him a social outing, and those ten Bucks can then be spent on a special two hours of gaming without little-sibling interference.

The point here is that he's going somewhere he wants to go (amusement park) but doing it with friends (a social challenge). So then he can revel in some good feelings of having accomplished this with a bit of game time. This scenario is quite a change from being caught in feeling upset and anxious over social situations.

Step 6: Ready, Set, Go

As your child builds his staircase for social anxiety, start with relatively easy situations that your child is likely to accomplish. At the bottom of the staircase could be:

- Waving to a friend in the hallway
- Calling a friend on the telephone
- Calling to order a pizza for the family

As your child moves up the staircase and masters each step, you can work to put more challenging situations into the mix:

- Sitting with a group of friends in the cafeteria
- Attending a club meeting after school by myself
- Raising my hand to answer a question in class

Work with your child to come up with a list of difficult social experiences and choose which ones to work on first. Let your child move up the steps at her own pace, gently encouraging her to keep moving rather than getting stuck at any one point. Confronting her lesser fears will give her a sense of mastery and accomplishment, which in turn will help her to be better able to tackle the bigger ones. Reinforce her for her efforts to ensure that she'll continue this path of brave behavior.

Creating a Fear Staircase

To help create a fear staircase, use this work sheet to determine the order of your child's fears. Let your child help you come up with the list of fears. If your child can come up with the situations he fears most himself, he'll have a better chance of confronting them. If he refuses to sit down with you and work on the staircase, come up with some of the steps for him.

ANXIETY FEELINGS SCALE

0	Piece of cake
1–2	Makes me a little anxious, but I can muscle through it
3–4	Makes me anxious and I try to avoid it sometimes
5–7	Definitely makes me anxious and I do my best to get out of it
8–9	Makes me scared and I avoid it like the plague
10	No way! Not doing it!!!!

SAMPLE FEAR STAIRCASE OF AN ANXIOUS TEN-YEAR-OLD GIRL

0	Smiling at a friend in school
2	Talking to the teacher privately after class
4	Volunteering to answer a question in class
4	Going to a party when I know all the kids
8	Eating in the cafeteria with a group of kids
10	Going to a party where I don't know many people

SAMPLE FEAR STAIRCASE FOR AN ANXIOUS FIFTEEN-YEAR-OLD BOY

1	Asking a store clerk for help
3	Making plans with friends
4	Disagreeing with the teacher during a discussion in class
7	Talking to a girl I find attractive
8	Walking into the school dance by myself
10	Asking a girl out on a date

FEAR STAIRCASE (TO BE FILLED IN BY PARENT AND CHILD)

0	
1–2	
3–4	
5–7	
8–9	
10	

Parental Prescriptions

Now that you've got some guidelines to help your child relax, problem-solve, and develop a coping plan, I want to give you some general rules to follow to help your child with social anxiety.

Give Your Child as Many Social Opportunities as Humanly Possible

Your child may not want to go to dance class or join the soccer team, but that's just what she needs in order to practice her social skills. She also needs plenty of unstructured social time, so be sure to schedule playdates for younger children and encourage your older child to call friends on days she's free. Start with one-on-one playdates (or, if your child is older, "hangouts") at your house. Get some board games or other structured activities for the children to play so your child will have a framework to work around. As she gets more comfortable with having friends in the house, try to invite three at a time (always work with even numbers of children, so there are four total). After that, try even more children, even hosting a party or two in the house. Encourage your child to say yes when she's invited to playdates and parties at other children's houses as well.

Practice Makes Perfect
(Or, at Least, a Bit More Comfortable)

Role-playing can be an extremely helpful tool for children with social anxiety. But first, do a little prep work yourself. Spend some time watching your child's favorite TV shows, so you can see common quandaries your child might face. And find situations in books and series written for children. Times have changed since you were in school. So what worked for you may not be on the mark for your child. In my day, I'd send invitations to friends through the post office. Now, children do this through texting or social media. You've got to be ready to go with what is socially acceptable and reasonable for your child at his age, and watching modern media will help you familiarize yourself with the ways that children are portrayed problem solving, and in turn, you can help your child come up with some realistic, current solutions. The more practice you give your child, the more prepared and in control he'll feel when the situation arises.

Help Make Things Happen

Don't sit around and wait. Help your child to make it happen! Make a deal with your son: If he asks some children to go to the movies or a pizza place, you'll drive them. If he invites some children over, you'll break out the video games and order Chinese food. If your child is in the teenage years, now's the time to talk about curfews and being out with friends. Be reasonable and flexible, letting your teen prove he's responsible while learning how to manage his anxiety. You might not be used to your child going places and doing things, so keep your own anxieties in check while you instill confidence in your child.

Stop Making Excuses for Your Child!

I've had the smallest of children tell me they can't do things with friends because "I'm shy." How does a five-year-old learn that label? One twelve-year-old girl wrote on my whiteboard, "I don't ever speak out loud to anyone but my family, so we'll have to write to each other." How did she come to own this no-talking identity, but yet she communicates perfectly in writing?

These children learned to label themselves because they were branded by others around them. When you take on a tone with friends and say, "Owen is shy, but he wants to play with your Benji, don't you, Owen?" you are not giving your child a chance to rise to the occasion. Instead, you're building an identity for him and allowing him to escape into it.

Watch what you say and where you say it. Drop these labels and, instead, encourage your child to move forward into the social world.

Special Situations

Your child will be bumping up against lots of social situations in his life. Here are a few, and how you can help him.

Participating in School

Make a deal with your child: She needs to raise her hand twice a week or to go up to the board to solve a problem. If she tells you she's trying but not being called on, suggest that she speak to the teacher about her efforts. If that doesn't help, speak to your child's teachers to let them know that your child is working on increasing her participation in class. You don't want her grades to suffer because her teacher thinks she's being willful or stubborn by not contributing to class discussions.

At the same time, you don't want the teacher to start calling on her again and again, which will only backfire and make her shut down even more. Brainstorm with the teacher on how to up your child's class input without overly increasing her anxiety. You might also ask the teacher to make sure to assign partners during class projects so that your child doesn't get left out.

For a younger child, ask the teacher to reward his efforts with positive attention. And play "school" at home. Practice with your child with a chalkboard and some homework papers, so that he can raise his hand and you, as the teacher, can call on him and make comments ("That's not quite right, Kevin, try again." "No, that's wrong. Let's see if someone else knows the answer." "Right! Good answer!"). Ask him how he feels after each practice and focus him on coaching himself to reward his effort and keep practicing!

Stage Fright

My brother, Joe, has a video of his daughter in her kindergarten holiday pageant. It shows her sitting onstage surrounded by her classmates and everyone is singing holiday songs. Everyone, that is, except Jackie. There she is, wide-eyed and tight-lipped, not a peep coming out of her. Not even an attempt to lip-synch with the others. It's adorable in its own way, and watching it now, we all laugh. Of course, that's because Jackie eventually found her voice on her own and started participating in classes, music, sports, and all the usual activities.

You may not be so lucky with your child. So how do you deal with an upcoming class play, concert, or spelling bee? Break out the family camcorder and role-play the situation with your child in front of the camera. While it can be anxiety-provoking for anyone to see himself on tape (admit it, you feel this way as much as your child does!), if you keep replaying the scene, you get used to it. Practice and record different scenarios and then get out the popcorn and watch the videos with your child. He will feel less anxious over time, but more important, he will know what to do when the real show starts!

Facebook: A Blessing or a Curse for the Socially Anxious Child?

Children today use Facebook and other social networking sites to announce good news, share jokes and photos, and get groups of friends together for hanging out and for parties. So for your socially anxious child, social networking sites can be an easy way to keep up with his friends' goings-on and practice his social skills in a less threatening environment.

We've also all heard terrible or even tragic stories about Internet dangers: Cyber bullying, stalking, or even suicides can be a result of children interacting on social network sites. So, for all the good there is in Facebook, is there enough bad to put the kibosh on the entire subject?

Absolutely not. With some easy safety rules and appropriate monitoring, your socially anxious child can use Facebook and other Internet sites to her advantage.

Gauge to your child's age: Start by checking with other parents what they think about social networking sites. Does your child's school recommend any sites or have cautions against specific sites?

- If your child is under the age of twelve, I suggest very careful monitoring. Sit with your child when she is on the site until you get to know it yourself and see how your child manages. For extra comfort, make sure your privacy and parental control settings are activated.
- If your child is between the ages of twelve and fourteen, firm limits and monitoring are in order. Make a condition of your child joining Facebook that she must accept your friend request. You can decide how to handle this, but some parents sign on as themselves and others will use a pseudonym. My preference is to be yourself so you can observe while your child's friends know that you are there. Your child must also give you a list of all of her sign-in names and passwords. And sign in as your child every once in a while to keep tabs on what she's doing.
- If your child is closer to fifteen or sixteen, this level of involvement may not be necessary or appropriate, but

base your actions on your child's level of maturity, honesty, openness with you, and ability to problem-solve. You may decide to just leave things as they are and stay full-on. Or, if you feel comfortable, decide together on a reasonable plan for keeping you informed while still giving her some leeway to handle her online relationships. Discuss in advance potential problems you may face (What if someone posts your child's SAT scores? What if someone is spreading nasty gossip about your child? What if your child is a victim of cyber bullying?). The more you discuss beforehand, the more prepared you will all be.

Check it out yourself: Ask your child what sites he'd like to visit, and go to the sites and poke around as a guest. Find out what kinds of privacy settings are available, look at what's being discussed, and see which other applications are available at the site. Red flags include things like "comparing people" (where users upload pictures of two people and ask for polls on who's prettier, or who they'd want to date) and "honesty boxes" (where users ask others to tell them something they wouldn't have the nerve to ask face-to-face).

Set the ground rules: Find some common ground and use this to help your child make good decisions. If you think he or she is too young or immature to visit a particular site, then what does he need to do to prove he's ready? Can he go on it with certain limits? Do you want to approve everything he posts in the way of pictures and personal information? Can you help him to present himself without identifying for the world exactly who he is? Whether you're approving every post or not, make sure he knows that he should never use his school name, town, last name, and so on.

Talk to your child about the realities of Internet privacy and life span. Nothing is really private and everything leaves a trace. Keep it local and real:

- You may share something with a friend today, but that person may turn out not to be your friend tomorrow.
- You can't always trust others to hold your private information for the long term.
- Things on the Internet have a way of surviving in one form or another . . . and being misused and misunderstood. (Do you really want those pictures with your freshman boyfriend showing up later in a new boyfriend's e-mail?)

For more information on Internet safety and your child, here are a few good websites I recommend:

http://www.cyberbullyhelp.com/
https://www.facebook.com/help/parents
http://www.cyberbullying.us/resources.php
http://www.atg.wa.gov/InternetSafety/Teens.aspx
http://www.ncpc.org/topics/internet-safety/social-networking-
    websites

Now you've gotten an overview on anxiety, as well as more detailed insight into the three major types of anxiety—what they are and how to parent a child with them. I've shown you how to parent a child with anxiety; in doing that, I introduced you to my area of specialty, CBT. Many children can be helped sufficiently by the advice I've given in these chapters. However, some of you may have to take it a step further. In the next chapter, I'm going to give you insight on whether or not you may have to seek outside help for your child. If you find that you do, I'll give you guidance on how to find a qualified therapist.

11

Finding and Getting Help

By now you should be well schooled in understanding the three most common forms of anxiety in children and adolescents—separation, social, and generalized—and the ways they hamper your child's life. You also know how your child's anxiety gets under your skin and affects the way you parent your child and take care of (or, more likely, don't take care of) your own self.

Hopefully some of the techniques I've shown you have helped you manage on your own. But you may still be struggling. If your child's fears and worries are causing too much distress, are chronic, and are still causing serious problems in your child's daily life and the lifestyle of your family, it may be time to reach out for professional help. I've already shown you that cognitive behavioral therapy (CBT) is the best type of therapy and I've explained how you can utilize it yourself. In this chapter, you're going to find out

- When it's time to look for outside help
- How to find the right CBT therapist for your child

- What to expect when you get there
- What to expect from CBT

Many parents I've seen tell me that they were initially hesitant to seek outside help for their child's anxiety issues. They imagined another person would now be in charge of their child and that they as parents had failed in their essential parenting role.

I'm going to stop you right here and make this perfectly clear: You play a critical part in this process. You're the one who decides when to seek treatment and you are the one to choose the type of treatment and the provider. You know your child better than anyone else in the world and you're uniquely qualified to provide crucial information about your child's behavior and the ways that anxiety is cramping her style. You're most familiar with her past development and your family history.

Nobody can expect you to know everything. You're reading this book—give yourself a huge pat on the back for doing that. You're following the advice I've been giving you—another deserved pat. You still need some help. That's okay. I've had more than fifteen years of schooling and specialized training and, along with my clinical teams, have treated thousands of children over twenty-five years. You cannot possibly expect to know what I do or have the experience I do. Going outside your family for help is not admitting failure or defeat. I would argue that you're doing exactly the opposite. You're empowering yourself, your family, and your child by doing what's best for all of you.

One Step Further

You've already used CBT in some of the previous chapters to help your child face his fears, and hopefully you've had some success with it. But a therapist may be able to push the line even more. A therapist has much more experience treating children with anxiety than the average parent. He's seen many different children with dozens of different types of fears, and he'll be able to apply CBT in a much more creative, skilled, and precise way.

Remember that as the parent, you're seeing your child through your eyes. So first, you may have blind spots yourself that you're not aware of—habits that you've sunk into that may be stalling you in helping your child. Anxiety tends to hide in common and everyday routines, and things that may be helpful habits may actually be, for me, little telltale signs of anxiety in a parent. Do you rearrange the dishes in the dishwasher a certain way or else you feel they won't really get clean? That's anxiety. Do you record your bill payments in a check ledger but also in a separate file, just in case one gets lost? That's anxiety. If your child has a party coming up, are you the one losing sleep while thinking through all the things that need to get done before the party starts? That's anxiety.

So, while your anxiety may be helpful to you in many ways, it's still there and might just skew your view of your child's anxiety and how much he or she is actually struggling with it. And second, a therapist will be seeing your child with fresh eyes and may be able to explain things to you and your child in a way you've never heard before.

Questions, Questions, Questions

By the time I meet parents in my office, they're usually at their wit's end. Their efforts to allay their child's anxiety may have reached heroic proportions, yet nothing seems to help. They've tried all sorts of methods and taken advice from aunts, teachers, friends, and maybe even plumbers, but nothing has worked for any reasonable length of time. You may have reached this frustrating juncture as well.

Most often in our practice, we see parents who have waited too long before moving to the next and potentially most helpful step: seeking a consultation with a professional. I know this is not easy for many families. Some may feel confused: *See a doctor for this? Therapy? How did we get here?* Others may be concerned with the stigma attached: *What will my in-laws think? Will the school find*

WHEN DO I KNOW IT'S TIME TO SEEK OUTSIDE HELP?

Ask yourself these questions:

- Is my child often upset and distressed because of worry, fear, or anxiety? Yes/No

- Are the reasons for his anxiety things that he should be able to handle at his age? Yes/No

- Do others (e.g., teachers, grandparents, friends) notice the problem, and have they suggested we seek help? Yes/No

- Is my child feeling down and lacking self-esteem because of his anxieties? Yes/No

- Have we tried taking the advice and steps in this book, and found that it's just not enough to settle him? Yes/No

- Am I getting more and more frustrated because I just can't seem to help him? Yes/No

If you're still answering yes to two or more of these questions, it may be time to go to a professional.

out? How will my child feel about being a "patient," and will that scar him even more than the anxiety? Others feel hopeless and defeated: *What's the point? Nothing will change, so why bother?* Financial concerns weigh heavily for some: *Will insurance cover this? How much will we have to pay out of pocket?* And most, if not all, parents wonder: *Who can help us? Will this person know what to do? Am I putting my child in the right hands?*

Once you've decided it's time to see an expert, here's what you need to know.

Before You Start

Find the right therapist. Ask your pediatrician or call your health insurance company for a referral. Make sure any therapist you choose is a licensed psychologist or mental health provider experienced in CBT. Set up a meet and greet with a few therapists and ask questions, such as:

- What type of degree do you have?
- Do you have any certifications, such as from the Ameri-

can Board of Professional Psychology (ABPP) or from the Academy of Cognitive Therapy (ACT)?

- What is your experience in CBT?
- How many children have you treated using CBT?
- Do you do other treatments (if they say yes, they may not be true CBT providers), and if yes, what do you do?
- What are the goals of treatment?
- What will my child be doing in the therapy?
- How will I be involved?
- What will the length of each session be?
- How many therapy sessions do you think my child will need?
- How will you assess progress in treatment?

Be aware of the costs. Contact your health insurance provider to familiarize yourself with what coverage it provides for psychotherapy. Some cover only a certain number of visits per year. If you're not covered, speak to any therapist you're considering about fees and payment options. And know your therapist's cancellation policy.

Bear in mind that university-based clinical psychology programs often have sliding scale, fee-for-service clinics where graduate students see clients under the supervision of the faculty. The same goes for clinical psychology internship sites, which may be housed in medical schools, community mental health centers, and other mental health service clinics. Check out whether there is a training clinic in your area and if the clinic is steeped in CBT. I say "steeped" because not all clinical programs are evidence-based, nor do they all train their students in CBT.

If you do live near a good program, don't hesitate to have a trainee as a therapist for your child. Trainees are all supervised by a mentor who may well be someone like Dr. Kendall, or Dr. Silverman, or Dr. Beidel, or any of the other colleagues whom I've mentioned in this book (and me, too!). Trainees are held to a very high standard, one that you won't often get in the private practice world, where a clinician is free to practice as she wishes.

In other words, the trainee won't drift from CBT into a non-evidence-based approach or go off on a tangent. In Resources, at the back of the book, you'll find some websites that will help you search for clinicians and also psychology training programs that may be helpful to you and your child.

Before your first appointment: Make a list of the issues you'd like to speak to the therapist about. Let's start with a few things he will want to know to make the correct diagnosis:

BACKGROUND INFORMATION

- Your child's prenatal development and early childhood development: Were there any problems? Were milestones (babbling, talking, walking, toilet training) met on time or delayed? Any major illnesses, hospitalizations, accidents, or surgeries?
- Your family and home situation: Who lives at home? Who cares for your child(ren) during the day? What are his routines? What are your parenting strategies?
- Family history of the biological parents, siblings, grandparents, aunts, and uncles, and especially any history of anxiety or other mental illnesses.
- Has your child had any prior counseling or treatment for behavioral or emotional issues? Any special education, speech therapy, or occupational therapy?

ABOUT THE PRESENT PROBLEM

- What is your main concern?
- When did this problem first start and how long has it gone on?
- What makes the problem worse or better?
- What have you tried to do to help manage this situation?
- Why are you seeking help for your child at this time?

Be sure to bring copies to the clinician of any prior reports (educational evaluations, psychological testing, relevant school reports) that may be helpful in understanding your child. You will also want to sign a release-of-information form for the clinician to speak to any current or previous therapists who might offer some insights as to their opinions and what they have tried in working with your child. If your child is currently or has been on medication, let the therapist know who is prescribing the meds, when the medication started, and what dosage your child takes. With the release-of-information form the therapist will also be able to collaborate with your child's treating physician.

When You Get There

You, your spouse, and your child will probably meet in the therapist's office for forty-five minutes to an hour for the first session, though it could be longer. Initially the therapist will need to figure out why you're coming to therapy with your child right now. He will zero in on the type of anxiety your child has and how severe it is, which will lead him to assign a diagnosis.

For some parents, the word *diagnosis* makes them nervous because they think that from now until eternity, their child will be "labeled" with a condition. But a diagnosis should not make you shiver in any way. Assigning a diagnosis is not only helpful to ensure the most targeted treatment plan, it's also required: Health insurance agencies need a diagnostic code to pay for services.

At our clinic, we see the parents for upward of ninety minutes (or more), and then we meet for one hour with the child. We use a diagnostic interview I developed with Dr. Silverman called the Anxiety Disorders Interview Schedule, Child and Parent Versions (ADIS). That's a long title (and a long interview), I know. However, the ADIS is an organized and detailed guide that covers every aspect of anxiety and other conditions necessary to understand your child and how to develop a CBT plan to meet her needs.

The interview itself is quite lengthy and needs to be administered by a trained professional: someone who is thoroughly familiar with development, who understands the full range of diagnoses in the *DSM* (*Diagnostic and Statistical Manual of Mental Disorders*), and who is skilled in giving the interview in the way it was meant to be given. The questions are designed to find out what type of anxiety your child has, how deeply it's entrenched, how it affects your child's life, and what your child has tried in order to overcome it.

The ADIS is organized into sections. Each section covers one of the twenty-five different diagnoses relevant to children, ranging from social anxiety to generalized anxiety disorder (GAD) to oppositional defiant disorder to eating disorders. I often see the parents' eyes widen (or roll!) when they see me take this huge booklike questionnaire out of my desk drawer, but I set their minds at ease when I tell them that each section has an introductory question that allows us to determine whether or not that section is relevant to the child. If not, we can skip it and go to the next section.

For example, to make a diagnosis of social phobia we ask, "When your child is in certain social situations, such as at school, in restaurants, at parties, or when meeting new people, has she told you, or have you noticed, that she is afraid that people might think something she does is stupid or dumb or that they might laugh at her?"

If they answer no to this question, we can skip the social anxiety section altogether. If the parent answers yes, we then ask the parent to tell us about it. This and similar questions lead us through a list of different situations where children are socially challenged, from speaking up in class to answering the phone to initiating conversations. We get parents' ratings of how anxious their child is in these situations and how much their child avoids them.

To meet diagnostic criteria, the child must have a certain number of symptoms (a minimum of three of eight possible symptoms for separation anxiety, for example), the symptoms must be present and stable (meaning unchanged, always there) for a certain minimum period of time, and we must see that it's interfering with the child's everyday life.

Why This Type of Interview?

You know your child. Ask her, "How do you feel?" and she may say, "I don't know." Ask her what frightens her and she shrugs her shoulders and cries. The ADIS makes use of age-appropriate methods to help children answer questions as easily and accurately as possible, without putting words into their mouths. For example, it includes a pictorial "feelings thermometer" that allows the child to rate "how much" they feel a certain way, such as how scared, worried, sad, or angry a situation makes them. Often, we find that once the child becomes comfortable with the thermometer, she finds her voice through the interview and starts expressing herself in words.

While time constraints prevent many therapists from using such a comprehensive diagnostic interview as the ADIS, you and your child will likely be asked to complete some questionnaires that assess symptoms and different feelings or moods. These questionnaires do not result in a diagnosis, but they provide the clinician with important information that will add to his understanding of your child. Some well-studied and widely used scales include

- *Child Anxiety Impact Scales, Child and Parent Forms (CAIS-C/P):* A twenty-seven-item rating scale for parents and children used to assess children's anxiety-related difficulties and functioning in multiple areas, including school, social, and home/family.
- *Multidimensional Anxiety Scale for Children (MASC):* A thirty-nine-item child self-report scale with four factors: physical symptoms, social anxiety, harm avoidance, and separation/panic anxiety. Items are rated on a four-point scale. There is also a parent version of the MASC that assesses your thoughts about your child's anxiety.
- *Screen for Child Anxiety Related Emotional Disorders, Parent Form (SCARED-P):* A forty-one-item parent-report instrument assessing symptoms of panic disorder, separation anxiety disorder, generalized anxiety disorder, social phobia, and anxiety related to attending school.

Most therapists will ask you and your child to complete these rating scales—or scales like them—at the first session and then they may ask you to do so again after six or eight sessions, to track your child's progress.

If you've read this far in the book, you probably have a good idea that your child indeed has anxiety, and even what kind of anxiety he has. You know from chapter 2 whether your child's anxiety is normal or something that may be diagnosable. But any expert you see will have to go through his own formal process, as he should.

Although you've no doubt learned a lot from this book, only a trained expert truly knows when anxiety has reached the level of a diagnosis. And as I said earlier in the chapter, you also may be seeing your child slightly skewed (because you're seeing him through your eyes), so a therapist can question your child in a more objective manner. In order to best deliver the treatment, he'll need to know exactly what he's dealing with.

All therapists do things differently. At our clinic we try to see each of you alone first to gather information, and then together to offer our opinion on a diagnosis and discuss the goals and treatment plan. This varies depending on the child, the situation, and the therapist's approach, so there's no hard-and-fast rule on how this will go. The first session is often longer, so the therapist can gather information about your child and how this problem plays out within your family. When speaking with the therapist, don't hold back. Believe me, nothing you say will surprise the therapist, and the more you share, the more you all will benefit.

How Long Will Therapy Take?

CBT is considered short-term therapy. The actual number of sessions will depend on several factors, including:

- The type of anxiety your child has
- The severity of his symptoms
- Whether the problem is in one specific area or over several
- How long your child has been suffering
- How and in what ways your child's life and functioning are disrupted due to these issues
- How quickly your child progresses
- How much and the type of support your child receives from you and other family members

If your child is younger, you'll likely be more involved in the sessions than you would if you had a teen. For example, if your child is eight, you'll probably come in for the first half hour with the therapist, then your child will be alone for another half hour with the therapist. When I work with families of teens, we usually meet all together up front to establish goals for treatment and talk about how the parents and I will communicate while still respecting the teen's need for confidentiality, and that determines how long each session may be split between you and your child or how often you'll come in for parent sessions.

Regardless of your child's age, every four to six sessions you will be going to the therapist—whether on your own or with your child—to work on how to be an effective coach. That means help-ing your child work through the anxiety at first, but you'll also need to learn what to do when your child gains more freedom. The goal is not for you to forever be your child's coach—it's to help your child take the responsibility for coaching himself out of the anxiety.

KEEP YOUR FOCUS

Since we've already discussed how anxiety can be influenced by family factors, such as genes and parenting styles, it's very likely that you may be struggling with your own issues. Sometimes when a parent is in front of a therapist, he thinks, *Hey, what a perfect opportunity to work out some of my own angst.* While a therapist may turn the attention to you to make you aware of these issues during a session, you don't want to monopolize the session by working on your own problems. While it's fabulous that you want to face your own stuff, let your child's therapist work with your child, and ask the therapist to direct you to someone who can focus on you.

When the Ball Gets Rolling

Things are going to start changing in your child and in your household. You may like it, you may not like it, or you may completely hate everything about it. That's understandable. Parents feel a wide range of emotions when their children begin with a therapist. Some feel extremely uncomfortable entrusting their most prized possession—their child—to a person whom they barely know. Some feel anger when they watch this almost stranger getting their child to open up in ways she never has, which causes her to feel troublesome emotions she's tried her best to avoid for years. Others feel a twinge of jealousy if their child begins talking about the therapist nonstop ("Mom, Dr. Albano says I have to do it this way!"). And still others find themselves second-guessing the therapist and catching themselves wondering, *Is this really working?* or *It's not working fast enough,* or *It's working too fast!*

If you feel any of these ways, do not let your child know. You never want your child to feel torn between you and the therapist or feel that he's doing anything wrong. If you have questions, concerns, or even doubts, communicate with your child's therapist while out of earshot of your child. A good therapist will have already prepared you for the timing and the pace of therapy and will have let you know that you're going to be doing things with your child you've never done before. I always tell the parents of my patients with social anxiety to start a pizza fund because they'll soon have a bunch of children over on a Friday night demanding dinner. A good therapist will also welcome your questions and refer you for a second opinion if you're still concerned.

A RED FLAG TO WATCH OUT FOR

CBT always needs to be practiced at home. If your child's therapist isn't giving you and your child homework, including detailed instructions on what to practice, how many times, what to look for, and what kind of notes to keep, you may not be dealing with a true CBT therapist.

Signs of Success

At first you'll probably see your child getting more upset. Believe it or not, you want that. It proves that the therapist is hitting your child's anxiety where it hurts, so to speak, and is bringing his triggers to the surface. Buckle up—your child may complain even more that he doesn't want to go to school or he doesn't want to go to that party, and he may not want to go to therapy. Stand firm! Now is not the time to let him slide—nudge him toward the anxiety, not away from it.

During the initial stages and throughout therapy, you'll start to see your child keeping a diary, allowing herself to confront her feelings on paper. Then you'll see her doing things she's never done before. She may be practicing her breathing on her own or she may come to you and ask for help with a problem. Remember what we learned in some of the earlier chapters—help guide her to the answers, don't give them to her. The great thing about CBT is that your therapist will be giving you measurable goals along the way—your son will sleep in his own bed for three nights in a row, your daughter will hand in a school paper on time—so you'll know exactly how the therapy is working because you'll be able to see your child achieving his goals.

THIS CHAPTER HAS GIVEN you a real flavor of what to expect in therapy. But what if CBT doesn't do enough for your child? What if he's making gains, but he's still suffering? Or, what if he won't even go into the therapy and no matter what you do, nothing gets him there? In the next chapter I'm going to give you an overview of medication therapy, which can be used in conjunction with CBT.

12

Medication Therapy: Weighing the Benefits and Risks

If you're considering medication therapy for your child, you may be deeply ambivalent about your next move. You may feel nervous, uneasy, and possibly even panicked. You may be afraid that your child will become dependent on the medication. You may fear that other children will find out and think differently of him. You may be concerned about potential side effects. And you may have heard about the Food and Drug Administration warnings about suicidal thoughts and behavior, which has you shaking in your shoes about even entertaining the thought of putting your child on anti-anxiety medication.

Let me assure you, these are all normal feelings. Making the decision to try medication with your child is an exceptionally weighty issue, fraught with concerns from every angle. In this chapter I will address all those concerns: addiction, side effects, as well as the FDA warnings. And I'll help you weigh any risks against the benefits your child may get from being on medication.

Keep in mind that if medication does become part of your child's treatment plan, you'll play a key role by making sure your child takes the medicine as prescribed, and by being on the lookout for any side effects your child may experience. As with any treatment plan, you are the best advocate for your child, and you have the final word.

I told you in chapter 3 that I was involved in a landmark study sponsored by the National Institute of Mental Health (NIMH) called the Child/Adolescent Anxiety Multimodal Study (CAMS). We found that an astounding 81 percent of those receiving a combination of medication and CBT were significantly improved. So, while CBT works, and it works well, adding medication to the mix gives more children a better chance to recover from anxiety.

We don't fully understand why, but the combination of medication and behavioral therapy packs a one-two punch, possibly because at the same time that the child is learning these new CBT skills, the medicine is helping her overall nervous system to calm down.

Many of you may be hesitant to put your child on medication, and that's understandable. There are several factors to consider in deciding what to do for treatment—CBT, medication, both, or nothing. We'll look at these questions in this chapter. But what I must admit at the outset is that where medication is involved, we don't yet know everything that happens over the long term. Our own CAMS trial was only nine months long, and no studies have looked at children on antianxiety medication for any longer than that.

Neither do we know what happens when we take children off the medication, as no controlled studies have been done with children after they stop their medication. So we can't make any solid statements about what happens when medication treatment ends. That's why careful monitoring is crucial during treatment as well as on an occasional basis afterward.

Is It Time to Consider Medication?

I am not an advocate of streamlining right to medication. As I've said previously, I always recommend trying CBT first, as do many of my colleagues in both psychiatry and psychology. However, sometimes a child simply cannot function, and medication may be the best option to get her to the path where CBT can then take over.

When trying to decide whether or not to use medication, ask yourself the following questions:

- Have you and your child tried CBT *faithfully* . . . following the therapist's recommendations as closely as possible, for at least eight weeks? Yes/No
- Is your child refusing to go to school and no matter what you've tried, he simply will not go? Yes/No
- Is your child getting depressed or increasingly irritable? Yes/No
- Despite your efforts, is your child continuing to lose friends and fall behind in school? Yes/No
- Does your child seem unable to do what we ask in CBT? In other words, does he refuse to practice the breathing or complete the forms that ask about his thinking? Yes/No
- Is your child simply unable to participate in therapy because even talking about his anxiety makes him much more anxious? Yes/No

If you've answered yes to any of these questions and your child's symptoms are continuing to interfere with his home life, school life, and his friends, you should discuss medication with your child's therapist. Most therapists are not actually M.D.s, so you will need to go to a psychiatrist or psychopharmacologist who will work in close concert with your child's CBT therapist in order to find the best medication for your child.

As I mentioned earlier, some children are so paralyzed by anxiety that medication is necessary to even begin CBT. Stacy was one of those children. From an early age she excelled in school and was the darling of every teacher. In the sixth grade, everything changed. Stacy began to refuse to do any "lame" assignments that she claimed didn't challenge her. She stopped answering questions in class, and she'd often just put her head down and not respond to the teachers.

By seventh grade Stacy refused to go to school, missing three or four days per week. On the advice of the school, Stacy's parents started her in talk therapy, three times per week.

But things continued to worsen, and Stacy's father began to scour the Internet, where he found our clinic.

We quickly uncovered the fact that underlying Stacy's school refusal and anxiety was a festering and untreated generalized anxiety disorder (GAD), where she doubted herself every moment of the day. Nothing she did was good enough, and by the end of seventh grade she was in the throes of depression, completely refusing to attend school at all.

We began CBT, and Stacy got worse, not better. She had been in talk therapy for two years and had little confidence that therapy could help her. My clinic's assistant director, Sandra Pimentel, Ph.D., tried to teach Stacy how to monitor her thoughts and work through feelings identification, and at the same time I worked separately with the parents to firm up their knowledge of child development and the need for parental guidance and limits on behavior.

Slowly, the family began to change the way they related to one another and Stacy's parents began coaching her toward health. But Stacy's anxiety was so entrenched and clouded by depression that she refused to try even the simplest of exposures, even after eight solid weeks of therapy. At that point, Stacy's parents agreed to a consultation with our clinic's medical director, Moira Rynn, M.D., who took her own careful history of the situation and worked with Stacy and her parents to understand what would happen if they began medication treatment. They agreed to try treatment with a selective serotonin reuptake inhibitor (SSRI) in conjunction with CBT.

After four weeks on medication, Stacy felt ready to begin exposures. There continued to be some fits and starts, and it took a bit of work on Dr. Rynn's part to find an optimal dose of the medication for Stacy, but by the fall, she went back to school part-time, and by the end of her eighth-grade year, Stacy was caught up in her academics. More important, she and her parents had tackled the biggest components of her anxiety—perfectionism and fears of failure and embarrassment—and her mood lifted and she was no longer depressed. We're happy to report she's currently a thriving high school student, and taking everything in stride while managing the potholes that her anxiety vulnerability will throw at her along the way.

Your child's problems do not have to be as severe as Stacy's before you add medication to his treatment for anxiety. Let's take a look at some of the medications available to us for use in children.

Meds for Minors

The most common class of medication used for anxiety in children and adolescents is SSRIs. SSRIs were originally developed to help treat depression, but doctors have discovered that, like many other medications, they're useful for other disorders as well. Studies in adults have found SSRIs to be beneficial in reducing anxiety, particularly panic disorder, obsessive-compulsive disorder (OCD), and social phobia. In addition, over the past fifteen years SSRIs have been found to help the treatment of children and adolescents with anxiety or depression. Most of these studies are clinical trials, comparing one of the SSRI medications to a pill placebo. Some studies also examined the benefits of combining medication and CBT, such as the CAMS trial that I described earlier in this chapter. However, our understanding of the efficacy of SSRIs for anxiety in children lags behind research conducted with adults. As a result, many questions remain regarding their long-term benefit, overall safety, and optimal ways of prescribing these medications to young people.

The name may be a mouthful, but SSRIs work in the following way: Serotonin is a neurotransmitter, or chemical messenger, used to communicate between brain cells (called neurons), and one of its functions is to help regulate mood. Cells are constantly releasing serotonin into pathways, called synapses, and each time the serotonin goes from one cell to the next, it fits itself like a key into a lock on the new cell. Any unused serotonin is then reabsorbed by the previous cell. The SSRIs block the reabsorption (or reuptake) of this neurotransmitter, keeping it "active" in the synapse for a longer period. For reasons we don't fully understand, having serotonin active may be the way that the SSRIs improve mood. SSRIs are called selective because they seem to primarily affect serotonin, not other neurotransmitters.

An Important Warning

In October 2004, the FDA issued a strong warning that antidepressant medications, including SSRIs, may increase suicidal thoughts and behaviors in a small proportion of children and teenagers who are treated with them. The warning was based on a review of twenty-four different short-term studies of nine antidepressant medications involving over forty-four hundred children and teens with major depressive disorder, OCD, or other psychiatric disorders. As compared with other children and adolescents who were not treated with antidepressants, those treated with antidepressants had approximately twice the rate of suicidal thoughts and behaviors (4 percent on SSRIs compared to 2 percent on placebo). It should be noted that no suicides occurred in any of the studies. In 2006, the FDA extended the warning to include young adults up to age twenty-five.

The FDA warning indicates that antidepressants may increase the risk of suicidal thinking and behavior in some children and adolescents with major depressive disorder (MDD). The warning also cautions that children and adolescents taking SSRI medications should be closely monitored for any worsening in depression, emergence of suicidal thinking or behavior, or unusual changes in behavior, such as sleeplessness, agitation, or withdrawal from normal social situations. Close monitoring is especially important during the first four weeks of treatment. SSRI medications usually have few side effects in children and adolescents, but for unknown reasons, they may trigger agitation and abnormal behavior in certain individuals.

Results of a comprehensive review of pediatric trials conducted between 1988 and 2006 suggested that the benefits of antidepressant medications likely outweigh their risks to children and adolescents with major depression and anxiety disorders. What does this mean for you and your child? The warning should not by itself persuade you to refuse to give your child medication or take your child off medication if she's already started and appears to be benefiting from it. The warning does, however, mean that you should be alert for any signs of emerging depression and talk to your child's doctor or therapist about your concerns. I advise my patients taking medication to keep in contact with their psychiatrist and to allow us as a treatment team to work together to monitor their behavior and symptoms. Remember, the ongoing risks of not treating your child often outweigh the potential safety risks of antidepressants. As we've discussed in previous chapters, untreated anxiety disorders in children increase the risk for depression, social isolation, substance abuse, and suicide.

MEDICATIONS PRESCRIBED FOR CHILDREN WITH ANXIETY

The most popular SSRIs used to treat anxiety include

- fluoxetine (Prozac)
- sertraline (Zoloft)
- paroxetine (Paxil)
- fluvoxamine (Luvox)
- citalopram (Celexa)
- escitalopram (Lexapro)

Another medication, venlafaxine (Effexor), is an antidepressant that inhibits the reuptake of serotonin and norepinephrine (a separate neurotransmitter involved in the fight-or-flight response) and has been found effective in treating GAD and social phobia in youth. Now less commonly prescribed, tricyclic antidepressants (TCAs like imipramine) were developed in the 1950s and have been generally replaced by the SSRIs, which are better tolerated by patients and have less concerning side effects, and are prescribed mainly for significant school refusal behavior and OCD.

Yet another class of medications, benzodiazepines (e.g., lorazepam [Ativan]), are also occasionally used to treat children with anxiety, mostly when there are panic attacks or disabling episodes of heightened generalized anxiety. You are likely familiar with benzodiazepines such as Valium or Xanax, especially if you've ever been prepped for surgery. These medications work by boosting the effect of the neurotransmitter gamma-aminobutyric acid (GABA), which causes sedation, induces sleep, and reduces anxiety.

Although benzodiazepines have long been found to be useful in the treatment of adults with panic disorder and GAD, many child psychiatrists are hesitant to use them in children due to their sedating effects. Also, children and adults can build a tolerance to benzodiazepines if they're taken over a long period of time, so the dosage may need to be increased to get the same effect. Some people may become dependent on them as well, so they tend to be prescribed for a shorter amount of time than the SSRIs.

Keep in mind that the FDA has approved the use of only fluoxetine (Prozac), sertraline (Zoloft), fluvoxamine (Luvox), and clomipramine (Anafranil) for the treatment of pediatric OCD. SSRIs are prescribed "off label," meaning that physicians prescribe the medications for the range of anxiety conditions based on studies in adults and in their usefulness as found in clinical practice.

Speak to Your Doctor

Controlled clinical studies provide the necessary information for the FDA to determine whether medications will be approved. Unfortunately, as we've already said, studies of the use of medications in children lag behind studies of adults, and more research is sorely needed in this area. My advice is to always discuss the risks and benefits of all medications prescribed for your child, whether FDA approved or not, with your physician.

How to Give Medications to Your Child

When it comes to medications and younger children and adolescents, parents most certainly will be in charge of when and where to take the medicine. Some children have difficulty swallowing pills because they're afraid of choking or simply because they don't like the taste. But never take it upon yourself to crush the pill or put it in your child's applesauce. Crushing or mashing the pills may change some of the properties of the medicine, so it's not always okay to do this.

Speak with your child's physician. Some medicines may come in liquid form as an alternative, and doctors can often work with the children to teach them how to swallow medications without fear, using a desensitization approach, or the doctors may refer them to someone who can do this type of work (again, a CBT therapist). Combining swallowing with small reinforcers such as stickers, a special ice cream treat, or extra playtime is a common strategy we use with younger children.

And don't forget those refills. You don't want to run the risk of missing days because you've run out of the medicine, so make sure to give yourself plenty of notice to have a refill called in to your pharmacy before you (or your doctor) go off on vacation. And always inform your child's school nurse about any medication your child is on, particularly if your child needs to take a dose during the school day.

Scouting for Side Effects

In general, SSRIs are well tolerated. The most commonly reported side effects include headache, stomachache or nausea, and difficulty sleeping, and these usually go away within a few weeks. However, no medication is 100 percent risk-free, so it's crucial that you speak to your child's doctor about any physical symptoms that may be related to the medication. You also need to review all the medications your child is taking with the doctor, including antibiotics and allergy medication, which may interfere with certain SSRIs.

I also urge you to inform your physician about any natural or herbal remedies that you may give to your child, such as Saint-John's-wort or fish oils. These compounds may be found in nature, but they still have their own neurochemical effects and interactions in the brain. To be clear, they work in ways that have not been systematically studied in clinical trials, and they may interact with any prescribed medication. Always discuss any remedy, prescription, or homeopathic treatment with your child's doctor.

Questions to Ask the Doctor Prescribing Medication

❖ What is the name of the medication you're prescribing?

❖ Is it available in a generic form (which is much less costly) and, if so, what's the name?

❖ How will it help my child?

❖ How long will it take before I start to see a change?

❖ How will we know it's working?

❖ What are the common side effects? Are there other, less common side effects I should know about?

❖ What should I do if my child misses a dose?

❖ What do we do if my child has difficulty swallowing pills? Can we crush the medicine or get it in liquid form?

❖ Is this medication addictive?

❖ If so, how can I prevent my child becoming addicted to it?

❖ How will you be monitoring my child while he's on this medication?

❖ Will he have to take any blood tests or other tests before starting or during the time he uses this medicine?

❖ Are there any foods or drinks he should avoid while on this medication?

❖ Are there any other drugs or herbal supplements he should not take while on this medication?

❖ Are there any other precautions I should know about while my child is on this medication?

❖ Does my child's school nurse need to be informed that he's on this medication?

❖ What if we want to stop the medicine? How do we do that?

How Will I Know It's Working?

Starting your child on an SSRI will not produce any overnight miracles. Remember, your child has been living with symptoms for years, so it may take awhile for them to lessen. For most children, it will take at least four to six weeks to start to see an improvement.

Just as we measure success when treating with CBT, we want an objective way to measure the medication's success. In our treatment program, we collaborate with the child, the parents, and the psychiatrist about the symptoms that we have targeted to change with our combined treatment. It's a pretty straightforward process that helps figure out how everything is working.

To try it yourself, identify two to four target behaviors with your child and his therapist. For example:

- Speak up with friends and teachers
- Call friends to get together
- Go on playdates
- Get on the school bus without complaining
- Do my homework without rechecking more than once

Rate each situation using a feelings scale:

- You rate how much anxiety your child has in each situation upon starting treatment

- Your child rates how much anxiety he feels in each situation upon starting treatment

Share these target symptoms with the child's psychiatrist:

- At each visit to the clinic, you and your child will again rate how much anxiety is present for each target symptom, as well as how much your child is avoiding these situations
- Plot your child's progress on a graph that we share with the child psychiatrist

After the first several sessions with the psychiatrist, your child will typically see her on a less frequent basis than he sees a CBT therapist. So charting with your CBT therapist and then giving the results to the psychiatrist will help the doctor keep her pulse on what's going on in your child's treatment, as well as insight into whether or not the medication has to be increased or decreased (or *titrated*), or changed in some other way.

Another benefit of charting is to make sure that exposure doesn't begin until the doctor finds the best medication at the most beneficial dosage. Keep in mind: Exposing your child to his fears is going to increase his anxiety to some extent. But because we've been teaching him coping skills and we're using exposure in a gradual way, it won't be anything he can't handle.

That being said, his heart is going to beat a little faster when he starts raising his hand, asking someone for a date, sleeping in his own bed, and handing in homework that isn't double-checked by you. That's not a bad thing. Your child actually *needs* to experience some of the anxiety that happens on these types of challenging tasks, so he can learn how to manage it. So you see, we don't want his medication to work *so* well that he feels zero anxiety at all.

MEDICATION PROGRESS CHART

As we've explained, the central work of CBT is exposure therapy, and at our clinic, we use an Excel chart to track how well it's working in conjunction with the medication. How we do it: Each week before we start a session, I ask the parent and child to give a rating from 0 to 100 for each situation, which I then enter into the Excel chart (0 means no anxiety and 100 means total terror). I send the chart to the child's prescribing doctor as often as she'd like it, which is typically every week at first, then we go to once a month. This allows the doctor to see a quantitative rating of any changes.

The chart on page 244 has a line for the parents' rating and one for the child's rating. Parents tell us what they observe; children give us both their inner feelings and what they are doing behaviorally. Notice how exposure increases anxiety a bit while the child faces his fears, but it is done in a way that he can manage it. Hence, the child's anxiety ratings are slightly higher than the parents' because he's tackling his biggest fears.

Notes: CBT and medication were started in session 1, week 1.

Changes in the medication dose occurred through session 6, at which point no more medication changes were made. Exposure sessions began in week 6 based on the psychiatrist's decision to stop increasing the dosage of the medicine and to allow exposure tasks to begin.

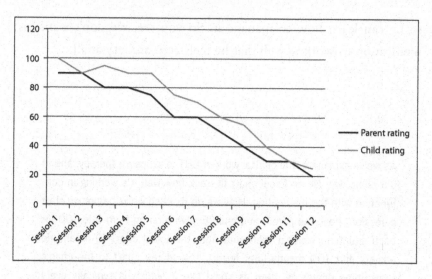

Parents' and child's rating of child's fear of inviting friends to get together. Fear is rated on a 0 (none) to 100 (worst ever) scale.

How Long Will My Child Have to Be on Meds?

Of course, every child and every situation is different. But as a general rule of thumb, I want to see my patient functioning well for an entire year on medication before his psychiatrist starts tapering it off. The anxieties a child will feel in the fall—starting school, going on the school bus, meeting new friends—will be quite different from those he'll feel in the winter or the spring. In fact, winter often brings a lull in anxiety because everyone is naturally stuck inside the house, so although the anxiety is always there beneath the surface, it tends not to show itself as much. But come spring and summer, when final exams loom, the pool opens, and people are out of the house, those anxieties have a tendency to creep back up.

A Word About Medication Adherence

I met recently with sixteen-year-old Robin and her parents, whom I'd been seeing on and off since she was around ten, when she'd successfully overcome a surge of GAD. Now Robin was in the throes of a depressive episode, irritable, withdrawn, and, in general, just not interested in engaging in the world. Robin and her parents decided to do a combination of CBT with me and medication with a psychiatrist in town.

As bright as Robin was, she rarely followed the directions her psychiatrist gave her for taking the medication. "I can't always remember," she complained, and she didn't seem to be taking anything seriously. So with Robin in the room, I dialed up her psychiatrist, my colleague Melvin Oatis, M.D., and put him on speakerphone. He went over why it was so crucial that Robin take her medication as prescribed. If she didn't, Dr. Oatis explained, he wouldn't be able to tell why she was or was not getting better, she wouldn't get the benefit of the medicine, and she could be messing with side effects and her mood. From there, I took over, and Robin and I brainstormed strategies that could work to remind her to take her medicine. A few we came up with:

- Take the medicine as a part of a daily routine at the same time each day (e.g., after brushing teeth, before a meal)
- Keep a tally sheet of doses
- Mark "take pill" on a calendar that's taped to the mirror
- Use a day-of-the-week pillbox
- Paste a note reminder on the medicine cabinet or refrigerator
- Ask a family member to remind me

- Set an alarm on my clock, phone, or watch
- Use a paging system with a beeper

Robin decided to go with taking the medication each morning after brushing her teeth. Since she had her own bathroom, she was able to keep her medication right next to her cup and toothbrush. And since she would never run out of the house without brushing, this reminder worked well for her.

When thinking through adherence issues with teenagers, it's important to find the most effective and confidential means to remind them to take their medications. Luckily for all of us, new technologies are constantly being developed, such as text, e-mail, or cell phone message reminders.

WHEN THE TIME COMES to decrease your child's medication, plan ahead with your team. It's normal for both you and your child to feel some apprehension at that point. By slowly tapering off your child's medication and getting some extra attention from the CBT therapist to bolster your child's coping skills (and yours), your child will be in a better position to move forward in a healthy and happy way.

13

Dealing with It: Living with a Child with an Anxiety Disorder

When you have a child with an anxiety disorder, it takes over every aspect of your life. You may spend hours a day on the phone with your child's school trying to sort out his plunging grades and nonexistent social life. I've met parents who have quit their jobs, shortchanged their other children, sacrificed their marriage, and given up their sex lives. When you have a child with anxiety, it reverberates throughout the entire family structure.

In this chapter I'd like to give you some concrete strategies on how to deal with day-to-day life when you have a child with anxiety. I'll also discuss how to create a healthier family dynamic and improved lifestyle and well-being for you, your spouse, the rest of your family, and, of course, your child.

All in the Family

Being the brother or sister of a child with anxiety can be as frustrating, if not sometimes more frustrating, than being the parent of a child with anxiety.

Most non-anxious siblings feel like they're getting the shaft at some point in their lives. It's only natural—you're spending all of your energies on the child with anxiety, so the typical child feels ignored and uncared for. What's more, the anxious child gets to skip school or duck out of (boring!) family functions, while the typical child gets chewed out for bringing home a C in biology or even mentioning that she doesn't want to go to Great-aunt Sally's ninetieth birthday party.

It's emotionally taxing to be the sibling of an anxious child, not to mention infuriating at times—the anxious child's sibling may not be able to go on family vacations, catch the bus on time, get his parents' help with his homework, have friends over, or even get a good night's sleep because of his brother or sister.

And you, as the parent, feel torn. You can understand your child's frustration. It's not his fault. Why can't he have friends sleep over? Why do you have to drive the long way to school because his brother doesn't like to go over bridges? Why don't you have time to help him with his homework? After all, if your life had to revolve around your sibling, you'd be frustrated and angry, too.

Other siblings may suffer in silence. Everything may seem fine on the surface, but underneath their feelings are brewing, and those feelings may come out later in other ways. The siblings may suffer from depression, they may act out, or they may perform attention-seeking behaviors.

QUIZ: ARE YOU SHORTCHANGING
THE SIBLINGS?

When you have an anxious child in the house, it's easy to overlook your other children. Could you be doing that? Answer yes or no to the following questions.

- Do you spend hours with your anxious child on homework, while you tell your non-anxious child he's a big boy and he can do his homework himself? Yes/No

- Do you spend a lot of time putting your anxious child to bed but tell your non-anxious child, "Just go to bed!" Yes/No

- Have you canceled family trips because your anxious child threw a fit about going away from home? Yes/No

- Are you saying no to a dog, cat, or other animal because your anxious child doesn't want one in the house? Yes/No

- Do you give rewards when your anxious child brings home good grades but just expect good grades from your other children? Yes/No

- Do you not allow parties in your house because your anxious child doesn't like to be around groups of children? Yes/No

If you answered yes to any of these questions, it may be time to reexamine how you're treating all of your children.

The Attention Trap

Your non-anxious child has been used to taking a backseat to her brother's anxiety, which means she is waiting and waiting for your attention. And by watching her anxious sibling, your child is learning a very important (and dangerous for you!) lesson: All I have to do to get Mom or Dad's attention is cause some ruckus, get upset, throw a tantrum, break down, or otherwise act out. After all, tears and fears have worked for the sibling.

Children learn very quickly, so I urge you to listen up. If your non-anxious child is complaining, use that as a wake-up call to take a step back and say to yourself, *This is not good for anyone—not for me, and certainly not for any of my children.*

Instead of always attending to your anxious child, tell her, "Dorothy, I'm working on homework with your sister now. Why don't you sit and read until I'm done. Then I can help you." This gives a very important message to your children—they are *all* worthy of your attention and you want to spend time with each of them, and everyone has to respect your time and their siblings' time. When your children feel that they all have equal access to you, they will all be better off.

Expect an Extinction Burst

If your anxious child is used to getting her way again and again, she's going to be unhappy now that the rules have changed, at least for a while. And that unhappiness will translate to even more beastly behavior than what you've seen so far. In other words, it's going to get worse before it gets better.

In psychology speak, we call this the extinction burst. Think about it: If someone's gained a reward every single time for a particular behavior, that behavior will continue. If suddenly the reward stops coming, the person doesn't stop the behavior right away. Instead, he'll try it again, and more vehemently than he did before, hoping to get the reward. If the payoff never comes, he'll eventually stop. We call that worsening of the behavior the extinction burst—the explosion of behavior before it goes extinct.

Imagine you go to a soda machine every day. Every day, you put in one dollar. And every day, the machine spits out a soda can. One day you put in the bill and nothing comes out. Do you just walk away? No sir, you push the button again. Then you push it again, even harder. You might hit the button again. And then you might even kick the soda machine (and utter a choice word or two). That's the extinction burst. With your child, you've got to outlast the extinction burst. It may be tough, but it's the only way he'll learn that no matter how much he kicks, he's not going to get any soda.

Don't Use Your Anxious Child as a Scapegoat

When you don't want to do something, like get your children a dog, or you can't afford a family vacation, it may be easier sometimes to let your child's anxiety take the fall. But telling your non-anxious child that you can't get a dog because of Bobby's anxiety is just about the worst thing you can do. Instead, be honest with yourself and your family. Explain: "I don't think we're ready as a family for a dog," instead of saying it's because Bobby's scared of dogs. Same with the vacation: Be honest that this isn't the right time for the family, but don't throw the anxious child under the bus.

Sibling Rivalry

How can you help your non-anxious child feel as important as your anxious one? Here are a few pointers.

Don't be stingy with the compliments. Make sure you tell your non-anxious child that you love her. And give her a specific compliment here and there: "I like how you were kind to your little sister. That means a lot to her!" "You've done a nice job on that social studies essay. It shows that you really know the history of the Revolution!" And let her know that you value the help she's giving you. "Thank you, Tania, for putting the dishes in the sink for me!" If she feels that she's choosing to help you rather than being forced to, it may make her feel better about what she's doing.

Focus on the positive. Children don't distinguish between good attention and bad—to them, any attention from you is good attention. As I've mentioned before, if you're spending a lot of time with the anxious child, the non-anxious one may begin to act out just to get your ear. React to any rogue behavior in a neutral voice— he knows what he's doing is wrong, and spending time scolding will only reinforce it. Catch your child doing something good, and give that plenty of positive attention.

Always be honest. It's crucial to be straightforward without being defensive when dealing with your non-anxious child's questions, comments, and concerns. Bottom line is, you and your spouse may not be able to give your children equal attention. Be up front about it when your child complains. Tell her, "I know I'm spending a lot of time with Bailey and that's really frustrating. I would feel the same way if I were you." Acknowledging your non-anxious child's resentment won't necessarily make it go away, but she'll feel better knowing she's being heard.

Use rewards and reinforcers. All of the strategies you've been using with your anxious child can work with your non-anxious child as well. You may be giving Tyler stickers for sleeping in his bed a whole night, but you could create a sticker chart for Alex for helping Mom set the table every night or helping Dad take out the trash.

Use the same problem-solving strategies with your non-anxious child as you do with the anxious child. When Alex comes home from school upset about a test, for example, you can say, "I understand it's upsetting not to do well on a test. What do you want to do the next time to improve your chances of a better grade?" Make this a natural way that you parent, not something unique for the anxious child.

Set out the rules clearly. While you understand that being the sibling of an anxious child can be difficult, you will not tolerate bullying, teasing, or taunting. "Cry baby," "Mama's boy," "Whiner!" are all nasty names that get thrown around in frustration by the non-anxious sibling, often out of anger that Teddy gets all the attention. But these types of attacks will only increase Teddy's attention seeking. Make "No personal attacks allowed" a rule throughout the house for everyone to follow. Period.

Small Acts, Powerful Reinforcers

Parents often fall into the trap of thinking they need to do something big to reward a child's coping behavior, but this simply isn't true. The most powerful type of reinforcement for most children is attention, and this is very simple to deliver. When you catch your child coping with his anxiety, simply:

- ❖ Smile at him

- ❖ Tell him what you like that he's doing

- ❖ Give a pat on the shoulder or back

- ❖ Walk by and just drop a note on the table with a smiley face

- ❖ Engage him in conversation

- ❖ Later in the day, tell him that you noticed him coping so well

- ❖ Pack a note in his lunch box telling him you are proud of his bravery

Friends, Family, and Buttinskies

When there's a child with a problem, everyone has an opinion on the best way to handle it. You've probably heard from many relatives about what you're doing wrong and what you could be doing better. You've no doubt had more than your share of:

"If you'd just be a little tougher on Robert, he'd get over his fear of dogs."

"Oh, let Sharon skip school. Once in a while won't kill her."

"You know, if you forced Lily to get on the phone when I call, we'd all be a lot better off."

Although friends and family mean well, they haven't lived in your shoes. So instead of trying to justify what you're doing or engaging in a discussion (which will only lead to frustration), smile, say, "Thanks, I'll take that under advisement," then pick and choose among the unsolicited advice at your leisure.

If the polite thanks is not enough to shut it down, tell your well-meaning buddy that while you appreciate the attempts to help, what will actually help you and your child is for your buddy not to keep bringing it up. You're reading this book, you're going to the professional—you know the best way to handle things with your child.

More drastic measures may have to be taken if friends or family members are going directly to your child with unconstructive, or even hurtful, remarks—something simple and straightforward, like: "Aunt Fran, Maggie is already stressed and your comments only reinforce the negative feelings she's having about herself." And suggest some alternate phrasings. For example, if Aunt Fran insists on saying, "Come on, Maggie, you're spending way too much time on that homework. Come downstairs and spend time with the family," suggest instead that she say, "Maggie, why don't you work for another twenty minutes and then join us."

A United Front

What if you've tried to follow the plan I've laid out in this book and someone else, despite your pleas, continues to overprotect your child? Jason was a not-atypical nine-year-old who developed generalized anxiety and worry about his performance in school situations. He gave up easily, complained, and begged his parents to let him stay home from school. We worked with Jason and his parents on a plan that integrated effective behavioral strategies, and within a short three weeks, Jason's complaints about school decreased and his grades were picking up.

Just about that time, Jason's grandmother came back from her winter vacation in Florida and settled into her apartment, located around the corner from Jason's home. His mother extended her work hours now that Grandma was there to greet Jason after school, and Jason enjoyed all the wonderful things that grandmas like to do: Hot baked cookies waited for him when he got home from school, he put off homework until after their daily walk to the park, he helped Grandma cook dinner for the family, and together they watched television until all hours . . . and, well, you get the picture. While Jason's mom had told Grandma all about the behavioral plan, Grandma had other ideas: "What? He's been in school all day and needs a break! He's only a baby! Let him have a rest and some fun!"

Not surprisingly, things started to slip. Jason began to complain again about school, and the teacher called to say that Jason hadn't turned in homework.

And so, inconsistency in the plan by a well-meaning and loving grandmother helped undo all the good work Jason and his family did in my office and at home.

So how do you prevent this from happening? The first step is to listen to Grandma (or Uncle Jimmy, or Aunt Alice). Ask her, "Tell me about your grandson. What are his strengths? Does he have difficulty with anything?" See if she recognizes anything herself. If not, then ask, "Have you heard about his struggles in school? Have you heard him crying over his homework?" Grandma may tell you that she never sees that in her house, and that's where you can gently point out the differences between when he's at home and when he's at Grandma's. You as the parent want him to get dressed by himself, do his homework within a certain amount of time, and sleep in his bed by himself all night. Grandma doesn't want to see him upset so she lets him get away with a lot more than you would.

Grandma thought she was helping by making Jason feel better, for the moment, at least. But once we explained what needed to be done and why, Grandma recognized that consistently following the plan, putting his work before his play (remember the Premack principle or "Grandma's rule" about using reinforcers *after* a desired task is completed?—see page 161), and using her lovingly baked cookies as reinforcers for finishing homework, she got on board immediately and became a vital member of the team. When you start laying out the differences and focusing on the outcomes for the child, Grandma will begin to see the benefit of being a part of the program.

Even Closer to Home

You and your partner need to be on the same parenting page as well. One parent does not get to play the good cop and the other play the bad. If there's any disagreement between the two of you, get a babysitter for the children, take a walk to the park, and hammer it out. What are your biases? What are his or hers? What kinds of families were you both raised in? What are you both afraid of?

As parents we all behave differently. You may like to talk things through while your husband uses a wait-and-see approach before plotting his next move. Disagreements in parenting styles, especially around parenting the anxious child, can lead to frustration, tension, and outright fights. But the bottom line is this: You both want your child to be healthy and if you're trying to meet that goal along two completely different courses, your child will be utterly confused. And he'll run for cover through the path of least resistance—the parent who coddles and comforts.

To get on the same parenting page, both parents should first read and review the information on anxiety that I've laid out in this book: where it comes from, what keeps it going, and how to change its course. You both have to be in synch in terms of knowledge and understanding.

Next, figure out your strengths and weaknesses. You may be great at setting limits and getting up in the middle of the night to march your child back into his own bed, while your husband is better at asking questions without jumping in to give the answer. Split tasks according to your strengths. But don't disappear on each other—your husband might not be best at setting a limit, but you want him standing next to you to affirm your authority in the matter. You've got to appear as a unified front, ready to help your child meet and master the anxiety.

Finally, get a handle on your own anxiety and that of your partner. When I meet with parents for the first time in my office, I always conduct a structured interview that goes through all aspects of anxiety and the way it manifests itself in a child. I cannot tell you how many times I've asked the question, "Have you ever noticed that your child, for no apparent reason, suddenly has waves of panic and fright?" and one parent begins to nod and point to the other as if to say, "Our kid doesn't have panic attacks, but my partner does!"

You've got to determine whether your own anxiety interferes with your ability to help your child manage his. If so, agree up front that your partner is going to do more of the work than you are.

Parenting Partnership

1. Present a united front.

2. Size up your strengths.

3. Split up tasks.

4. Figure out (both of) your fears.

Divorce Dilemmas

If you're co-parenting from two homes, such as in the case of divorce, it's probably even more important to work this out together. I can't stress enough how everyone has to work in concert to assist the child. While we don't necessarily expect the exact same rules for junk food or television watching in both houses, when there's a child with anxiety, we *do* expect consistency. If co-sleeping is the problem, the child can't do it at either house. If social anxiety is the problem, Mom can't call the teacher about a problem sixteen-year-old Jerry is having in school after Dad told Jerry to speak to the teacher himself.

No matter how acrimonious your divorce may have been (or still is), this is your child and you both need to be on the same parenting page. If you see your child regressing after he comes home from a visitation, I strongly suggest mediation or co-therapy. There's no use getting angry. Again, as in any parenting situation, there needs to be discussion, education, and a coming together on common goals.

Consistency Is Key

There's a very famous experiment, done by the late Harvard psychologist B. F. Skinner, Ph.D., that demonstrates the importance of consistency. He taught pigeons to peck a button; every time they did, they got a piece of corn. Giving the corn after every peck is called "continuous reinforcement." Then, the corn stopped coming and after a brief extinction burst, the pigeons stopped pecking the button. But when Professor Skinner taught pigeons that the corn came now and then, known as "intermittent reinforcement," and the pigeons couldn't tell how many pecks it would take to get the corn, those pigeons pecked and pecked for an extended period of time until they finally gave up.

This is because intermittent reinforcement is a powerful thing. Think about a slot machine: People stand and feed coins into them and pull and pull, not because they get a payoff every time, but because they don't! Every once in a while they'll get a little payout, and maybe even a medium-sized one, but they have no idea when that big payoff will come. So they keep putting in more coins and pulling and pulling.

You and your partner don't want to be a slot machine for your child. If you stand firm while your partner gives in every once in a while, or vice versa, together you're providing intermittent reinforcement to your child for doing what she's doing—her pulling and pecking. She views you two as a unit—one big slot machine. It takes only one of you to give in, just a little bit, to keep her behavior going. So until you stand firm together every single time, she's going to peck you to death to see which time one of you will give her that payoff.

School Daze

School-related anxiety is often what brings parents to my office. This comes as no surprise because many of children's strongest fears center around school: failing a test, not knowing the answer when called on in class, being ridiculed in gym class, having no one to sit with in the cafeteria. If your child has such fears, mastering them can help him make the most of learning opportunities and develop a sense of achievement. In contrast, if your child's school-related anxiety spirals out of control, the result may be plunging grades, social isolation, missed classes, and even total refusal to go to school.

You may worry that the effects of such problems will reverberate throughout the rest of your child's life. The good news is that you can promote success at school by teaching the educators and getting them on board with the treatment plan. In many cases, special classroom accommodations aren't necessary (though you should know your rights in case they are—see page 268 for information).

Let's deal with the most glaring problem I see in my office: allowing children to skip school. I know it can be frustrating to fight with your child day in and day out to get him on the school bus. But permitting your child to skip school only feeds on itself, getting worse and worse as the days progress. The longer your child stays out of school, the more difficult it will be to get him back there.

That being said, you can't simply force a child to go to school. Okay, I guess you could swing him over your shoulder and carry him in, but that probably wouldn't be very good for either of you unless it's indicated in a treatment plan with your therapist. So, short of channeling Tarzan, how can you get him back in the swing of school (no pun intended)?

First, you need to take a step back and figure out why he's dodging class. Is there something truly going on at school that needs to be addressed? Or is it simply your child's read of the situation that's causing him such agita?

- Is he panicked about speaking in class or getting called on by the teacher?
- Is he afraid that his grades won't be up to his expectations?
- Are you giving him positive rewards for staying home, like unlimited access to the television or computer?

The key to treating the behavior is to get to the root of your child's complaints. In other words, what is the purpose of his school refusal?

Before I go into more detail, I want to make sure that we're clear on the kinds of children and adolescents we are talking about here. These are not the children who are abusing substances or playing hooky so they can go to the movies with their friends or hang out on the street corner. These are not children with oppositional defiance or other behavioral issues. Those children are skipping school for reasons that are beyond the scope of this book. I'm talking only about children with anxiety issues.

That being said, my colleague Christopher Kearney, Ph.D., has devoted his career to understanding why children continue to side-step school. In the old days, we used the term *school phobia,* implying that the child had an overall phobia about school that was driven by some unconscious ideas. This led to inappropriate and unwieldy treatment, using long-term therapy to try to find some repressed cause for the problem. Dr. Kearney and his colleagues have led the field in groundbreaking research showing that there are four main reasons, or "functional conditions," for why children refuse to go to school.

Function 1: Escaping from Miserable Feelings. The child is trying to get away from some sort of negative emotion that he experiences in school. Manny's afraid of fire drills, Petra's too scared to ride the bus, and Scott is afraid of thunderstorms. Jack constantly frets that something will go wrong, that he'll fall far behind and never catch up to graduate on time. And Madison has panic attacks and feels uncomfortable in school. If these children go home, leave school early, or skip school altogether, they feel better, which makes them want to go to school even less.

Function 2: Keeping Out of the Limelight. The child is trying to escape being the focus of attention, judged and critiqued in school. Barry hates using public restrooms because someone will hear him and tease him, Cindy's petrified of changing in front of other girls so she doesn't want to go to gym class, and Eddie is so afraid that he'll answer a question incorrectly that he doesn't want to go to school altogether. The cafeteria is too overwhelming for Barbara, who is intimidated by peers. Peter freezes up on tests and doesn't turn in homework for fear of being judged as stupid. These children feel better when they don't go to school, so they continue to avoid it. Staying at home keeps them out of harm's way, and they, too, feel relief.

Function 3: Locking Up the Attention. I'll start with a story: A mother came to me because her daughter hardly ever left her side. School consisted of a series of missed buses, lateness, frowning teachers, and calls from the nurse. This mom sought help from a therapist, who said, "She obviously fears that you will abandon her. If she doesn't want to go to school, take her to the museum or shopping. Let her know you love her." Ahem.

Similarly, Crystal stays home from school. She loves being with her mom, and the more she begs to stay home, the more time she gets to spend with her. The more Matthew refuses to go to school, the more likely it will be that his mom will sit outside the classroom and volunteer to run the PTA book fair. For these children the school refusal is fueled by separation anxiety. They get all sorts of attention when they cry, whine, and beg to skip school, and the more their parents give in, the more these children are going to do it. They're learning, *If I act up, I am the center of the universe and I am safe.*

Function 4: Gimme, Gimme, Gimme! Ava doesn't even know why she's anxious anymore, but she does know that when she shakes her head at going to school she can sleep late, play video games, and eat whatever she wants. Mario loves to go with his mother to the office when he stays home from school. These children have forgotten why they were out of school in the first place, but they sure do like it at home.

Often children who sour on school have a combination of reasons 1, 2, or 3 with reason 4.

You may be asking yourself: Why does it matter what's motivating the school refusal? I'll tell you: Once we know the main reason, then we can tailor the right combination of behavioral and family strategies to get that child back to school. That is, much like a physician prescribes a certain type of antibiotic for different conditions, the prescriptive treatment of school refusal pioneered by Dr. Kearney does the same thing. It provides the optimal combination of treatment strategies to give the child her best chance of overcoming the problem.

It's important to note that while you're working on getting your child back to school, she must continue some type of connection with it. Perhaps she can go half-days, even quarter-days. You don't want her falling so far behind academically that it will be impossible to catch up. I tell all the parents I see: Even when your children are home, keep to a school day schedule. Yes, I mean it—wake 'em up and work 'em at 7:30 a.m. Give her some boring chores to do and she should work on all homework sent from school. If you have to go to work, bring her to work with you and assign her an unexciting task.

Even if she's old enough to stay home alone, do not leave her alone. Arrange supervision so she can't play video games all day. And continue to push her to go to school throughout the day. Once an hour, ask her if she's ready to go to school. Staying home from school isn't a license to go hog wild. On the contrary: no school time, no free time.

School refusal is a serious problem that, left untreated, leads to more complications and very upsetting consequences that are hard to turn around: school failure, dropout, depression, and long-term dependence on the family. I'd advise you to get professional help now if your child is missing one day or more of school each week.

Should You Let the School Know?

While working with your child, it's best to let the school know what's going on so that you, your child's teacher, and the school administration can all be on the same page. Contact your child's guidance counselor to let her know that your child has anxiety issues that you're working to rectify. You don't want your child isolated or called out in any way in school, but you do want his teachers to know that he needs support during the day. All of your discussions with the guidance counselor should be kept confidential.

The First Day of School

The beginning of the school year is tough for any child, but it's particularly thorny for a child prone to anxiety. To get through that first day:

- Lay clothes out and prepare lunches and snacks the night before so the morning can go as smoothly as possible. Let your child pick and pack what she's going to eat, or, if lunch is for sale at school, go through the menu (or have her go through it herself) and choose what she's going to buy.
- In the morning, keep her moving through the routine, even if she fusses. Have her get dressed, brush her teeth, and eat breakfast. The more you distract her, the better, and you never want to give her the idea that going to school is optional. She just has to muscle through what she has to do.

- Bring your child to school before it starts, particularly if your child is young. Show him his cubby, where he's going to eat lunch, and, with older children, the location of his locker. For younger children, take pictures of your child around the classroom, with the teacher if possible, and hang the pictures up around the house.

- If you want to take your child to school rather than have him take the bus on the first day, that's okay, but make the farewell fast. And let him know that this is the only day you'll drive him.

- If he's never ridden a bus before, do some practicing beforehand if you can.

- Bring her to the bus stop and introduce her to the other children. Pair her with another child whom she can sit next to on the ride.

- Set up a routine when he comes home. Have a snack waiting, and ask how his day went. If you hear any complaints, move past them with a terse, "Oh, I'm sorry that happened. What did you read? Did you play with anyone?" Give him plenty of attention for neutral or positive comments, and play down complaints.

- Use reinforcers (stickers, prizes, time spent with you) after he comes home that first day.

- Start a scrapbook right off the bat. Fill it with artwork and assignments she brings home, some stories she tells you about school, and pictures of her engaged in various activities. Go through it every few weeks to see her progress and always play up how great school is.

Teacher Talk

Bear in mind that your child's teacher may have twenty to thirty students to think about every day, so you want to create systems that work for your child, but don't put undue burdens on her. For younger children in preschool or elementary school, set up a meeting and ask the teacher what she thinks would be most helpful for your child. For example, would it be better if you walked your child to the classroom or dropped him off at the door? For children with social issues, ask about your child's playmates and whether you should set up some dates for them to come play. For older children who are having trouble with homework, does the teacher have a website where she posts assignments so you can look at them with your child?

A daily report card might be a good strategy as well, to target a few specific behaviors. For example, Melanie, who suffers from generalized anxiety disorder (GAD), asks the teacher dozens of questions every day. The daily report card could be, "Melanie will ask a question once before lunch and once after lunch." If Melanie succeeds, she gets a check on the chart and a certain number of checks earns Melanie a special reinforcer at home.

Most middle and high school students are changing teachers every class, so coordinate with a school guidance counselor or psychologist. Ask that person to observe your child so you and she can put your heads together to identify what makes your child the most anxious, and how you can work to help alleviate the anxiety. For example, if your child has GAD, tell the teacher in advance that your child is going to hand in an incomplete assignment so she can practice handing in something that's not up to her standards. She'll see that nothing catastrophic will happen if her homework's not perfect.

Academic Accommodations: Know Your Rights

Federal law protects your child's right to a free and appropriate education in the least restrictive environment. The Individuals with Disabilities Education Act (IDEA) oversees how states and public agencies provide special services for children with disabilities. In order to qualify for special services, IDEA requires that a child be evaluated to document that his anxiety is interfering with his school experience, and he must receive a label. In the past many children with anxiety were given the label "social emotional disturbance," but today many schools are recognizing anxiety as "other health impaired."

I feel mixed on labeling. I don't like a child to be defined as his anxiety. Being a child with social phobia is quite different from being the disorder. However, having special accommodations may help many children who would otherwise be unable to get to, and stay in, school. And in order to get those special accommodations, they must have a label.

If you feel your child would benefit from any type of special accommodations, speak to your school district about getting your child evaluated. If the tests show that his anxiety is hindering his learning process, he will receive an Individualized Education Plan (IEP) (which you must approve), which will include specific, measurable goals to be reviewed every year. It will also include the special accommodations for your child. Special accommodations include:

- Tests taken orally rather than written
- Tests taken in a separate room
- Reduced homework
- A specific number of breaks per day

- Preferential seating
- Social skills group
- One-on-one meetings with the school psychologist

Even if your child doesn't qualify for IDEA, he may still get special accommodations under Section 504 of the Rehabilitation Act of 1973, which protects the rights of children with disabilities and provides reasonable accommodations. A 504 plan can be written without the arduous testing of the IEP, but because there are no requirements for parental involvement or measurable goals, school adherence can vary greatly.

Live an Antianxiety Lifestyle

Everyone needs to live a healthy lifestyle, but for a child prone to anxiety, it's even more crucial. Good, healthy habits should be the norm for your whole family.

Eat an Antianxiety Diet

Drink plenty of water. Dehydration can make your child feel sluggish, keep her from concentrating, and just give her the general blahs. Many anxiety-prone children suffer from stomach ailments such as constipation and diarrhea, and ample hydration will keep things moving along the digestive tract and will replace any fluids that may be lost.

Keep blood sugar even. Make sure your child always eats before she goes to school and give her a small snack when she gets home. If your teenager's rushing to get out the door, hand her an egg white and veggie wrap or make a protein smoothie in a to-go cup.

Keep your child away from sugary snacks, which will send her blood sugar on a roller-coaster spiral and rob her of the nutrition every child needs. Choose snacks that are high in complex carbs and protein and have a bit of healthy fat. Some healthy choices: red pepper slices dipped in plain yogurt; baked chips and salsa; cheddar cheese; or whole-wheat toast with some almond butter.

Up his intake of omega-3 fatty acids. These "good fats" are also called essential fats because your body can't produce them—you have to get them from foods like cold-water fish and certain plant foods. Experts have long known that omega-3s hike up heart health in adults, but they may be helpful in keeping anxiety at bay as well. In a recent study, researchers gave healthy medical students a fish oil supplement containing either omega-3s or a placebo. They found that those taking the omega-3s showed a 20 percent reduction in self-reported anxiety from baseline compared to those taking the placebo. Now, don't run out to give your child supplements of omega-3s. The investigators of this study caution that it is much too early to make any recommendations about these supplements. However, they do recommend eating a diet containing omega-3 fatty acids. Make sure your child eats plenty of salmon, mackerel, cod, and tuna (particularly the albacore and bluefin varieties). If he doesn't like fish, look for eggs high in omega-3s, flaxseed, and walnuts.

Keep him away from caffeine. Caffeine can make your child anxious and jittery, neither of which you want. Caffeine can be in soda, other drinks, or chocolate. Check labels! Definitely cut off caffeine in the evening, so it does not interfere with your child's ability to wind down and get to sleep.

Practice Breathing Techniques as Much as Possible

We know how important proper breathing is. As I've mentioned before, anxiety often begins with quickening of the breath or subtle hyperventilation. When you don't take a deep breath, your lungs don't fully expand and fill with air, sending a signal to your brain that you're in danger. You're actually breathing much more quickly than the average person, which results in symptoms that perpetuate the anxiety, and a vicious cycle begins. As your breathing becomes even more shallow, the brain gets more of a danger signal, which increases the anxiety. Controlled diaphragmatic breathing can help. Keep reminders up around the house—signs like "Keep Breathing" or "Pause, and Take a Deep Breath"—so your child will be reminded to practice his breathing whenever possible.

Eat Together as a Family

Now that your child is involved in more typical childhood activities like soccer, baseball, Girl Scouts, and cheerleading practice, it may be harder to sit down as a family for dinner. Don't let your rush-rush life get in the way of family time, which is just as important now as it was before. Sit down for dinner with whoever is home, and once the busy child arrives home, then sit with him while he eats.

Family dinners are a great time to talk about what's going on in all of your lives. I love playing the "What were the highest and the lowest points of your day" game with children of all ages. We also ask, "What's in the news?" and "What surprised you today?" Make sure you turn off all digital devices and be present in the moment. On days when dinners together are impossible, try to get a family breakfast or lunch in instead.

Make Mozart Your Friend

Music is a great stress reducer. Research has found that listening to soothing music can decrease blood pressure, heart rate, and anxiety levels. Keep soft music playing throughout the house whenever possible.

Exercise as a Family

Working your body is one of the best antianxiety techniques we have available to us. Exercise releases endorphins—brain chemicals that help us feel good. Exercise can also increase lung capacity, to help your child breathe more deeply all the time. Make it a goal to do something physical for at least thirty minutes every day, whether it's a walk after dinner, a family game of football, or playing in the playground.

Make Sleep a Priority

When your child was more anxious, she was probably having more sleep problems, but just because she's not experiencing the same angst she was before doesn't mean she can skimp on sleep. Sleep is crucial for the body and mind to function properly, and for keeping anxiety at bay. Going to bed a little bit late may not seem like a big deal, but when it leads to a habitual behavior, it is a big deal, particularly for the child prone to anxiety.

To make sure your child sleeps soundly:

- She needs to go to sleep and wake up at the same time every day—and keep to this schedule as much as possible, even on weekends and during vacations.

- While exercise is crucial, it needs to be done earlier in the day and not within a few hours before bed.
- Create a nightly wind-down ritual for you and your child. For younger children, a warm bath, a massage with lotion, and a story is great. But keep your time with your child short, so as not to invite back separation anxiety! Older children can read a book by themselves, or even with you before lights-out.
- Shut down all electronics (television, video games, computer) thirty to sixty minutes before bed.
- Keep your child's room cool, dark, and quiet.
- Banish electronics (that includes TV and laptops) from your child's bedroom.

14

When Your Child
Gets Better

Whether you've helped your child overcome his anxiety solely with the help of this book or sought outside professional help, once things are getting under control, a whole new set of worries may besiege you.

How long will this honeymoon last?

What if something sets him off again?

She's heading into a new middle school next year that might start everything spiraling again!

Maybe we shouldn't have another child. That could just make things worse for my son again.

Do we have to report this anxiety on his college applications?

How do I tell if it's anxiety coming back or just some normal jitters?

These are all normal feelings when you have—or have had—a child with anxiety. Your life and the life of your entire family have probably revolved around your child's anxiety in one way or another for years, and although learning a different way of taking on life can be extremely exciting, it can also be a little (or a lot!) scary. In this chapter and the next, we'll look at

- How to reduce the risk of relapse
- How to spot the symptoms of the anxiety's return
- How to act at the first sign of trouble, before the anxiety has a chance to take hold again
- Advice on helping your child stay anxiety-free for life
- Tips for you to lower the stress level in your life

Revisiting Dan

Remember Dan, whom we met in chapter 9? He suffered with social phobia, causing him to white-knuckle it through each school day as he struggled to be invisible to others. You might recall that he spent each lunch period in the bathroom stall, not wanting to even venture into the cafeteria to get a spoon so he could eat the pudding cup his mother packed for him. As a junior in high school he was lonely, depressed, and isolated, all because he was petrified of making a fool of himself. From Dan's perspective, coming to our center was a last-ditch effort to try to find some help.

You might have wondered what happened to Dan. Well, he and four other teenagers met together with my co-therapist, Patricia DiBartolo, Ph.D., and me for sixteen CBT group sessions. The first two sessions included the parents, where we addressed goals and expectations realistically. In other words, these children's personalities were not going to do a 180. They'd probably never be stand-up comedians or head cheerleaders. But they could be free from anxi-

276 ★ YOU AND YOUR ANXIOUS CHILD

ety so they could begin to make life choices based on what they wanted to do rather than what they were afraid to do.

We then focused on teaching CBT skills. Once the teens mastered them, we began conducting and assigning exposures to put their newfound knowledge to the test. Dan was instructed to hang around school longer, to mill around at his locker, to walk through the cafeteria, and to attend the school basketball games: in other words, to stop being invisible.

Up until then, Dan's anxiety had always told him: You'll be teased, rejected, laughed at! But an interesting thing happened after he began applying the CBT strategies. In addition to feeling less anxious as he increased his time in school, Dan told us that a girl in his class had asked him to the junior prom. He hadn't even spoken to this girl in school. But apparently he'd been sending out enough confident signals that she'd taken a fancy to him and had made the first move his way. Obviously, she wasn't held back by any social anxiety!

Naturally, he was anxious. Who wouldn't be? And he wasn't yet prepared to do something he'd never done, so with just a few weeks to work on this, we held a mock prom. We exposed Dan to every which way that a date could go. The girls in the group took turns role-playing his date, and we instructed them to try all sorts of different things—be nice and talkative with him, to spill a drink on him, to ignore him, to step on his feet while dancing, to offer alcohol to him, and to tease him a bit. One exposure after another tested his coping skills and gave him experience with realistic challenges that happen repeatedly in the teenage dating world.

I'd love to tell you that when Dan came back for the session after the prom, he told us that he and the girl hit it off and now they're an item. But what actually happened was even better. His date left him for another guy! I know, I know, that doesn't sound better than

Dan getting a girlfriend. But it's what Dan did afterward that was so remarkable. Instead of running headlong to the bathroom stall, vowing never to venture into the school again, he took a deep breath, looked around the room, and decided he wouldn't crumble. And then? He asked another girl to dance. And she said yes. And then he asked another. And another! And he had a good—no, a great—time talking and dancing with new kids.

Dan didn't stop there. In a later group session to which we invited the parents, Dan played his saxophone for the group, something he had never done before. When he finished, he walked across the room to his mother and handed her a spoon—from the school cafeteria.

I'm tearing up as I write this, remembering Dan's mother's tears and those of his dad. From that time forward Dan took on high school just like everyone else. His calendar began to fill, the family's phone was tied up with calls from friends, and the family had to clear out of the basement when friends came over for take-out Chinese.

We spent the last few sessions of our group teaching the teens to watch for signs of setback, that anxiety is their Achilles' heel and when they feel relief from a canceled meeting or party, to examine why they feel that way. Relapse prevention strategies, which I will talk about in this chapter, enabled Dan and his group mates to expect challenges that were on the horizon and plan ways to deal with them—college interviews and applications, part-time jobs, more and more dating, and standing up to peer pressure.

I last heard from Dan as he was heading off to college, something he didn't think would ever be possible. CBT helped Dan reach his goals: to be a normal, productive high school student who could eat in the cafeteria, go to games and dates and dances, and take all the bumps and curveballs life throws. Of course, that didn't mean that everything would be coming up roses day after day. Like most things in life, beating anxiety goes in fits and starts and ebbs and flows. And he'd take things as they come.

Like Dan, your child may have gotten his anxiety under control. And I know you want to keep it that way. That means not slacking off when it comes to the new lifestyle habits you've formed.

Shifts and Slipups

Everyone has a setback now and then. Jillian first came to our clinic as an engaging seven-year-old who was inquisitive, funny, and playful. She also had separation anxiety and Jillian's mom, Sophie, rarely had a minute to herself. Jillian, along with Sophie and her dad, Rick, came for help after she adamantly refused to sleep in her own room, despite all their efforts. "I thought I'd at least get a break at night and have time with my husband, but she just wouldn't let up," Sophie told me with a sigh.

We set up a staircase of situations for Jillian to work through, from the bottom step—playing by herself for a few minutes—to the top—sleeping in her own room. It took just a few months for Jillian to reach that top step, and she and her mom checked in with us several times after she finished her CBT program.

But then, as Jillian was about to head to middle school, a backslide started to set in. When Sophie came to our office, she told us, "She started over the summer with a lot of questions, like, 'What would it be like in middle school?' 'Will there be many new children?' and 'Suppose that I get lost in that big school? Will that count against me?'"

Sophie thought it was just normal jitters at first, but then Jillian refused to go away to the summer camp she'd loved the year before.

Sophie enrolled her in a day camp, but Jillian ended up dropping out of that, too.

When school started back up, the tears and meltdowns began. Jillian was worried about every aspect of middle school and her parents could not keep up with the reassurance.

While Jillian's separation anxiety got under control for a while, a change in routine brought it back again. Remember that anxiety is a normal, natural emotion. When working correctly, it serves a valuable role in our lives. And so it's not possible to zap it entirely out of your child's life and never hear from it again. More likely you're going to see ebbs and flows as your child navigates her way through development. You may have a period of calm and average levels of anxiety—weeks, months, or even years—but your child will have a vulnerability, that Achilles' heel that will act up if too many things go awry.

When it does, you may be tempted to sound the alarm bell and think that all the gains you've made are completely lost, that you're all back to square one and the time and energy spent dousing the distress was all for naught. And you would be wrong. As with anything, you take two steps forward and one step back. What worked to turn around anxiety in the first place will work again, so you have to get back with the program. Sophie and Rick called us fairly quickly into the new school year and admitted that they missed the warning signs during the summer. "We gave too much reassurance rather than asking her what she was thinking," Sophie told me. And she realized that she missed a major warning sign—Jillian dropping out of her activities.

Because Jillian wasn't begging to come back into their bed, Sophie and Rick didn't realize that the same problem was settling back in. Anxiety doesn't always look the same over the years, even in the same child. At age seven, Jillian was sleeping with them. But by age eleven she started with worry, not separation anxiety, and this fooled her parents for a little while. The good news in this story is that Jillian got with the program fairly quickly. She saw me for a few weeks, and we worked on spotting the signs of her anxiety, doing some deep breathing, doing detective thinking, and developing a deal-with-it plan. Her parents set up a reward program, and by October she was feeling secure and confident in middle school. And now she's thriving in high school and did this without a hitch.

Relapse Rousers

Sometimes relapses are sparked by something specific. For example, your nine-year-old child worked through his separation anxiety and then your husband had to go on a two-week business trip out of the country. Your child might begin to cling to you—something you hadn't seen in months. Don't panic. Instead of throwing your hands up, allow the family some time to adjust and calm down. You may find that your child goes back to his more confident ways on his own. If not, begin putting some CBT exercises back into place, such as routines at bedtime, sleeping in his own bed, and deep breathing.

Keep a Watchful Eye

Although you shouldn't be obsessively watching your child, waiting for the day the anxiety returns, you do need to be mindful of how much anxiety is reasonable and how much is not, in order to determine whether she's experiencing a setback or a relapse. A setback is a minor bump in the road. Your child crawls into bed with you for a few nights while she's ill with the flu. Simply walking her back to her room should take care of that pretty quickly.

A relapse, however, involves more upset and a return of several symptoms at once. Again, you have to remind yourself of what worked to turn things around before and to get back in the program. You don't want anxiety to creep back in unannounced, so be on the lookout for these signs:

Excuses. Your child says he'd rather be with you than go with friends on a school trip. You son doesn't want to talk to the teacher because the teacher doesn't like him. Your daughter doesn't want to go to summer camp because she doesn't want you to miss being with her on your birthday. Your son doesn't want to go to his best friend's party because there will be too many kids there and his best friend won't be able to spend quality time with him.

Relief. When your child breathes a sigh of relief when something is canceled that may challenge him, that's a sign of creeping anxiety. For example, let's say you were planning a family trip to a new destination, but it turned out that Dad had to work so you canceled the trip. Most children would be upset, but if generalized anxiety disorder (GAD) is creeping back up on your child, he'll be relieved.

Questions. If you see the "what if" questions start again and are feeling interrogated ("Where are you going?" "What are you doing?"), be aware that GAD could be sneaking its way back in again. Same thing for separation anxiety disorder (SAD): "When will you be back, Mom?" "Will you call me?" "Can I wait up for you to come home?"

Physical ailments. If you see that your child is complaining about headaches, stomachaches, or not sleeping again, he could be heading for trouble. Be sure to keep him going to school unless there's a good medical reason (fever, vomiting) to stay at home.

Stick with the Program

If you feel yourself going back down the rabbit hole of enabling the anxiety, stop yourself right now. Remember all the things I've taught you in this book and do not turn back now. You've come way too far! Need a reminder?

First and foremost: Continue questioning your child. Don't give her the solutions. Ask her how she wants to solve the problem. As tempted as you are to swoop in and save your child from a struggle, don't! Put your hands right where I can see them and let her fend for herself.

Do not fall back on changing your schedule and that of your other children to accommodate the anxiety. Don't stay home, don't let him stay home, don't cancel plans. You rule the anxiety, it doesn't rule you. In fact, why don't you add *more* to your social and self-care schedule when anxiety is nipping at your child? See your friends for dinner, go to the gym on a regular basis, see a movie with your spouse, which will serve as exposures for your child and self-soothing for you.

Your child will always want to avoid and escape. Be proactive and set up practice exposures. For example, if your child is going from elementary to middle school and you think she'll be anxious, talk about what possible triggers might come up for her. Ask her, "You're going to be going to middle school in the next couple of months. How do you feel? How do you want to approach it?" If she feels she won't know any kids, set up some meetings with classmates in the area. If she's nervous about changing classrooms, go to the building and walk her through a typical day. If she doesn't think she'll know how to use the locker, ask a guidance counselor if she can practice. Let her familiarize herself with the route to school.

PROBLEM-SOLVING STRATEGY

Don't fall back into the old habit of solving the problem for your child. Remember to help your child come to the answers himself. To review:

1. Spell out the problem.

Help your child to identify the problem by asking simple questions: What is going on? Tell me what happened? What do you need to do?

Examples of problems that spark worry:

- Too many assignments at one time for school

- A conflict with friends

- Balancing social and school commitments

2. Define the goal.

Goals must be realistic, attainable, and something your child can own. Don't come up with them for him. Let him think of them himself.

- Example of a reasonable goal: It should take no more than five or six hours to do this project, which I will complete over the long weekend and not put it off until the last day.

3. Brainstorm ways to accomplish the goal.

Come up with any and all solutions, no matter how silly they may seem.

- Examples: I can pull a report off the Internet. My uncle can write the report for me. I can work a little bit at a time each day when there's not much going on at home. Mom can call me in sick on Monday and I can finish the project then.

4. Make a choice!

- Now is the time to evaluate each of the proposed solutions for how realistic they are and whether they will move your child toward his goal. For each one, lead your child through the process of asking,

"Will this really help me to get to the goal?" "Will this solve my problem or cause another problem?" "Does this make the most sense?"

- For example, here's a plan for the holiday weekend: Over this holiday weekend, I will work three hours each day on my project in the morning and then relax in the afternoon.

5. Take action!

- Put the problem-solving plan in place and work toward the goal. Assist your child in a reasonable way. For example, make materials available that he needs, keep siblings away if your child needs to do work, but let him work toward the goal as much on his own as possible.

6. Remember Grandma's rule!

- Plan some reasonable and desired reinforcement for following the plan. Then, talk with your child about how it feels to make progress on a goal. If he gets stuck on a step in the plan, use the problem-solving steps to retool and move forward.

WHEN TO SEE A PROFESSIONAL (AGAIN)

If your child is coming into your bed again, ramping up the tears, or starting to lose sleep, don't wait more than three weeks to see a professional. And if there is a refusal to go to school, go even sooner. Missing one day a week for two weeks in a row is already too much.

Growing Up and Letting Go

At every age and stage of maturity, children face a slew of choices and challenges. If you've just begun to loosen the ties that hold you to your child, how do you continue that letting-go process when the stakes are so high?

It's hard to trust that your child is going to do the right thing, particularly if you've been überinvolved in every aspect of his life up until now. But your child is going to have to make tough decisions without you at some point. Eventually he's going to have to take charge of his own health, his own money, and one day his own household. So you want him to have every opportunity to make those life-altering choices while he's still under your roof and has an all-access pass to you and your wise counsel if things get too rough.

What is and is not appropriate for him to do on his own isn't always clear, particularly if you tend toward the anxious yourself. How old should he be for drop-off birthday parties? When should he be doing his homework independently? At what age can he walk to school himself? When can he be in the house alone? When can she be allowed to babysit for other children? When can he use the oven? What's a reasonable curfew?

Here's where friends come in. Get a consensus, particularly from friends whose value systems are in line with yours. And put your head together with your child. What could potentially—and *realistically*—go south, and what true evidence do you have that that might happen?

Remember our rule—for anything your child wants to try, have him do this with you once, then twice on his own. He's eleven and wants to walk to school on his own? Walk with him the first time, follow a bit behind him the second, and then have him call you when he arrives the third time. She's thirteen and wants to bake a cake? Be next to her during the first run, but sit at the table nearby for the second, and then busy yourself in another room for the third. She'll yell if she needs you.

One Size Does Not Fit All

I've given lots of advice in this book, but let's bear something in mind: Every child is unique, every family is unique, every neighborhood and every school is unique. You get the picture. What makes sense regarding the age at which a child walks alone to school in Oxford, Mississippi, is very different from the age of a child walking to school in Washington Heights, New York. The difference in the amount of traffic alone causes the New York family to think twice. Are there crossing guards? How far does he have to walk? Are there other children doing this, too, at the same time? Is the neighborhood safe? I advise parents to allow their teenagers to meet alone with the pediatrician for their annual physicals, to learn how to speak to their doctor and take some control of their health care before going off to college. Parents from some Caribbean cultures thought I was a bit off. For many families it is customary for their daughters to be accompanied until the time of marriage. Think carefully through the advice in this book and think through what is reasonable, safe, and in line with your cultural, financial, and environmental realities.

Launching a Healthy and Responsible Young Adult

Recognize that your role during his teen years is to gently push him out of the nest. To that end, help him to think about his own decisions and his own plans. So, he's got SATs coming up. Ask him, "What do you need to get it done?" If it's time for his yearly physical and he's getting himself around town for social events, then ask him to make his own appointment, take the forms needed with him, and see the doctor on his own. Don't worry, the doctor will call you if there's something amiss. But this is your child's chance to learn how to handle things on his own, while living with you, before you set him free for the college years.

Many parents I've seen in my office assume that somebody's watching over every child in college, making sure he gets a seat at the lunch table and eats all his vegetables before he has dessert. But I'm here to tell you: That's not even close to the real world. At our clinic we actually have a huge program for kids who have gone away to college but dropped out or are on medical leave because they couldn't cope with everything they had to do on their own. High school is a preparatory time for what they need to do in college—talk to professors on their own, make their own appointments, do laundry, get to meals, exercise, assert themselves with rowdy dorm mates and more, never mind the academics. Make sure your child is prepared by letting him do these things on his own before he leaves you.

It's also tough to let go of the reins when the issues are drugs, alcohol, sex, driving, and other assorted teen dangers. Again, when you're used to having your child home every Saturday night, it can be disconcerting when he's staying out all weekend.

While I understand that the discomfort may be difficult, you must trust in your child. It's also okay to give your child some helpful hints on how he can get out of situations he's not comfortable in. For example, if he's at a party where there are drugs or alcohol, it's perfectly okay for him to go in the bathroom to text you to come pick him up.

Of course, when your formerly anxious child asks you to pick him up from a party, your antenna may perk up and cause you to think, *Hmm, does he want me to pick him up because there truly are drugs at the party (good!) or because he's feeling anxious about separating again (bad!)?* Here's how you can tell the difference: Is he saying, "Every-

one's doing drugs so I don't want to be at this party"? Or is he saying, "A few of the kids were doing drugs so I didn't feel comfortable
there"? Not every teen does drugs, so yes, my antenna would perk
up if he told you the former. And the more your child is getting out
there and learning whom he can trust and whom he can't, the more
he's going to be making smart decisions.

IN THIS CHAPTER we've discussed what happens once your child's
anxiety has begun to wane. Some parents want to forget all about the
former problem. Others go the opposite way, unable to shake that
ever-present nagging worry that the anxiety will return. The best
course of action? Strike a middle ground and be proactive. Make
sure you're doing what you can within reason to reduce the risk of
relapse, but don't feel like you have to constantly be looking over
your shoulder, wondering when the anxiety is going to catch up
with you again.

Continue with all the strategies we've talked about in this book
that promote a brave, empowered life. It's tough, I know. You've
been acting a certain way for years—many years if your child is
older—and some habits may run deep. But in order for your child
to continue to progress, it's crucial that you begin to trust him and
his decisions. In the next and final chapter, I'm going to talk once
again about how important it is to examine your own anxious ways.
You've focused on your child. Now let's focus on you.

15

Getting Back to You

We've spent much of this book talking about your child, and how her anxiety has influenced her as well as your entire family. Now, in this last chapter, I'd like to focus solely on you, something that may feel foreign and even uncomfortable. Parents, some would say moms in particular, are hardwired to think first and foremost about their children. But as I've illustrated, the way you think and the way you act play a direct role in how your child thinks, feels, and behaves.

As we've talked about many times throughout this book, anxiety comes from our own inborn alarm systems for handling a threat. And everyone experiences excessive anxiety from time to time. So, if anxiety is natural and necessary, why should we rein it in? Why should you, as a parent, control your natural tendencies to protect, comfort, and reassure your child?

I'll tell you why. Anxiety works best for us when enough is enough, or, to borrow a phrase from the poet Robert Browning,

QUIZ: ARE YOU STILL TOO ANXIOUS?

Even after all the work you've done with your child, you may still be putting your own spin on situations that raise anxiety reactions in both you and your child. Here are some questions to ask yourself.

Answer yes or no to the following questions.

- When a bill arrives, do you worry aloud and say, "Oh, I don't know where we'll find the money for this! What are we going to do now?" Yes/No

- If there's a sudden noise, do you jump and yell? Yes/No

- When leaving the house, do you go back to check and recheck the stove and locks? Yes/No

- If your child looks upset, do you immediately ask, "What's wrong? Did someone do something to you?" Yes/No

- When planning a trip, do you pack an extra suitcase filled with first aid, flashlights, extra food, battery packs—even though you're going to a hotel in a populated area? Yes/No

- Do you scan the newspaper and announce the dismal headlines first? Do you say things like, "Did you see this? They're cutting back on police and firefighters in the city!? How are we going to survive?" Yes/No

If you answered yes to one or more of these questions, you may still be focusing on the negative. Keep in mind, your "Uh-oh!" reactions are the first signal to your child that something is wrong. And you continue to show him there's something to be anxious about by your negative approach. Instead, you want to show him ways to cope with these situations, and perhaps you might want to think about some CBT for yourself.

less is more. The least amount needed to handle any situation is best. As you learned earlier in chapter 1, excessive anxiety is usually a product of multiple influences, from genes to temperament, to personality, to environment.

You've focused a lot lately on your child, and you've done a lot of work to help her face her fears. Want to keep it that way? You've got to get your own worries under wraps. While you've done some work in that area throughout this book, I want to emphasize the importance of taking care of yourself.

Let's start by thinking about before you had children. What set off your anxiety alarms back then? Did you tend to anticipate the worst? Were you jumpy or did you experience panic attacks? Did you worry about what other people thought about you? Were there certain situations that gave you that queasy feeling, such as riding in an elevator, being the center of attention, or getting those dreaded shots or blood tests? Based on what you know from this book, ask yourself whether you were more anxious than most as a child, a teenager, or as an adult before your children came along.

Or, perhaps the opposite is true and you weren't the least bit anxious as a child. If that's the case, ask yourself, "Have I changed in this regard since my child was born?" Did you become antsy about germs and cleanliness once your baby was in the house? Did your stomach lurch or chest tighten each time your child cried? Do you make sure things are all in place and just right so your child doesn't get stressed?

Children will resonate with their parents' emotions. From the very earliest days of their lives, infants will react to parental expressions of feelings and emotion. This is how they begin to learn to respond to the world. You can recall your child smiling in response to your smiles, his excitement if you were in a happy mood, and his furrowed brow if you were mad about something. Remember times when your child just seemed to know that you needed a hug? Your emotions transfer fairly readily to your child, from his earliest days. And so it's not a far stretch to understand that children will learn about emotions from their parents and those with whom they spend their time, from relatives to peers to teachers.

When you recoil with fear at the sharp crack of thunder, your child will react to this. If you express worry over safety and health concerns, your child will sense that something is amiss. In essence, you can transfer your anxieties to your child.

That's why it's critical to keep your own anxiety at bay. You've done a great deal of work throughout this book in order to control your child's anxiety. What have you done for yours? If you still don't think it matters, despite all the ways I've shown you in this book, let me tell you a story about my sister, Joanne, and her daughter, my sixteen-year-old niece, Erin.

Keep Yourself in Check

One day while poking around on Facebook, I saw an unsettling post written by one of Erin's friends on her wall. If you're not on Facebook, a "wall" is a page where you, or your friends, can post comments and pictures. The post on Erin's wall used some graphic language that would make anyone blush, and I was embarrassed on my niece's behalf. When I checked back after a few minutes, it was gone, so quite frankly, I didn't give it a second thought. Later in the week while on the phone with Joanne, I remembered the post and brought up the subject. My sister went ballistic.

"I told her exactly what I thought of that friend and that post, and laid into her about what others will think about her if she allows

her friends to post things like that on her wall!" She continued to
rant and rave about the subject for a solid ten minutes. When she
took a breath, I finally got the chance to speak. "What did Erin
think about the post?" I asked.

"What? Well, I told her—"

I interrupted. "Wait, Joanne, what did Erin think about the post
before you told her what you thought?"

"Well, I guess I didn't give her the chance to tell me."

What a lost opportunity for my sister. She was so quick to react
that she failed to even consider that Erin might have an opinion
about this herself. And it may not have been very different from her
mother's.

In fact, the reason the post was on her wall for such a short time
is that Erin had seen it, deleted it immediately, told her friend she
didn't appreciate the post, and changed her privacy settings to block
further postings from this person, all without hearing a thing from
her mother.

The incident reminded me of a study I'd been involved in. We
asked adolescents with social anxiety to tell us how they would feel
and what they would do in two different situations:

Situation 1: You go into the cafeteria and sit with a group of
kids. Some you know; some you don't know too well.
Some of them are popular. Everyone is talking about plans
for the weekend. How anxious would you feel? What
would you do?

Situation 2: You have been assigned an oral report that will
weigh heavily in your final grade. It can be about anything
you want, but you haven't been doing too well in that class.
There are some popular kids in the class. How anxious
would you feel? What would you do?

We tape recorded the teens' responses and then brought in their parents and said, "Discuss with your son/daughter how they can handle each situation." We taped these discussions as well, then we excused the parents and asked the adolescents to once again tell us how they'd feel and what they would do.

What we found was not encouraging. Essentially, the parents dominated the discussions. In fact, statistically speaking, the parents talked significantly more than their children. And when we identified the content and emotion in the parents' statements, we found that they were substantially negative and not focused on problem solving. Some of the statements the parents uttered included:

- Take out a book and read while you eat.
- Eat as fast as you can and excuse yourself.
- Think about vacation or something nice so you don't feel bad about being there.
- She said there were popular kids there. Won't you feel funny around these kids?
- You don't go out with any of these kids, so you really won't know what they like to do.
- Maybe you can do an extra written report instead of oral?
- I always hated oral reports and would be sick on those days.
- If someone laughs at you, laugh during *their* talk!

We also found that if the parents were anxious themselves, their children reported more negative feelings, less problem solving, and more avoidance of dealing with the situation after their talk with their parents. In other words, anxiety in the parents was associated with a teenager changing her plan to one of avoidance and escape!

So, to circle back to my sister. Joanne saw a real threat to her daughter—that she might be seen in a negative light due to the Facebook posting. In response, she reacted in order to protect Erin before any harm was done. Erin, however, had already taken matters into her own hands and solved the problem—very effectively, in fact.

The parents in our study acted similarly, though rather than acting on an objective threat (the Facebook posting), they were focusing in on ambiguous cues—things that were neither positive nor negative but felt to them like a threat to their children.

Let's look at the parents' misinterpretation of cues in the cafeteria scene:

AMBIGUOUS CUE	NEGATIVE MISINTERPRETATION
Some kids you know, and some you don't.	It will be difficult for my child. What if they don't talk to her? She's had trouble making friends.
Some of them are popular.	He's not a part of that crowd. They won't like him. What if they see him shaking and sweating?
Everyone is making plans for the weekend.	My daughter won't be included. She won't know what they like to do. She will feel terrible about herself.

The parents acted on these supposed threats by encouraging avoidance—eat fast and leave, do a written report instead of oral—in order to protect their children from some negative outcome.

Let me be clear about something: These parents were trying to help and wanted the best for their children. They are not bad parents; they are concerned parents. After many years of watching their sons and daughters suffer with social anxiety, the parents had trained themselves to be on the lookout for potential potholes and guide their children on the best ways to avoid them.

This is the overprotection trap. As a parent, you think that you're helping by preventing your child from potential upset. And while the adolescent might indeed feel better in the moment, over the long term he does not get the opportunity to try to manage these situations on his own, and he feels worse.

The take-home message here is to examine your own feelings. Are you worried about what could happen to your child? Do situations like the cafeteria and oral report scene cause *your* stomach to flip and *you* to think, *Oh no, he's going to crumble in that one!* Have you spent night after night worrying about what will prompt your child's anxiety and go wrong for your child next? This is where we need *you* to turn these CBT strategies around and use them on yourself—examine your own thoughts and think through a plan that will foster resilience and competency in your child. Always ask yourself the question, "How can I coach my child to handle this situation himself?"

Make Your House an Anxiety-free Zone

It's tough to keep yourself anxiety-free. I know that. The world can sometimes be a scary place. And there are a lot of things to worry about. But, just as you've been able to help your child see that she can take on anything life throws at her, you should feel confident in your own abilities. While life won't always hand you lemonade, you can always figure out how to make your own. And that's the attitude I want you to have, whether your child is around or not.

Here are some steps to help maximize your power over anxiety and to minimize the transfer of troubles to your child.

Stick to Reality and Be a Problem Solver

Listen to your own self-talk. Do you tend to coach yourself in a negative way? Are you typically telling yourself, "I shoulda, coulda, woulda" instead of, "Okay, that's what I chose to do and now what's next?" Do you blow things out of proportion in your own mind?

In the same way that we want your child to be a rational thinker, to focus on the realistic likelihood that something will happen, and to think through how to handle situations rather than run from them, that's what I need from you. Turn down the anxiety meter and turn up the coping mechanism. Look at what's in front of you, stay with what's reasonable and likely, and figure out how to deal with it. Remember my friend Dan? His date may have left him at the prom, but he looked out on the dance floor and told himself to go ask someone else to dance. And he danced. And danced some more.

Take Care of Yourself

Do you consider self-care to be that time late at night, when everyone is finally asleep, when you get to fall onto the couch and watch a bit of reality television before zonking out yourself? Do you think it's selfish to meet your own needs, or even to engage in small pleasures like a manicure or an evening with a friend, because your child needs you or it's unfair to leave things to your spouse for a while?

How is it I can guess that you put everyone else first and leave your own self-care to some later date, when things settle down, far off in the future when the children are grown and settled? Stop. It. Now.

Rethink this. You have to be refreshed, rested, and healthy in order to function normally. This is where you have to practice what you preach. Do you want your children to live healthy and balanced lives when they're adults? Then start them on that path by taking care of yourself and showing them that everyone deserves the best for themselves.

Getting sufficient sleep is a must for any parent. Eating right to give your body the fuel it needs to function optimally is essential as well. If you don't know what to eat, look for a nutrition class at the local Y or check the local bookseller for a good book on nutrition. And move your body regularly. I can't stress enough the importance of exercise in helping to ward off excess stress, keeping your body in good cardiovascular shape, and helping to regulate your sleep and improve your mood. Whether it's Jazzercise, Zumba, yoga, a treadmill, a bicycle, or a walk in the neighborhood, get moving to improve your own well-being. And see your doctor and dentist for checkups—at least annually. I'll bet you take your children for their checkups religiously. Don't forget about you.

Learn to Soothe Yourself

What do you do to comfort yourself? Do you have a favorite sweater to wrap in, a blanket that you love, a sachet with a soothing scent? Do you like warm baths, long showers, walking in the rain? Is there a piece of music or a song that always brings a smile to your face? Have you carved out at least ten or fifteen minutes every day, to close your eyes and just be alone and relax?

I've taught you relaxation strategies for your children, such as deep breathing and progressive muscle relaxation. Use them on yourself as well whenever you need a time-out. Also, I highly recommend that you take a yoga class. And then another, and another. Find the time to learn some mindfulness meditation strategies either from a class or a video. Mindfulness practices are incorporated into much of the CBT done with adults who have stress- and anxiety-related issues, and similar programs for children are emerging as I write this. Much research has demonstrated the benefits of these techniques in improving physical health and emotional well-being. Give it a try. And remember, too, to set aside time just for you and your favorite soothing activity, which is critical for emotional health.

Start Dating Again

Now, before I get in trouble, let me explain. If you're married or in a relationship, date your partner. If you're single, get out there and be available. Once the children come along it's easy to lose the romance, especially if you've had a child with separation anxiety sleeping between you and your partner. Now that your child is back in her room, snuggle up again to the one you love.

Anxiety in children often takes the romance out of the parents' relationship. Find ways to get it back. Send the children to Grandma's or a friend's house for the night. Plan a date night and stick to it—no excuses—it's for you and your partner and not for the children. Make a deal with some friends—you'll take their children for a weekend and then they can take yours, so you can get away. Children who are raised in homes where parents are warm, affectionate, and loving to each other tend to be more secure and happy.

Develop an Interest Outside of Your Partner and Family

It's important that you have something all to yourself that brings you a sense of pleasure, accomplishment, and satisfaction. Whether you're a homemaker or work outside of the house, you must have something for yourself. Perhaps it's volunteering at the community garden, or maybe you tutor adults learning English as a second language. Give time to a local food co-op or farmer's market or sit on a nonprofit organization's planning board. These types of activities can take you away from the hustle and bustle of work and parenting, and renew your sense of belonging in the wider world.

Volunteering gives you a sense of purpose that is solely driven by you and not by a need to earn or achieve. These activities can help you to prioritize and reflect on what's important in your life. At the same time, you're modeling altruism for your children, something we all want to instill in our kids.

WHAT WILL YOU DO after your child masters his anxiety and running around like any other child on the block? Remember Timmy's mom, Linda, from chapter 1? Linda went back to work. And then she joined a book club with some new and fun friends. She and Jon go out to dinner and every once in a while even manage to sneak away for a weekend night for some romance. And, she loves to ride her bike through the park, and she does this whenever she feels the urge.

Susan's parents, Kim and Len, whom we met in chapter 9, complain now that without social anxiety Susan's no longer their best friend. In fact, they don't hear from their college student for weeks on end. But they say this through smiles because they know their daughter is too busy with school and friends to keep them up to date on her life. And so Kim and Len, now empty nesters, revel in the quiet nights at home together that they wished for over many years.

There still are occasional bouts of anxiety for all the families. But everyone is ready to handle it. If the child falls off the horse, they know how to get right back on and ride away. These parents, as well as the thousands of parents I've worked with over the years, are now able to share stories of their children's accomplishments and ins and outs of Little League tournaments, dance recitals, teenage heartbreak, and pushing the limits of their curfews.

One of the most important pieces of information I learned from my mentors is that anxiety takes away a person's free will. That is, the anxious child and her family make choices based on fear rather than on desire or need. Freeing your child from anxiety gives back to you and your child the freedom to choose—to do what you want to do and to enjoy what you want to enjoy.

The lessons learned in this book and through CBT will work for you and your child for many years to come. The skills taught in this book are adaptable to whatever your child will encounter next— graduations, rejections and acceptances, romance, you name it. And oh, yes, these CBT principles will help you to adapt, too, as you move forward with your own life. My hope is that you've taken these suggestions to heart, made changes in the ways you parent that enhance your child and your family, and that you are all healthier and happier because of it.

Acknowledgments

My sincere thanks to Charles H. Madsen, Jr., Matt Jaremko, and Karen Christoff, influential mentors who taught me the theory and fundamentals of CBT. Special thanks to David H. Barlow, without whom I would never have pursued a career as an academic clinical psychologist and specifically in the anxiety disorders.

There are several incredible women, all advocates for children and families facing mental health challenges, for whom I have deep respect and admiration. Their selfless and unfailing efforts made tangible differences in the lives of many, and I had the great fortune to learn from each of them. Thank you to Midge Shailer and Jeanne Miley-Clark, former co-directors of Kids in Distress of Fort Lauderdale; the late Jerilyn Ross, co-founder of the Anxiety Disorders Association of America; Laurie Flynn, formerly of the National Alliance for the Mentally Ill and Columbia University TeenScreen; and Mary Guardino, founder of Freedom from Fear on Staten Island. And Mary, an extra thank-you for introducing me to Mark (and Emily and Rachel) and bringing much love to my life!

Thank you to my close colleagues, collaborators, and students from SUNY Albany, Louisville, and New York City, who worked side by side through grants and ADISs and no-shows and various deadlines. Many thanks to my good friend and collaborator Patricia DiBartolo, and to Michael Detweiler, who has opened more clinics for me than can be counted and is the best friend ever. My deep appreciation to John March and the TADS and CAMS investigators and teams for a great and stimulating run of research and collaboration.

Very special thanks to an exceptional group of clinicians who work with me at CUCARD: Sasha Aschenbrand, Kate McKnight, Joanna Robin, James Hambrick, Muniya Khanna, Teresa Piacentini, Jon Comer, Tony Puliafico, Matt Goldfine, and our postdocs and externs. You make our clinical practice a refuge for many families and your dedication to the work is inspiring. And to Sandra Pimentel, a very special thank-you for always being there, always finding a way, and for filling our clinic with camaraderie and laughter, and a practical joke or two.

Thank you to Tracey and Jon Stewart and Monique Gibson, for believing in CUCARD and for making our space beautiful and peaceful!

This book would not have been written without the wise counsel and encouragement of Lynn Sonberg and the collaborative writing and enthusiasm of Leslie Pepper. I am grateful to Lisel Ashlock for turning ideas into perfect illustrations. Anthony Puliafico, my good friend and colleague, and Elaine Glickman, my mother-in-law and a lifelong educator of children, gave careful and detailed attention in reading and providing editing and feedback on early drafts of the book. Gabrielle "Gigi" Campo and Lucia Watson at Penguin made this an enjoyable and stress-free experience. Thank you to what collectively is a wonderful publications team!

And to my husband, Mark Olfson, your love, support, teasing, kindness, encouragement, laughter, and beautiful mind bring me happiness each and every day.

Resources

I want to direct you to a very exciting website that is co-sponsored by the Society for Clinical Child and Adolescent Psychology, the Center for Children and Families at Florida International University, and the Children's Trust of Florida. This website, www.effectivechildtherapy.com, provides parents with up-to-date information for understanding mental health problems in children, how to identify these issues, and how to seek evidence-based treatment. There is much information on which psychotherapies have been studied and found effective for treating these disorders.

A companion website, www.effectivechildtherapy.fiu.edu, houses videos for parents and continuing education videos for professionals. Parents can watch free brief videos of experts describing specific problems experienced by children and adolescents.

Organizations and Websites

American Academy of Child and Adolescent Psychiatry
www.aacap.org
202-966-7300

American Psychiatric Association
www.psych.org
apa@psych.org
888-357-7924

American Psychological Association
www.apa.org
800-374-2721

Anxiety and Depression Association of America
(formerly Anxiety Disorders Association of America)
www.adaa.org
240-485-1001

Association for Behavioral and Cognitive Therapies
www.aabt.org
212-647-1890

Children with Attention Deficit Disorder (CHADD)
www.chadd.org
800-233-4050

Evidence-based Mental Health Treatment for Children and Adolescents
www.Effectivechildtherapy.com

International OCD Foundation
www.ocfoundation.org

National Institute of Mental Health
www.nimh.nih.gov
301-443-4513

Selective Mutism Group
www.selectivemutism.org

Society of Clinical Child and Adolescent Psychology
www.clinicalchildpsychology.org

Evaluation and Treatment Centers Specializing in Childhood Anxiety Disorders

Note: These clinics all have expertise in Cognitive Behavioral Therapy.

Anxiety Clinic at Virginia Commonwealth University
Co-directors: Michael A. Southam-Gerow, Ph.D., and Scott R. Vrana, Ph.D.
612 N. Lombardy St.
Richmond, VA 23284
804-828-8069
anxietyclinic.vcu.edu

Center for Anxiety and Related Disorders at Boston University
Child Program
Co-directors: Jonathan S. Comer, Ph.D., and Donna Pincus, Ph.D.
648 Beacon Street, 6th Floor
Boston, MA 02215
617-353-9610
www.bu.edu/card/

Child and Adolescent Anxiety Disorders Clinic
Director: Philip C. Kendall, Ph.D., ABPP
Temple University
Weiss Hall, B-1, Lower Level
1701 No. 13th Street
Philadelphia, PA 19122
215-204-7165
Fax: 215-204-0565
www.childanxiety.org

Child and Adolescent Mood and Anxiety Treatment
Program at the University of Miami
Director: Jill Ehrenrich-May, Ph.D.
5665 Ponce de Leon Blvd., Room 315
Coral Gables, FL 33146
305-284-9852, ext. 1
Fax: 605-284-4795
www.miami.edu/childanxiety

Child and Adolescent Psychiatry Outpatient Clinic
Director: Mary A. Fristad, Ph.D., ABPP
Ohio State University
1670 Upham Drive, Suite 460G
Columbus, OH 43210-1250
614-293-9600
psychiatry.osu.edu/patientcare/outpatient/

Child Anxiety and Phobia Program
Director: Wendy K. Silverman, Ph.D.
Florida International University
http://www2.fiu.edu/~capp
305-348-1937

Child Anxiety and Related Disorders Clinic
Director: Andrew R. Eisen, Ph.D.
240 West Passaic Street
Maywood, NJ 07607
201-880-7575, ext. 23
www.childanxieties.com

Child School Refusal and Anxiety Disorders Clinic
Director: Christopher A. Kearney, Ph.D.
University of Nevada, Las Vegas
702-895-0183

Child FIRST Program
Director: Bruce F. Chorpita, Ph.D.
University of California, Los Angeles, Department of Psychology
310-825-9445
www.childfirst.ucla.edu

Child Study Center
Director: Thomas H. Ollendick, Ph.D., ABPP
Virginia Tech, Department of Psychology
Blacksburg, VA 24060
540-231-6451
www.psyc.vt.edu/labs/csc

Columbia University Clinic for Anxiety and Related Disorders
Director: Anne Marie Albano, Ph.D.
3 Columbus Circle, Suite 1425
New York, NY 10019
212-246-5740
www.anxietytreatmentnyc.org

Duke University Program in Child Anxiety and Affective Disorders
Director: Scott Compton, Ph.D.
919-416-7200
www.mentalhealth.dukehealth.org

Johns Hopkins University School of Medicine
Division of Child and Adolescent Psychiatry
Child Anxiety Program

Director: Golda S. Ginsburg, Ph.D.
410-955-5335
www.hopkinschildrens.org/psychiatry/

UCLA Child OCD, Anxiety, and Tic Disorders Program
Director: John Piacentini, Ph.D., ABPP
Semel Institute
760 Westwood Plaza, Room 67-467
Los Angeles, CA 90024
310-825-0122
Fax: 310-267-4925
www.semel.ucla.edu/caap

Youth Anxiety and Depression Clinic
Director: Brian C. Chu, Ph.D.
152 Frelinghuysen Road
Piscataway, NJ 08854-8020
848-445-3905
Fax: 732-445-4888
yadc.rutgers.edu

Index